This planner belongs to

....

Weekly planner

Date:..../.../.....to..../.../....

MON

TUE

WED

THU

FRI

SAT

SUN

Date:..............

Gratitude

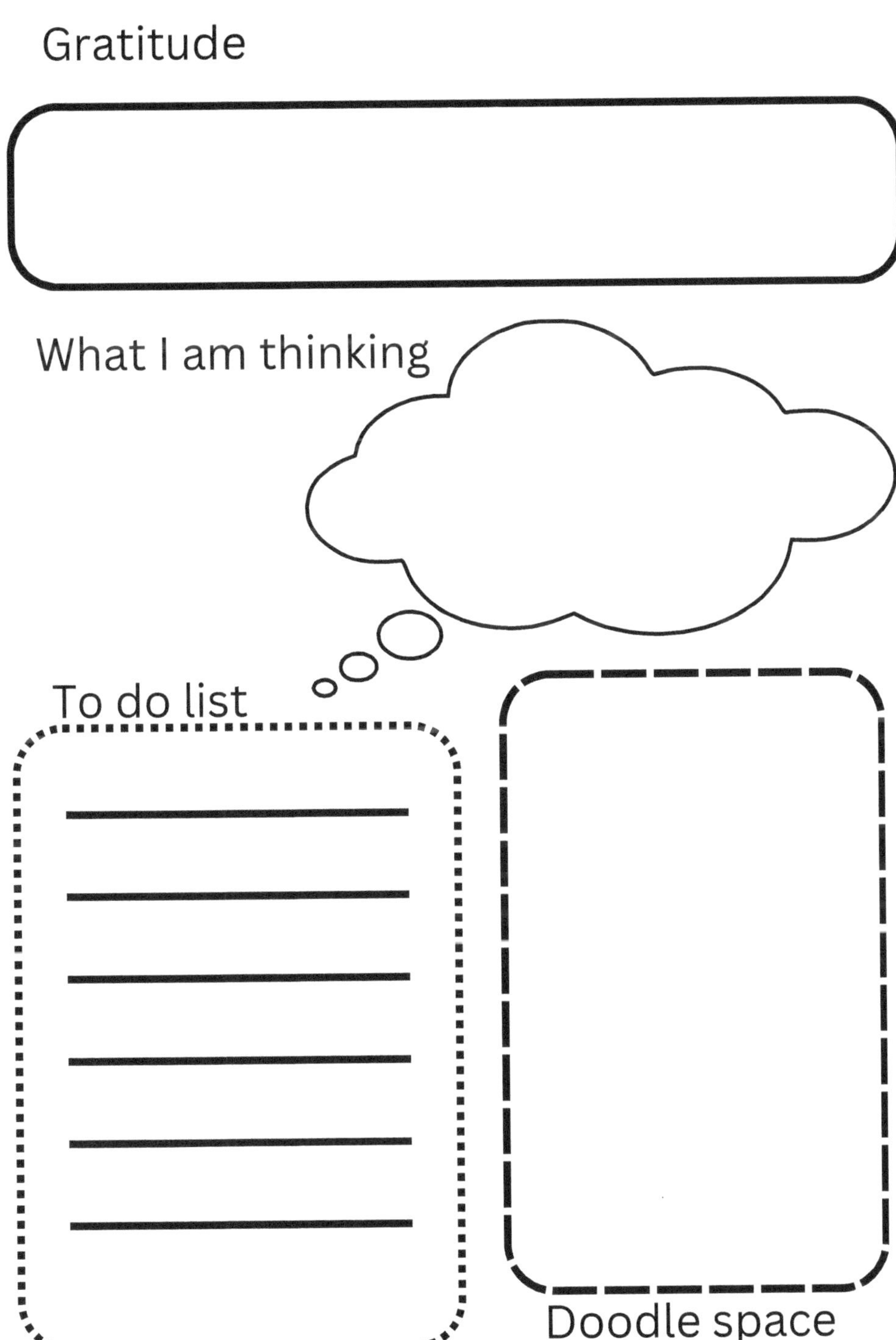

Date:..............

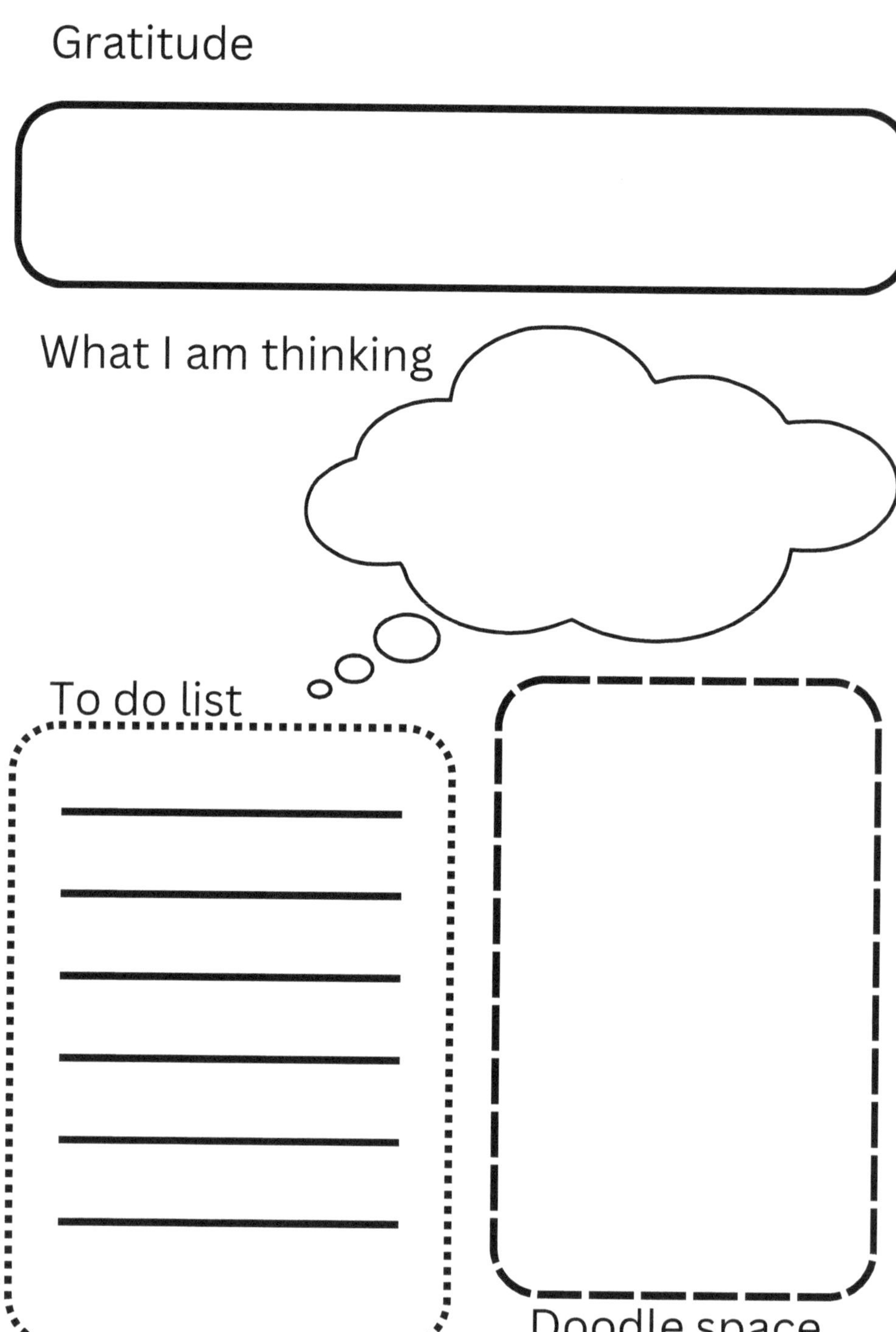

Date:..............

Gratitude

What I am thinking

To do list

Doodle space

Date:..............

Gratitude

What I am thinking

To do list

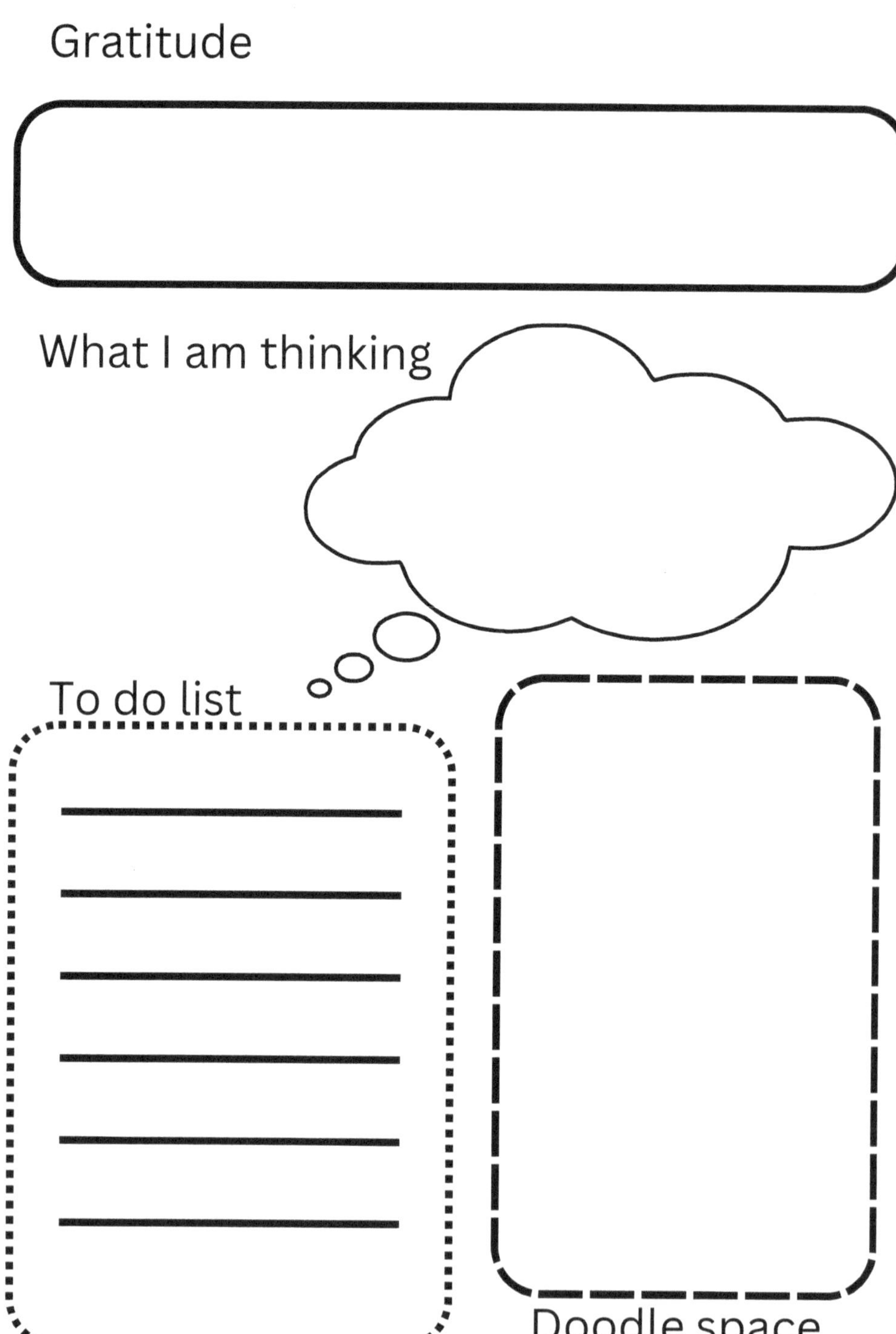

Doodle space

Date:..............
Gratitude
What I am thinking
To do list
Doodle space

Date:..............

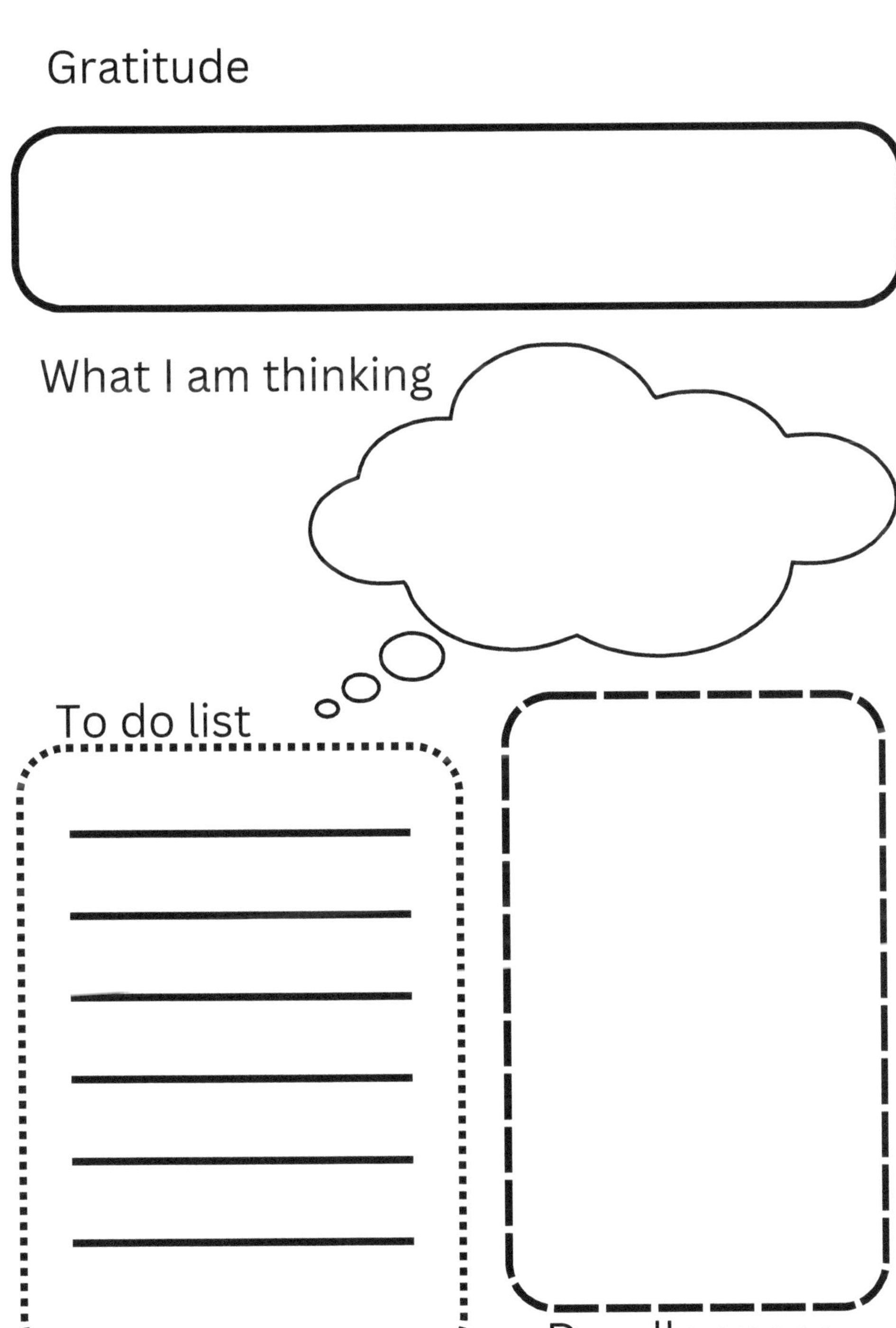
Date:..............
Gratitude
What I am thinking
To do list
Doodle space

Weekly planner

Date:..../.../.....to..../.../....

MON

TUE

WED

THU

FRI

SAT

SUN

Date:..............

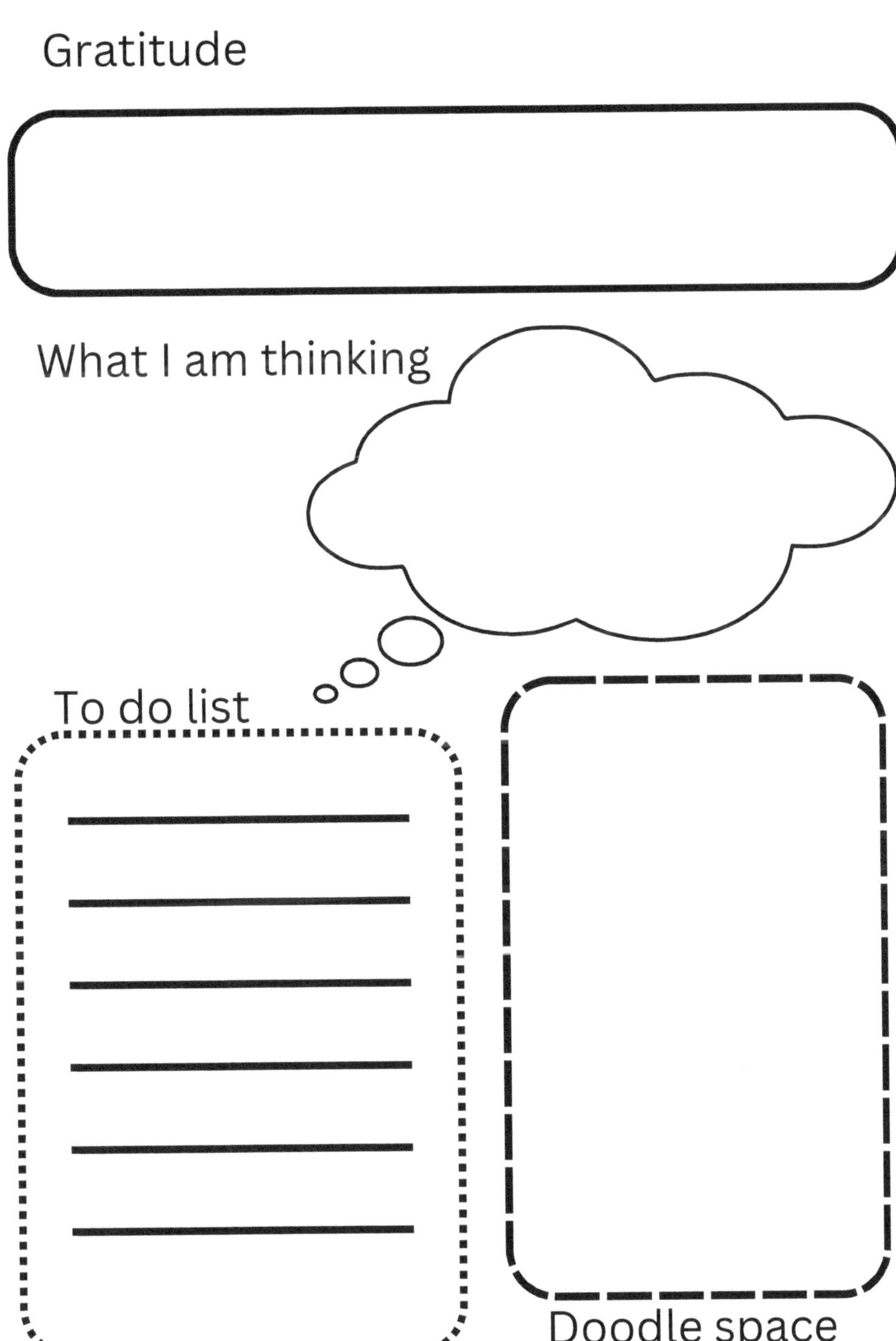

Date:..............

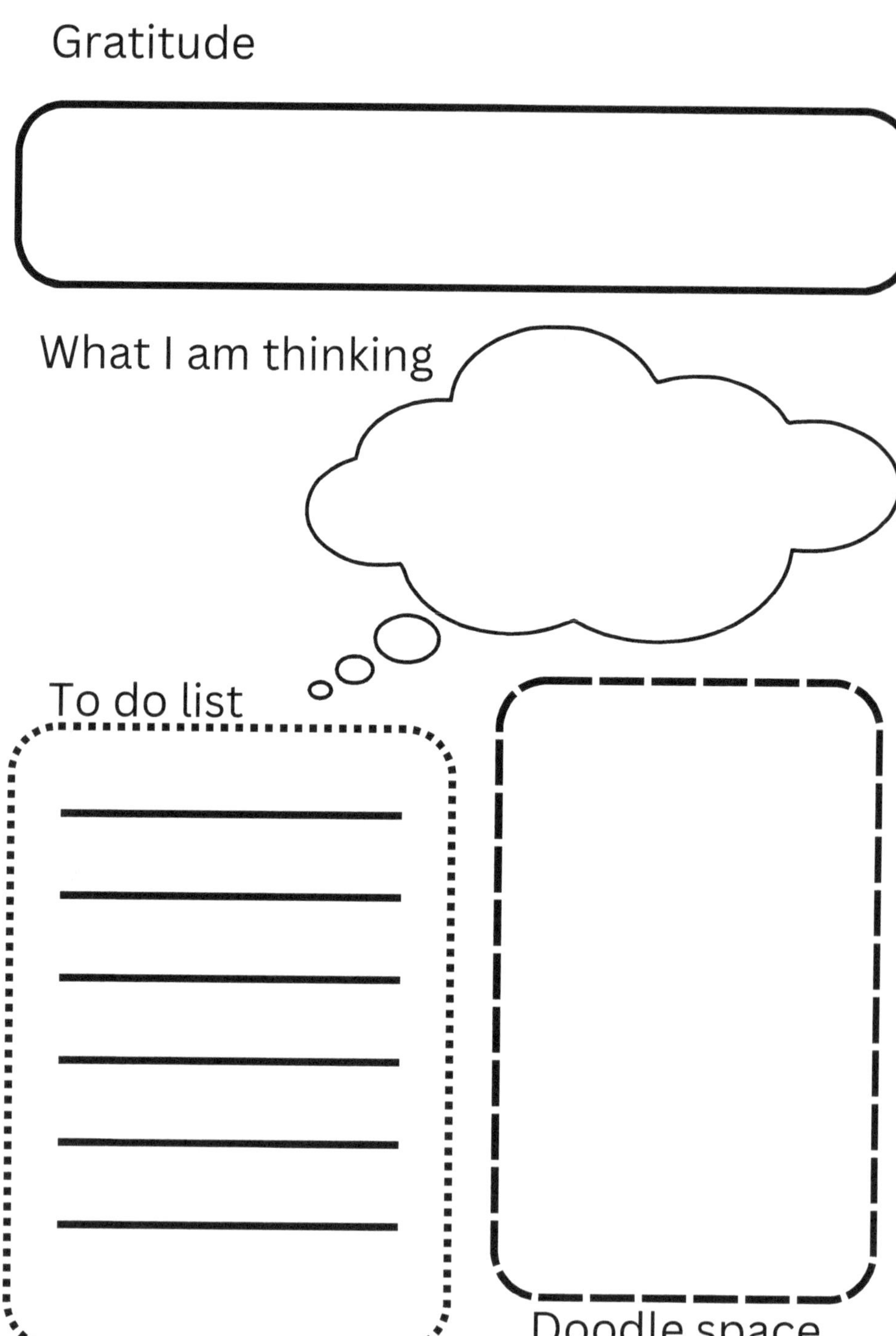

Date:..............

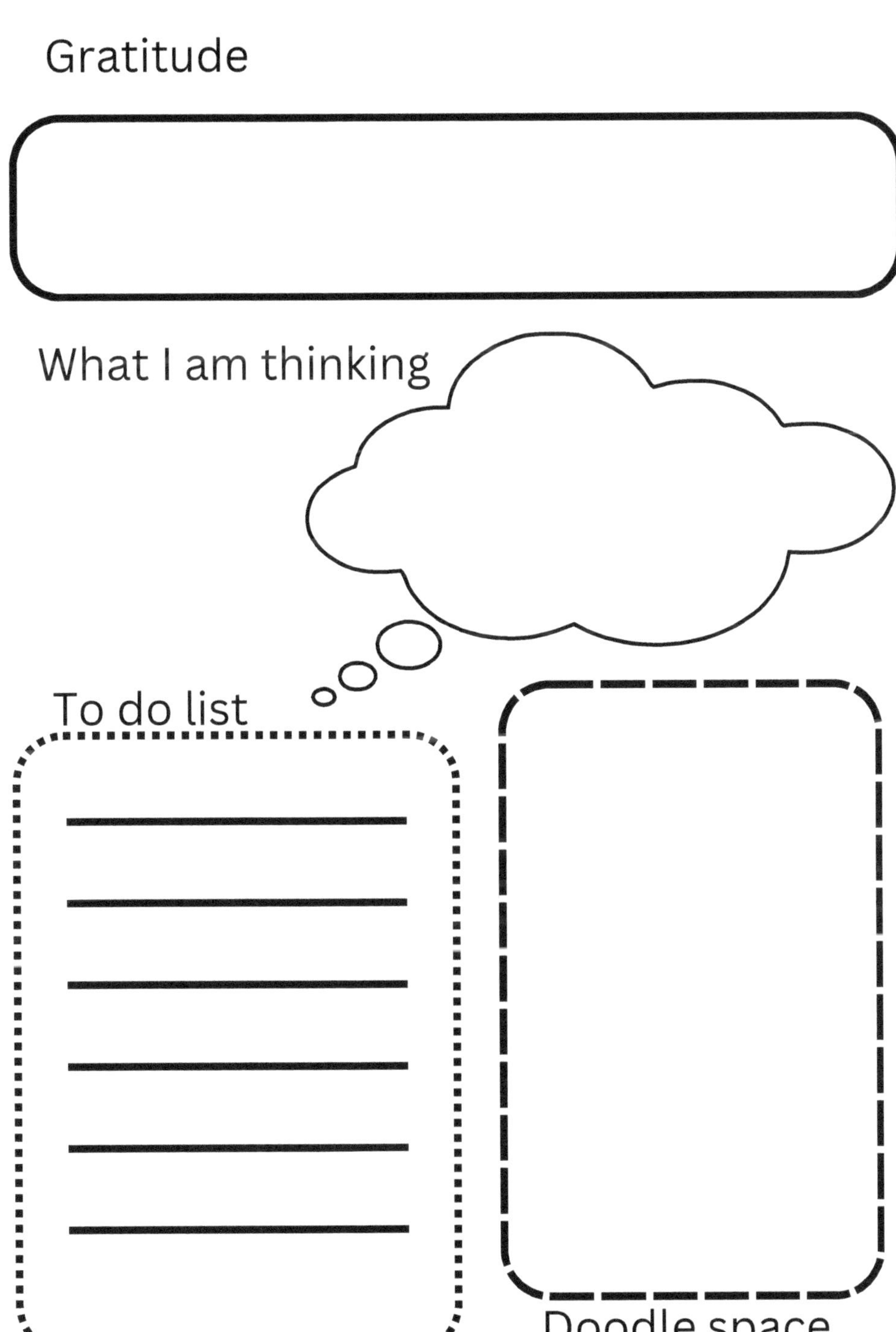

Date:..............

Date:..............

Date:...............

Date:..............

Gratitude

What I am thinking

To do list

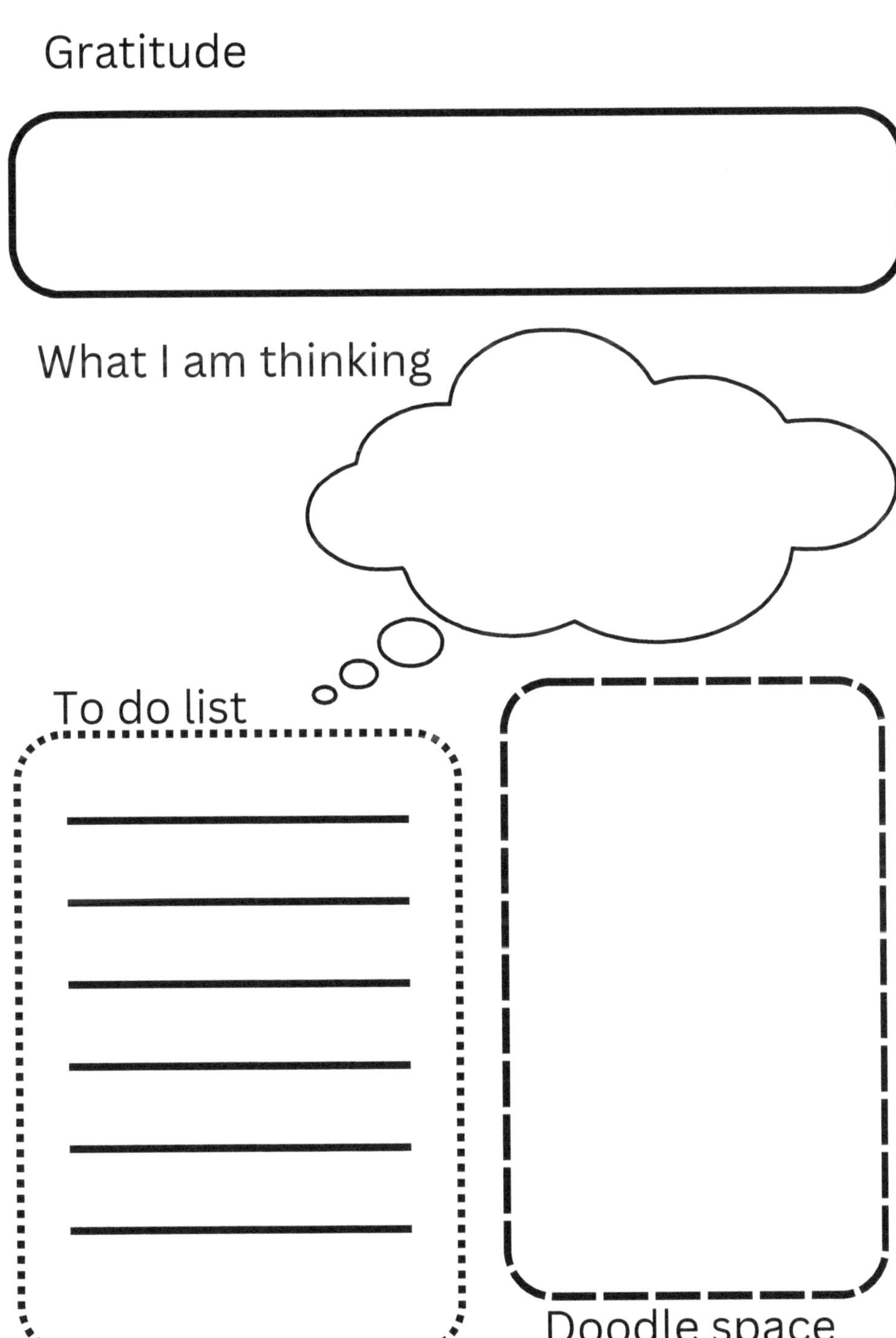

Doodle space

Weekly planner

Date:..../.../.....to..../.../....

MON

TUE

WED

THU

FRI

SAT

SUN

Date:..............

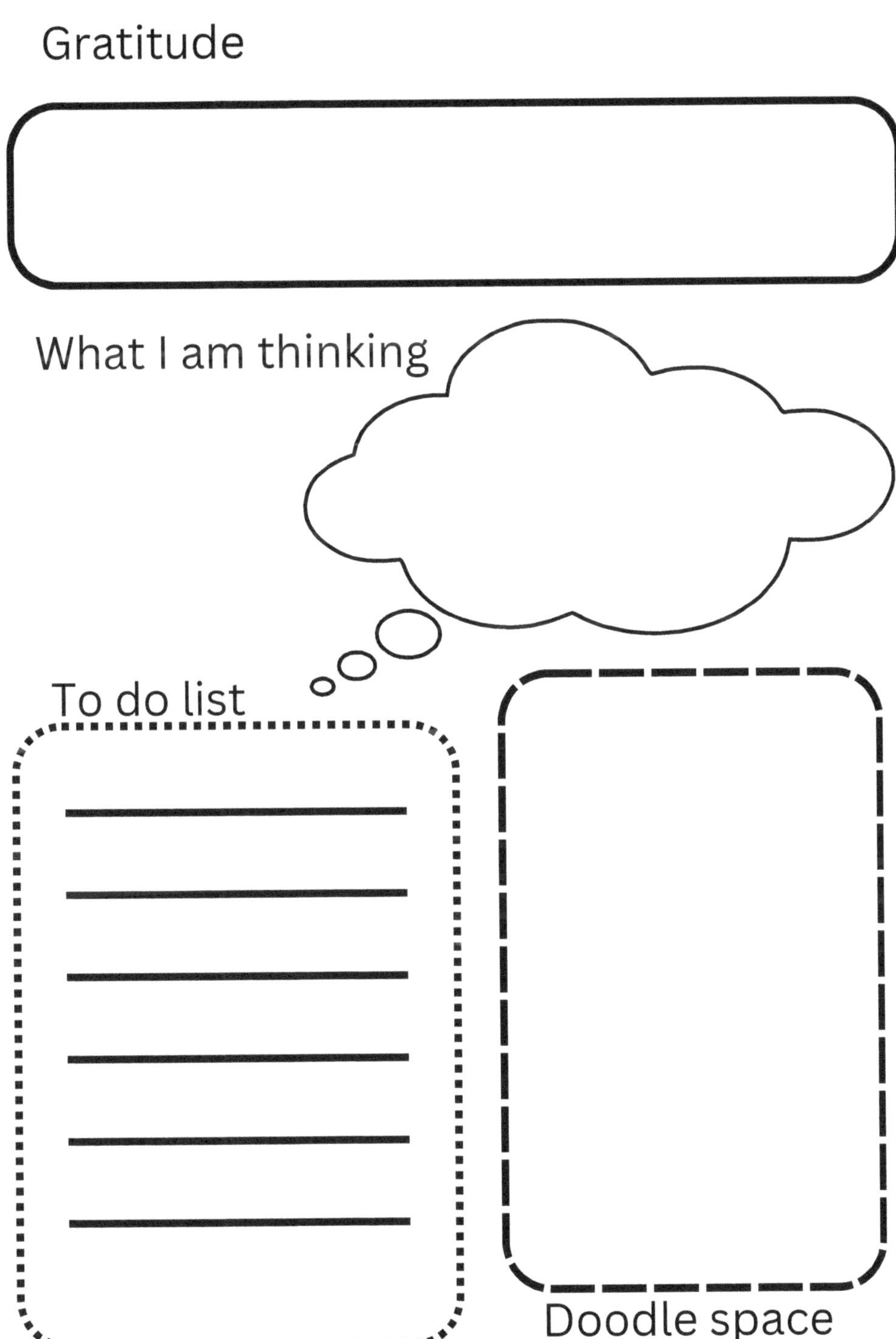

Date:...............

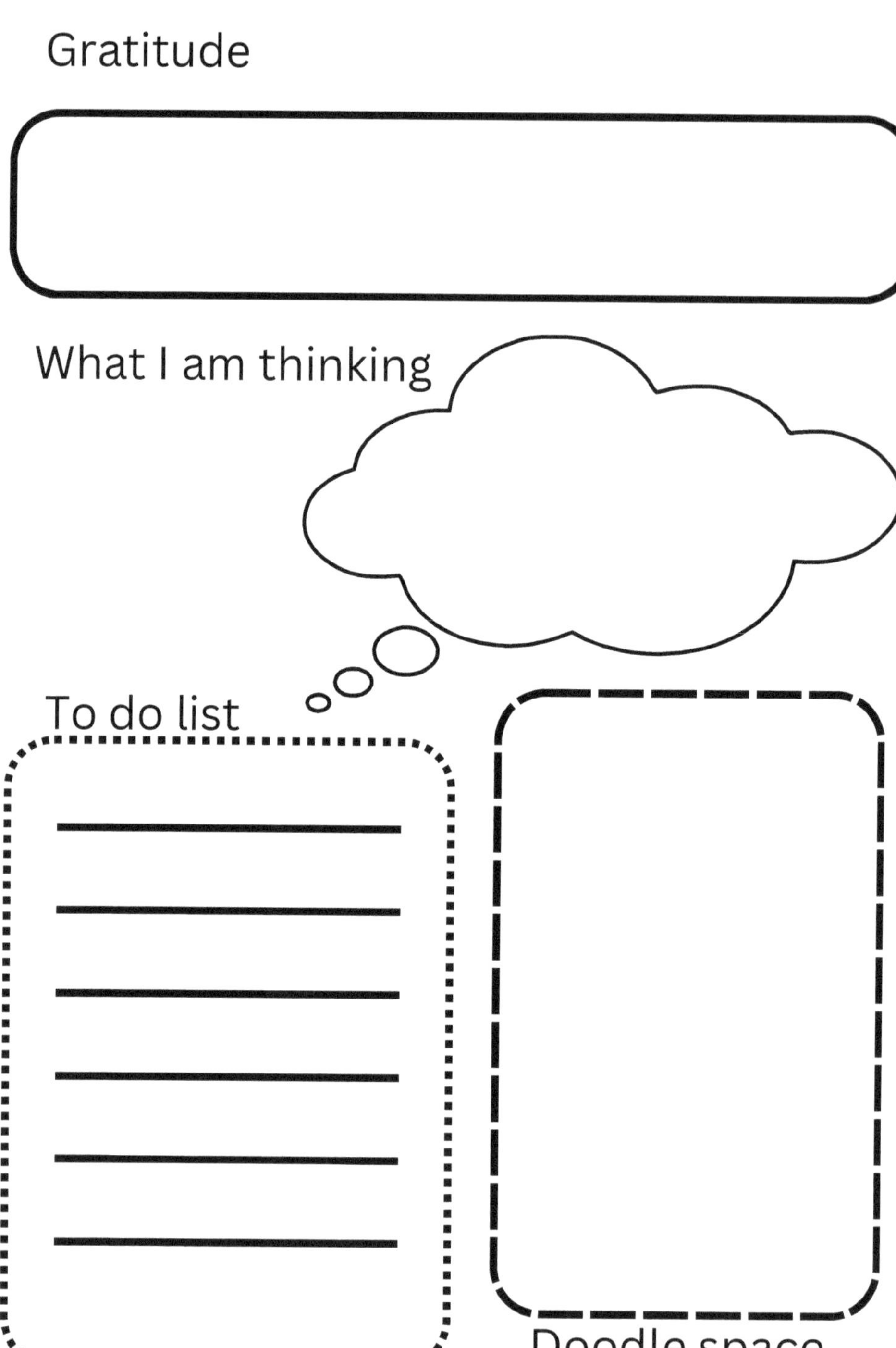

Date:..............

Date:..............

Gratitude

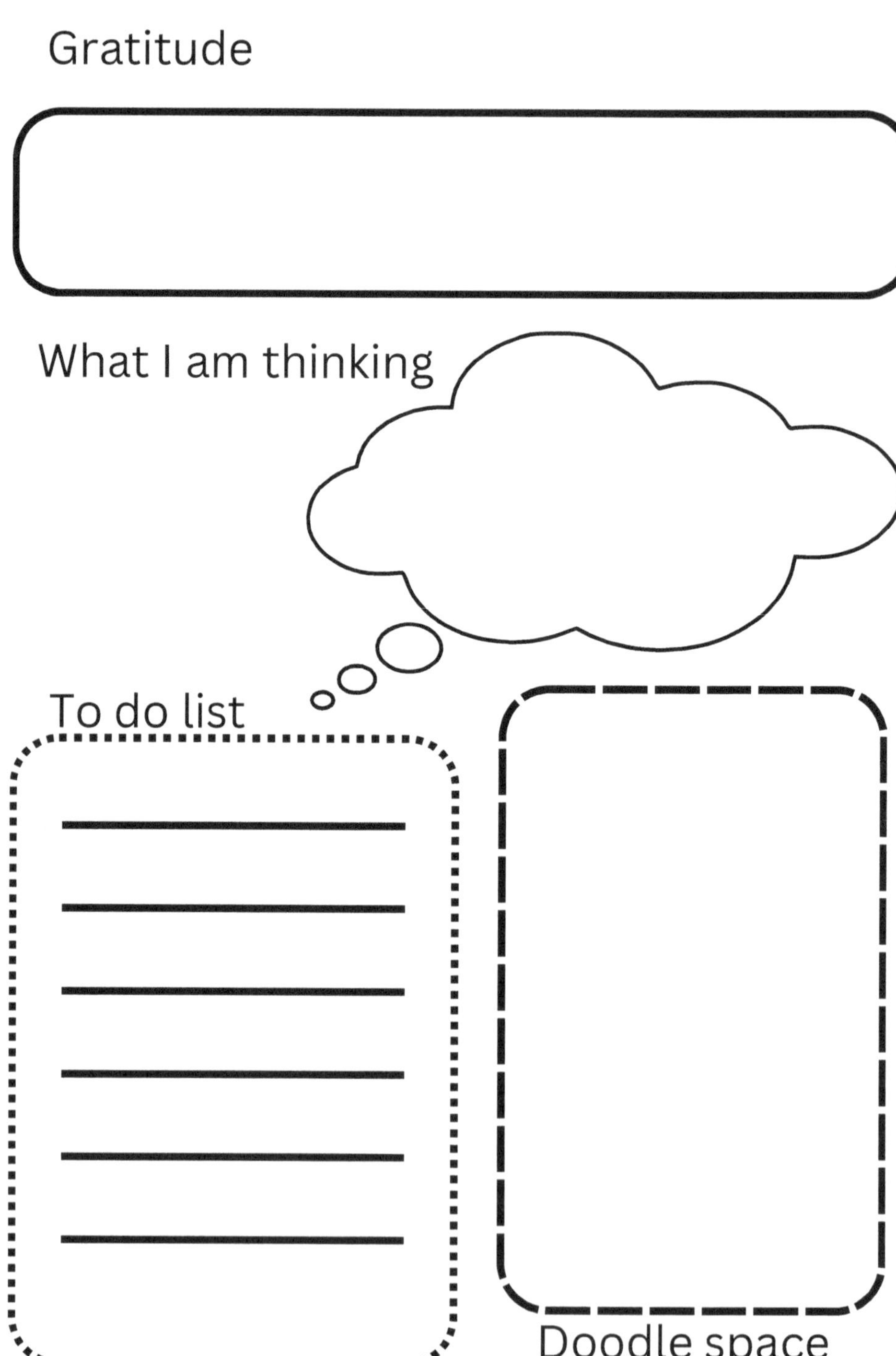

Date:..............

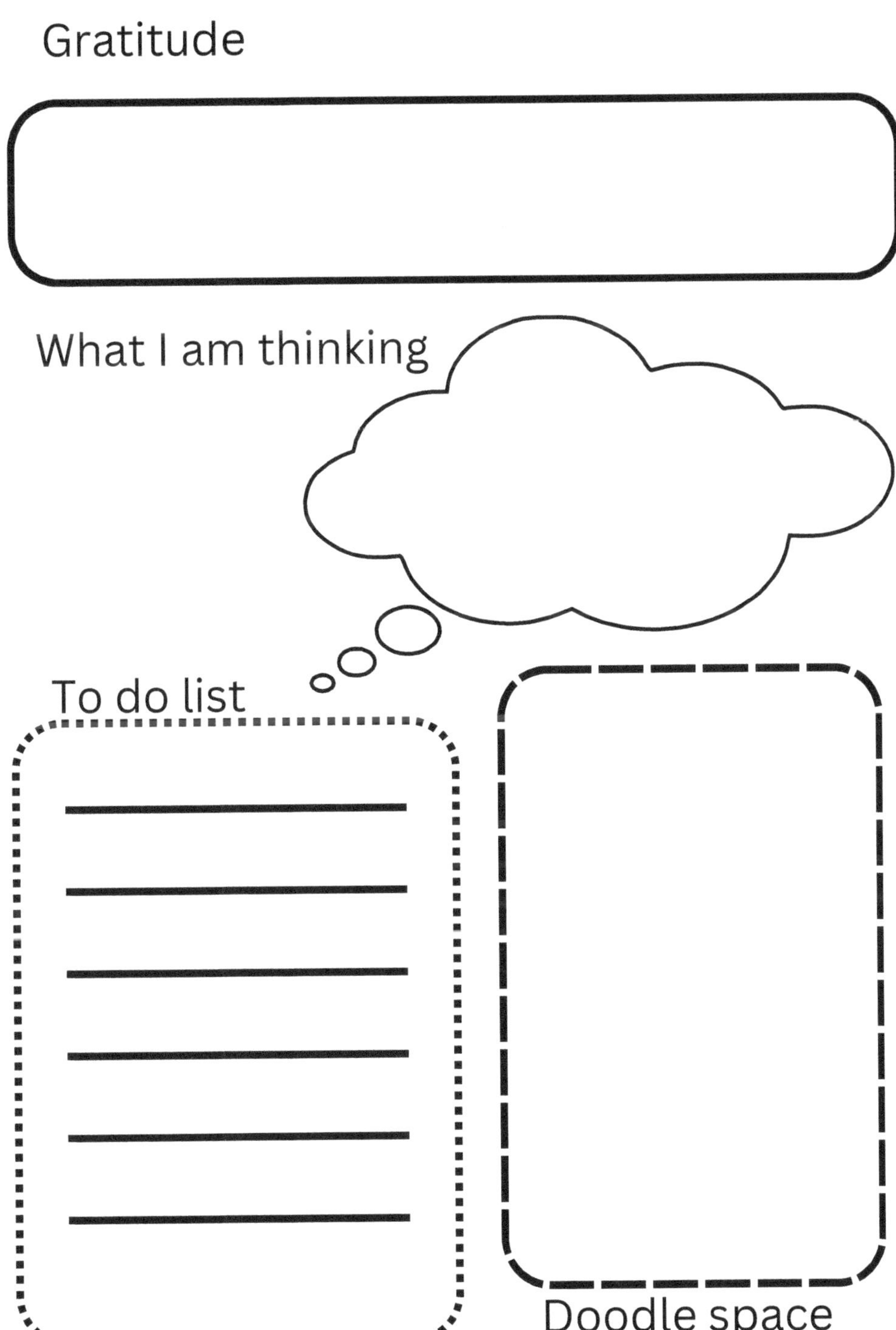

Date:..............

Date:..............

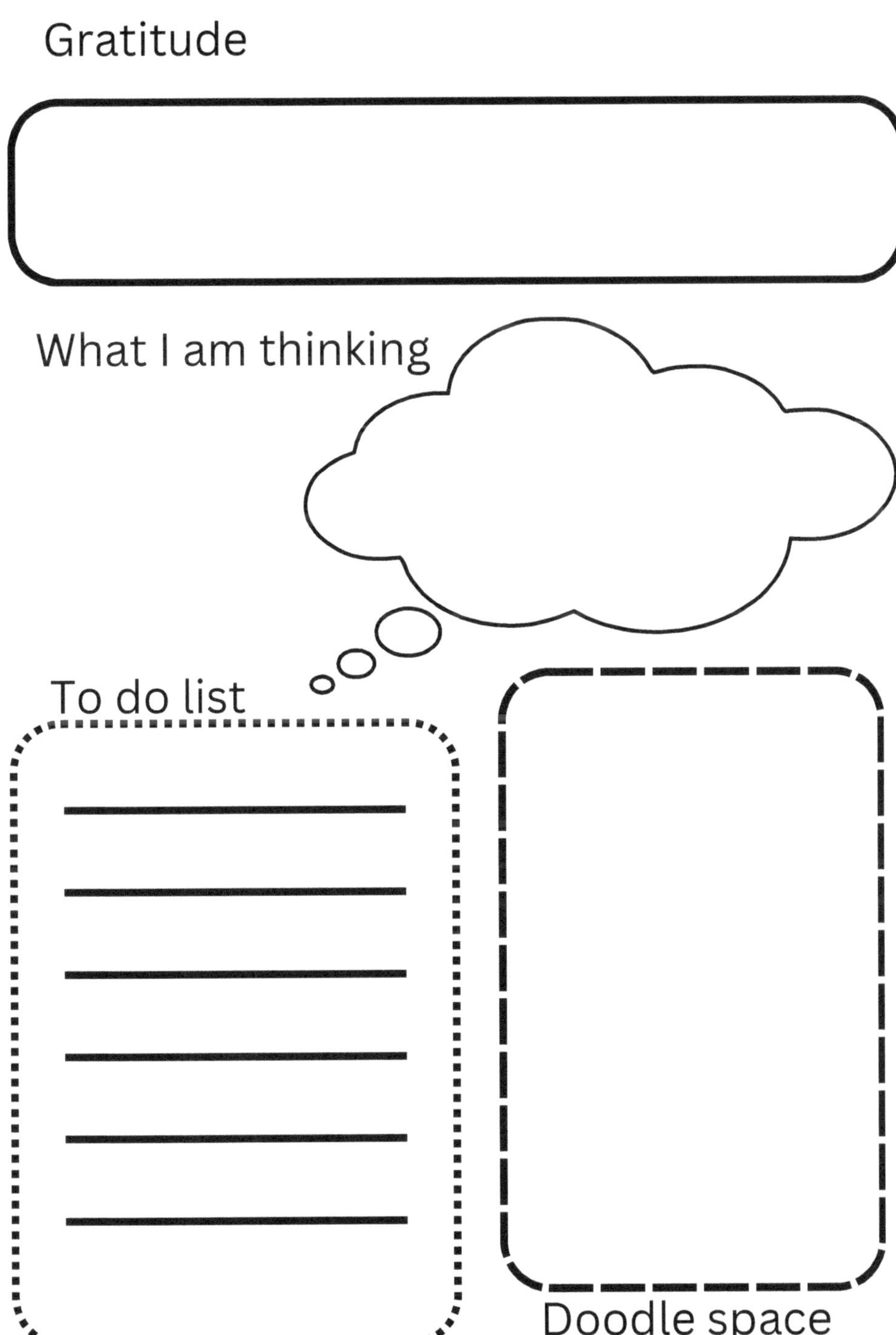

Weekly planner

Date:..../.../.....to..../.../....

MON

TUE

WED

THU

FRI

SAT

SUN

Date:...............

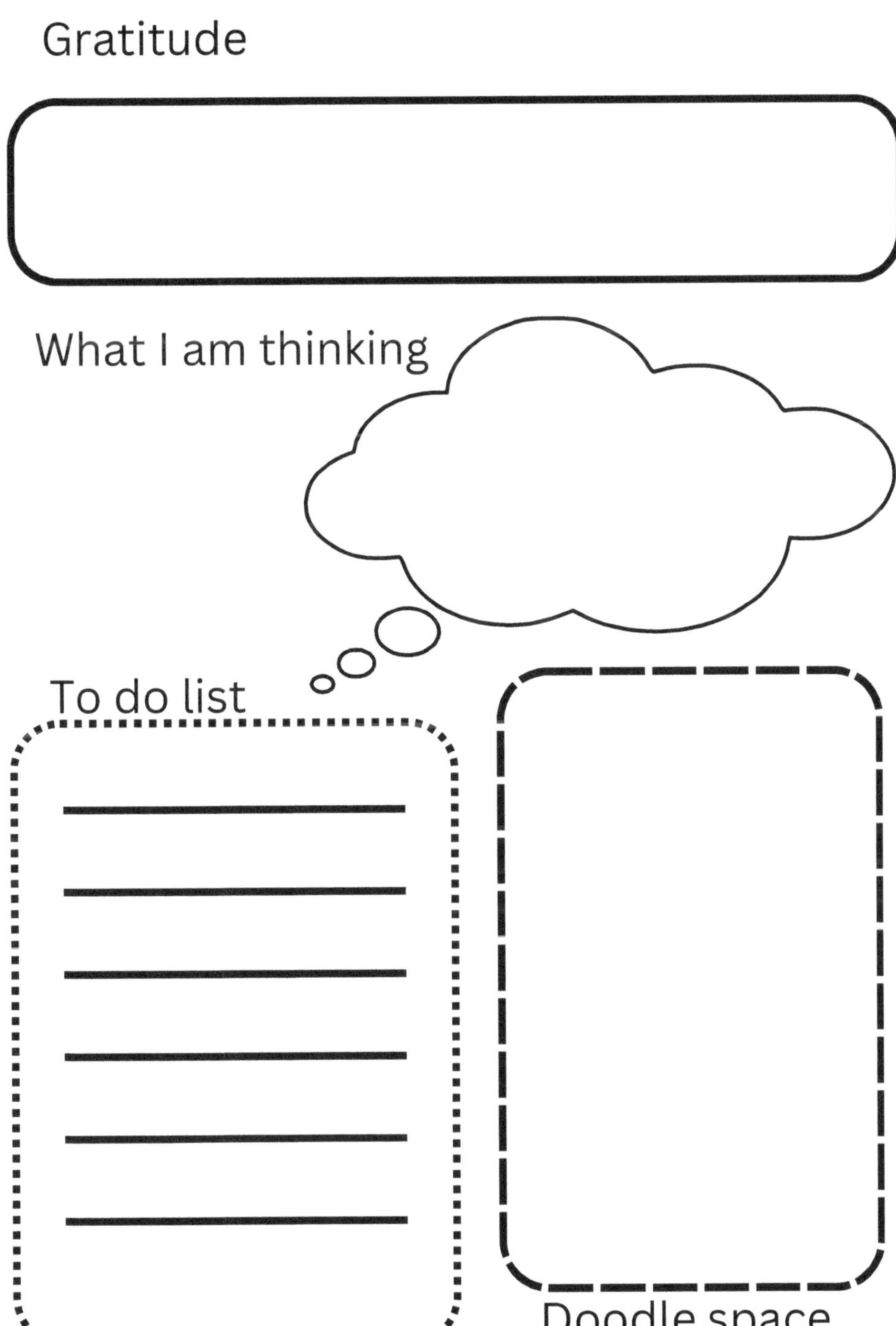
Gratitude

What I am thinking

To do list

Doodle space

Date:..............

Date:..............

Date:..............
Gratitude
What I am thinking
To do list
Doodle space

Date:...............

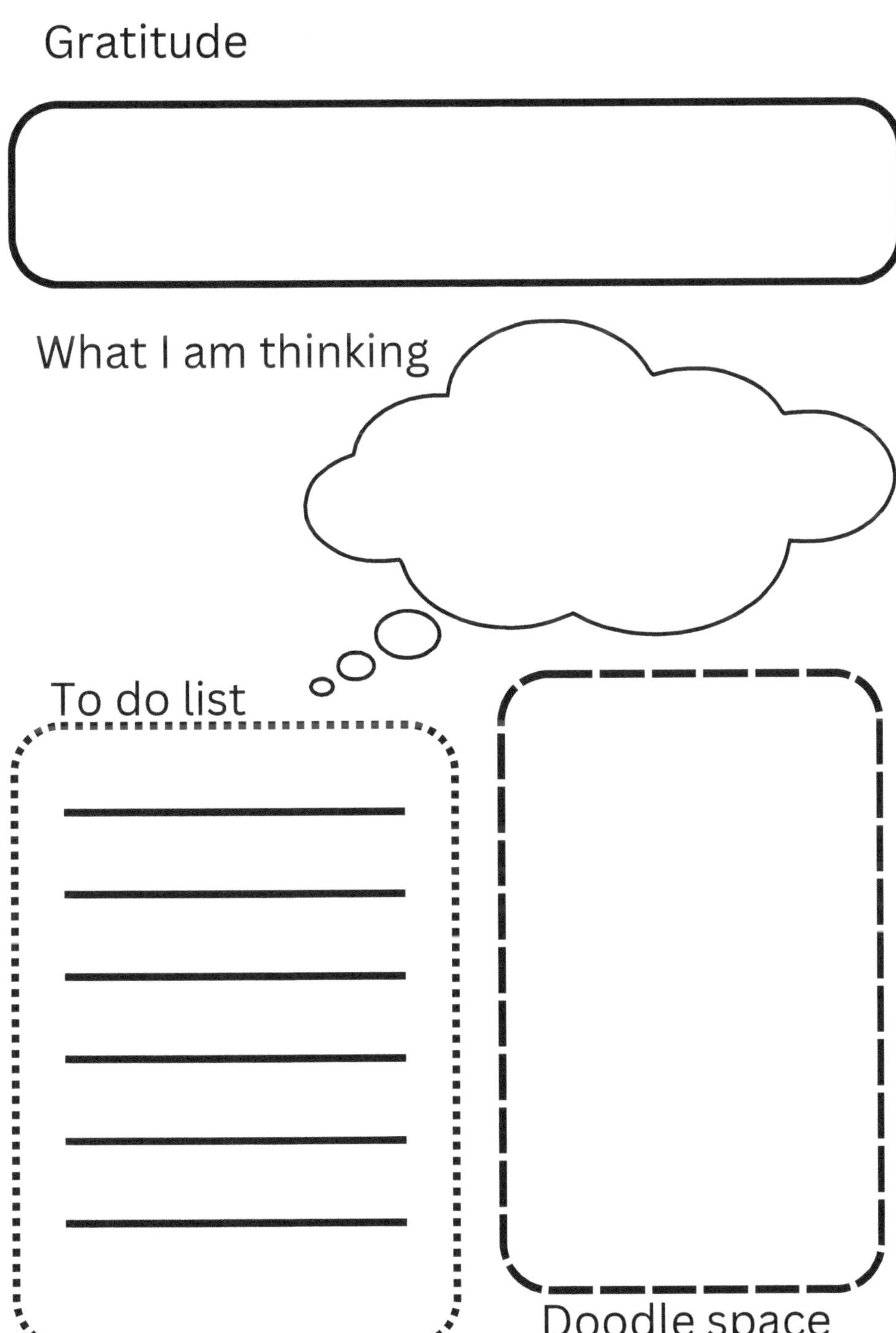

Date:..............
Gratitude
What I am thinking
To do list
Doodle space

Date:..............

Weekly planner

Date:..../.../.....to..../.../....

MON

TUE

WED

THU

FRI

SAT

SUN

Date:..............

Date:..............

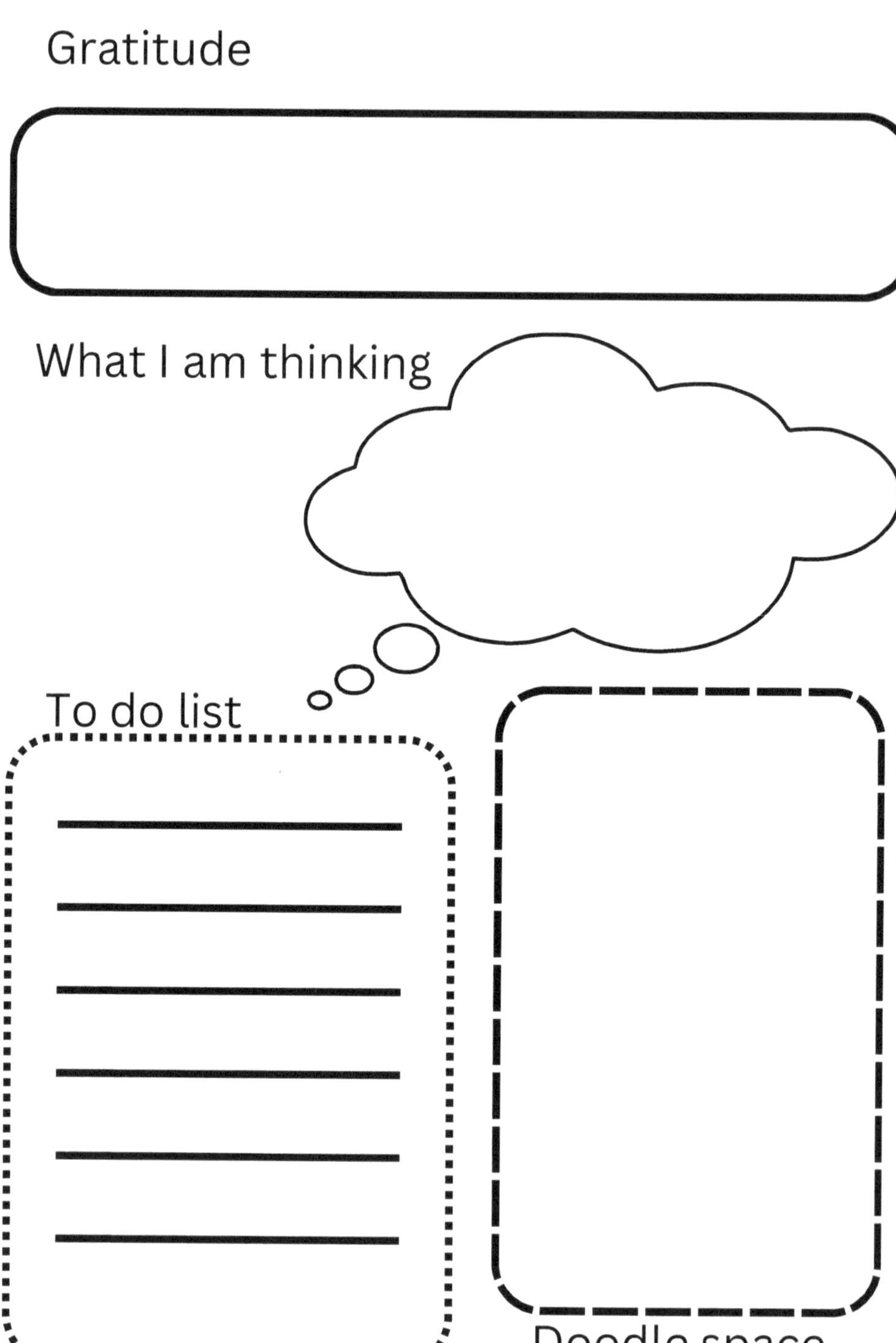

Date:...............

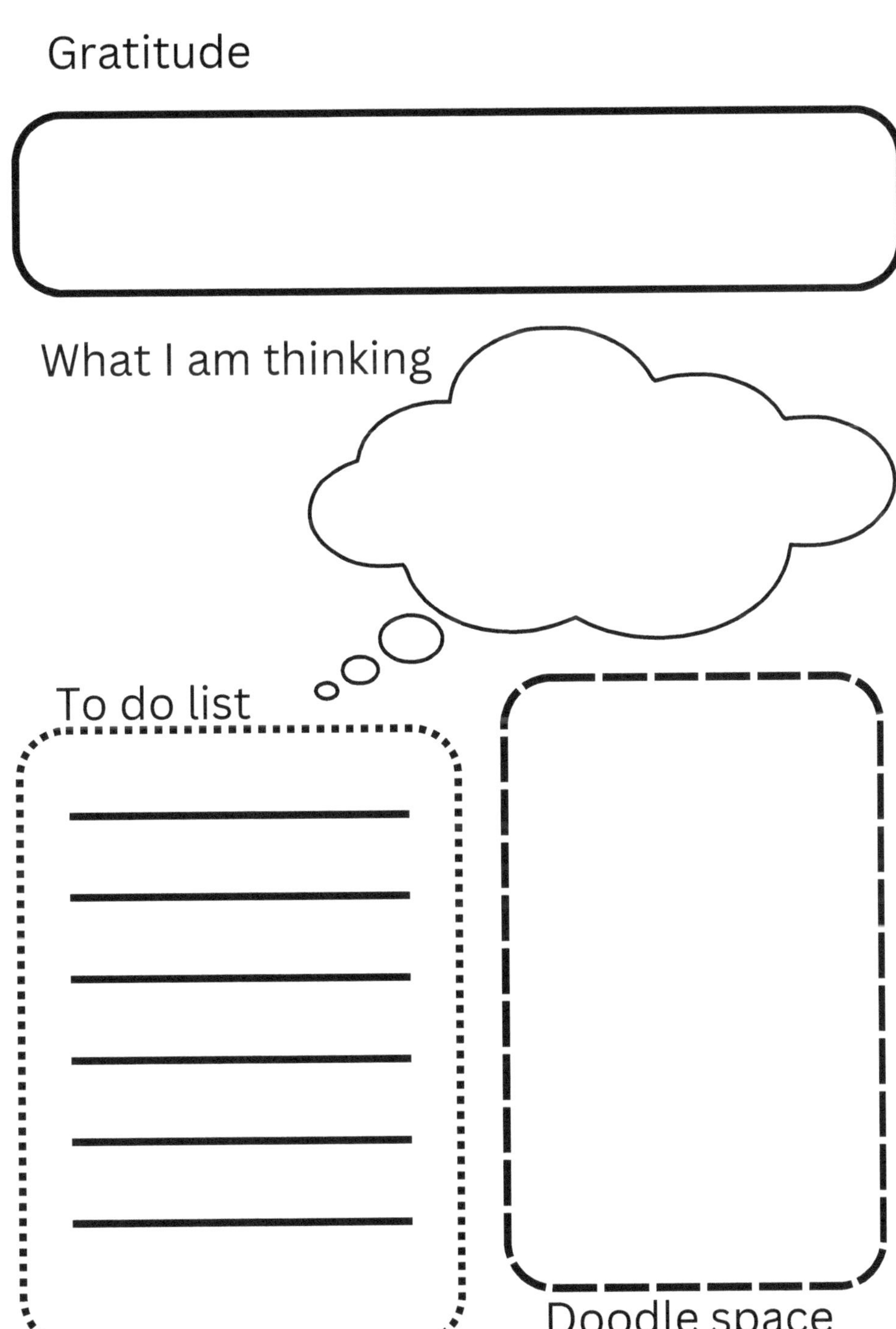

Date:..............

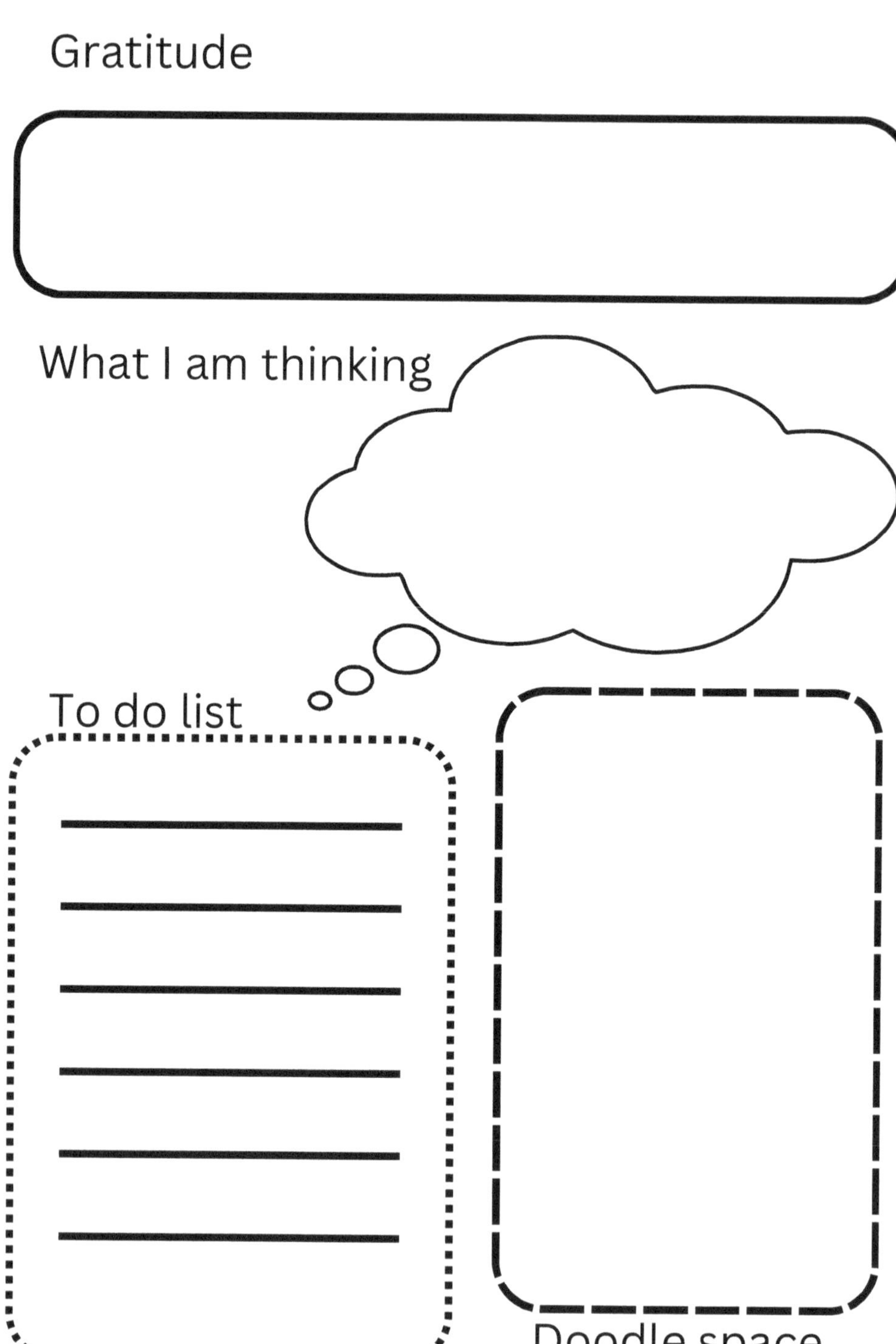

Date:..............

Date:...............

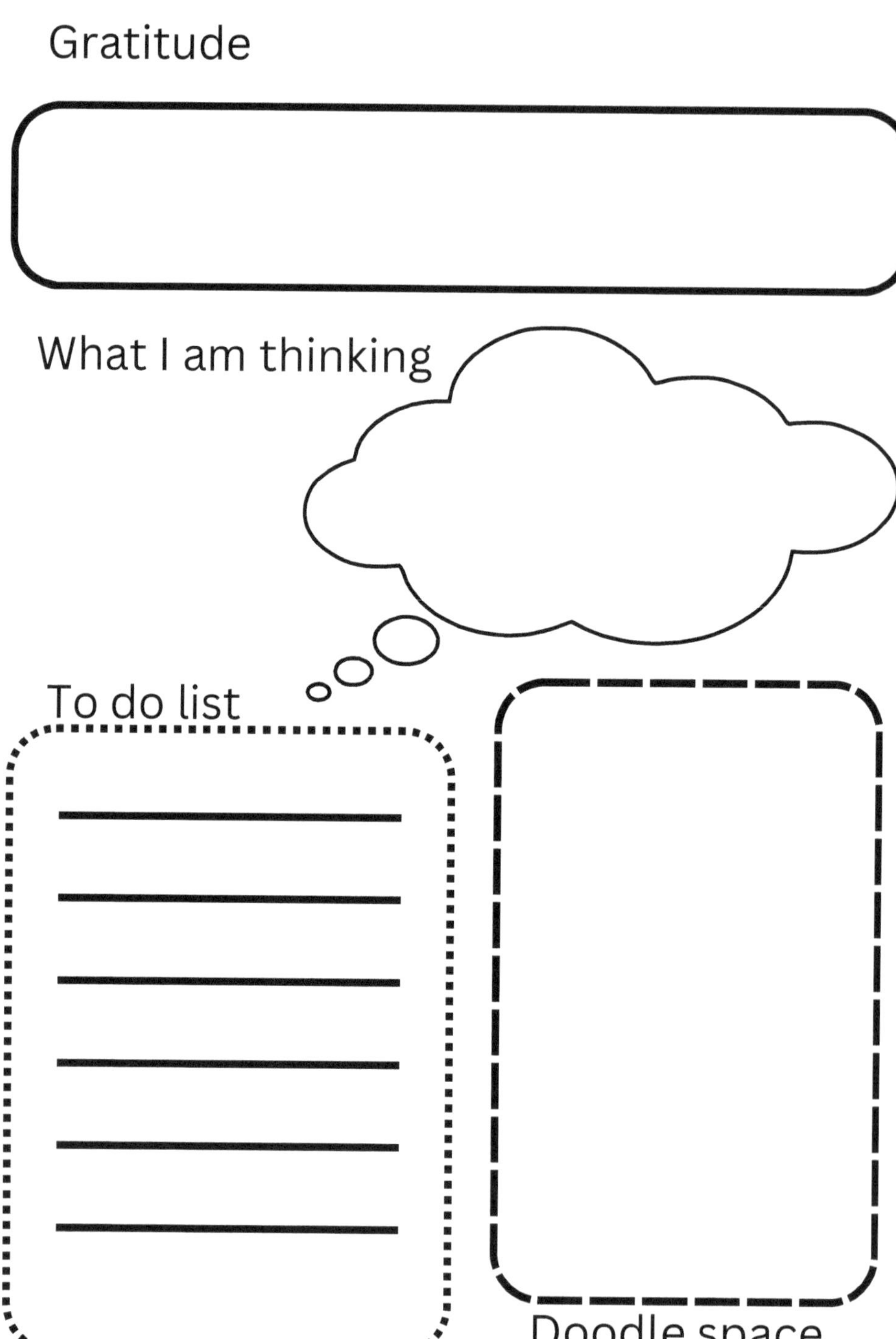

Date:..............

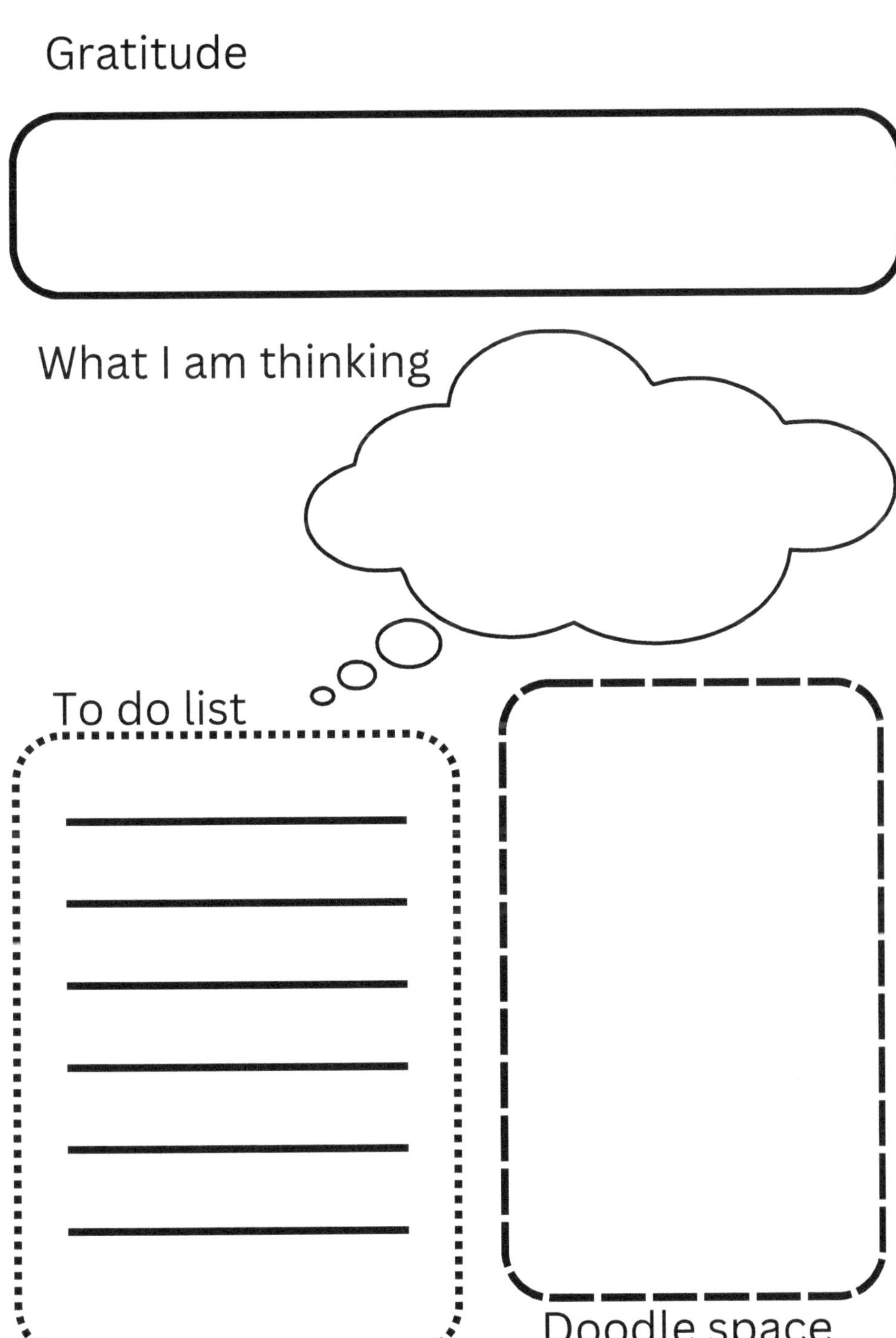

Weekly planner

Date:..../.../.....to..../.../....

MON

TUE

WED

THU

FRI

SAT

SUN

Date:..............

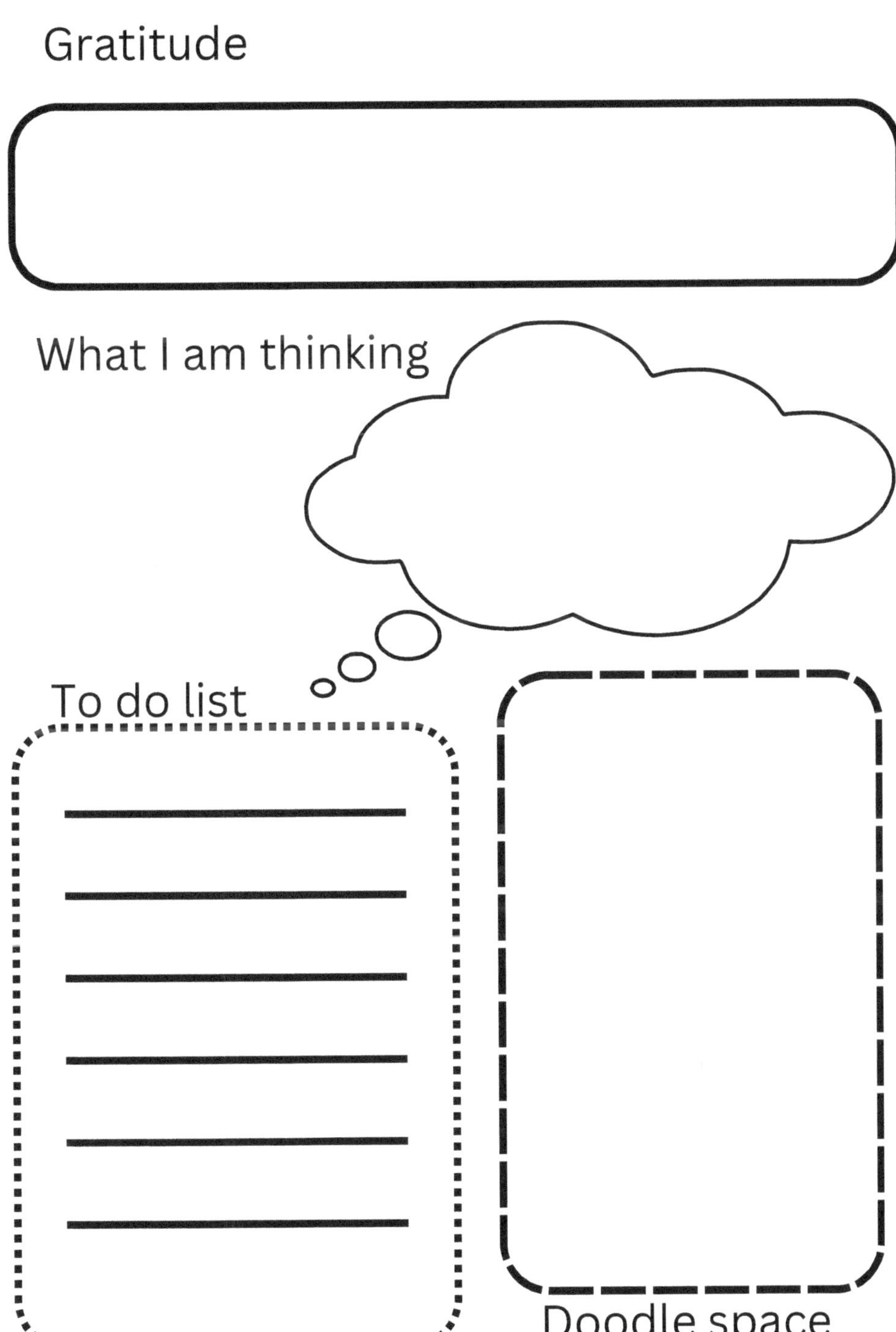

Date:..............

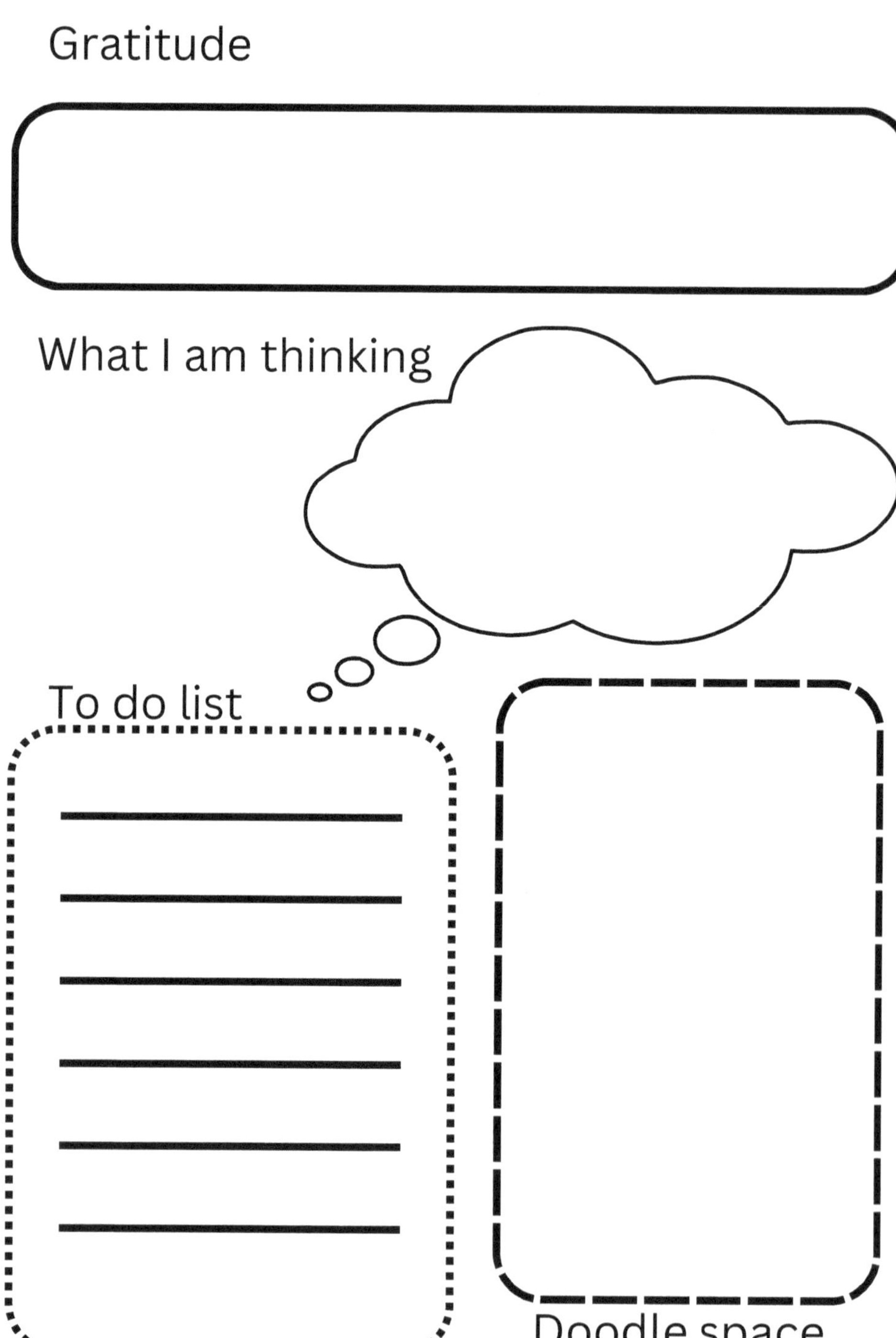

Date:..............

Gratitude

What I am thinking

To do list

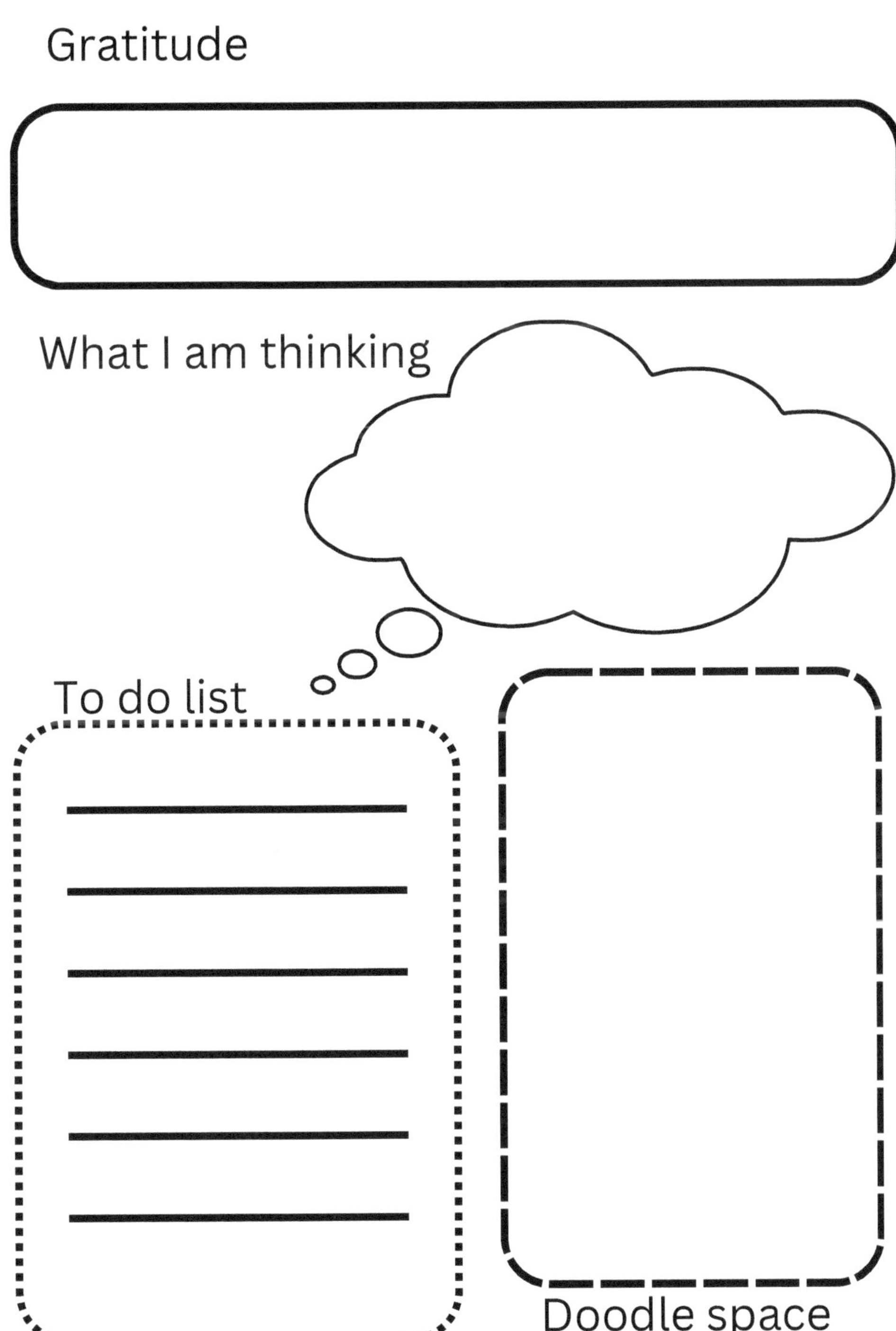

Doodle space

Date:.............

Date:..............

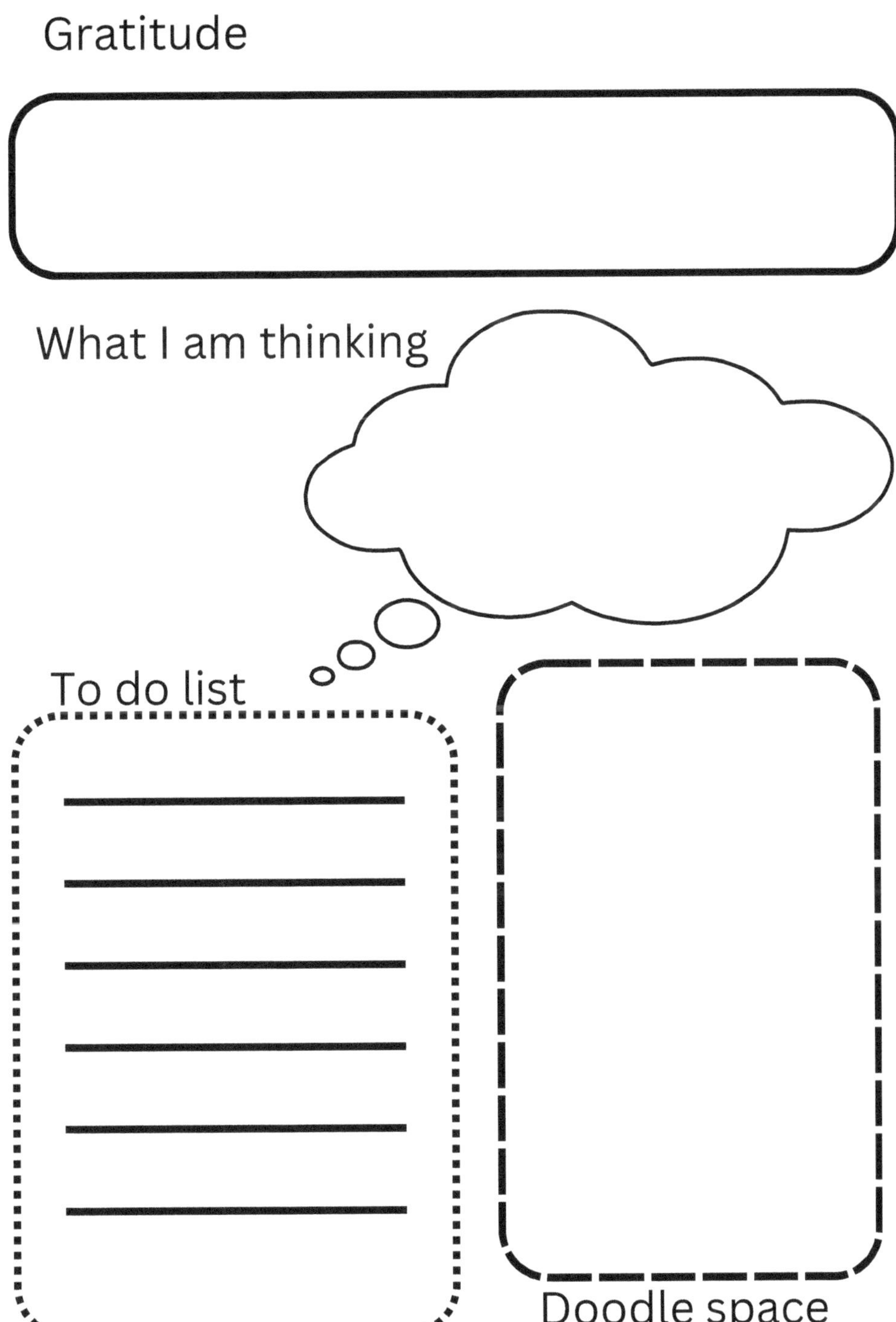

Date:..............

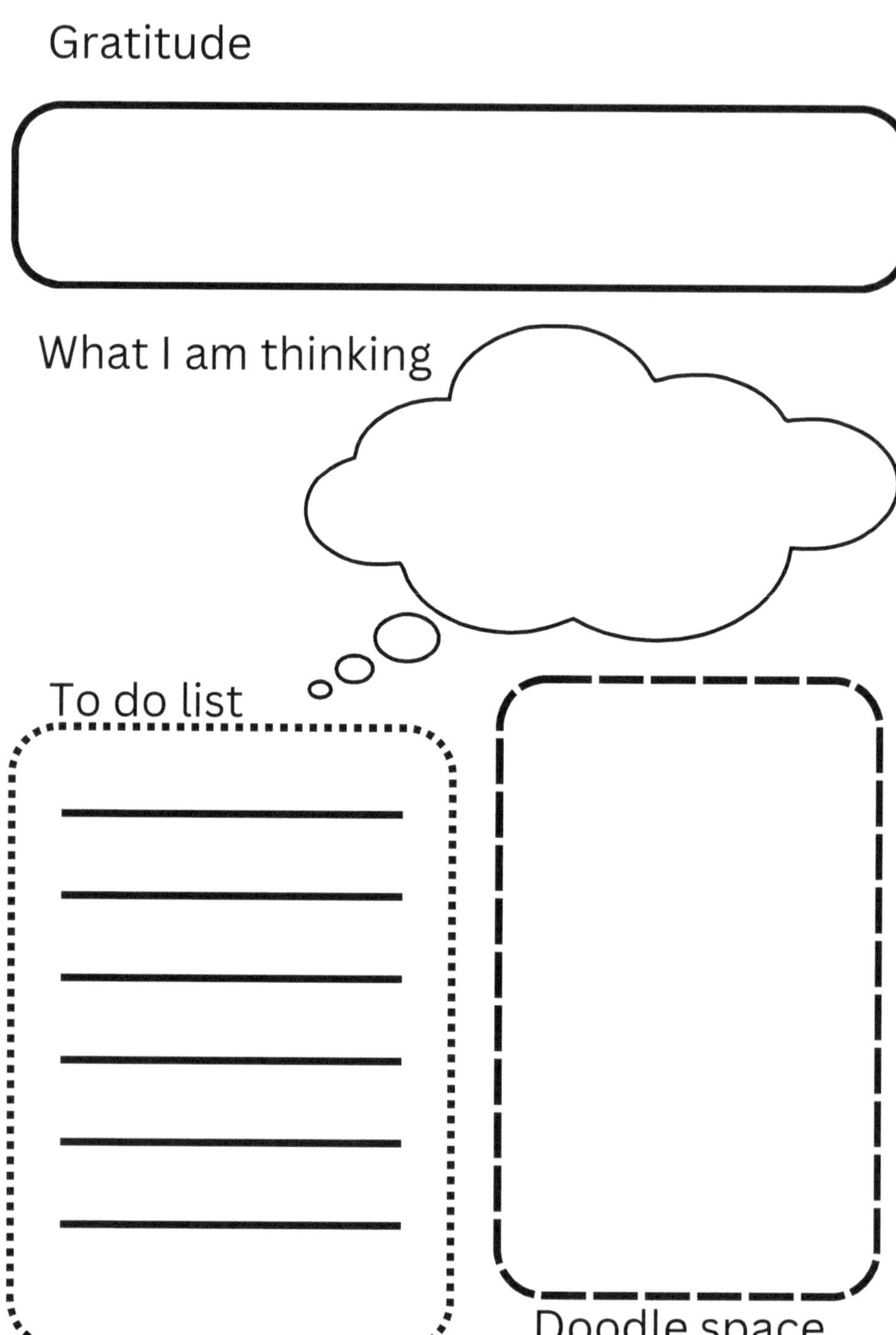

Date:..............

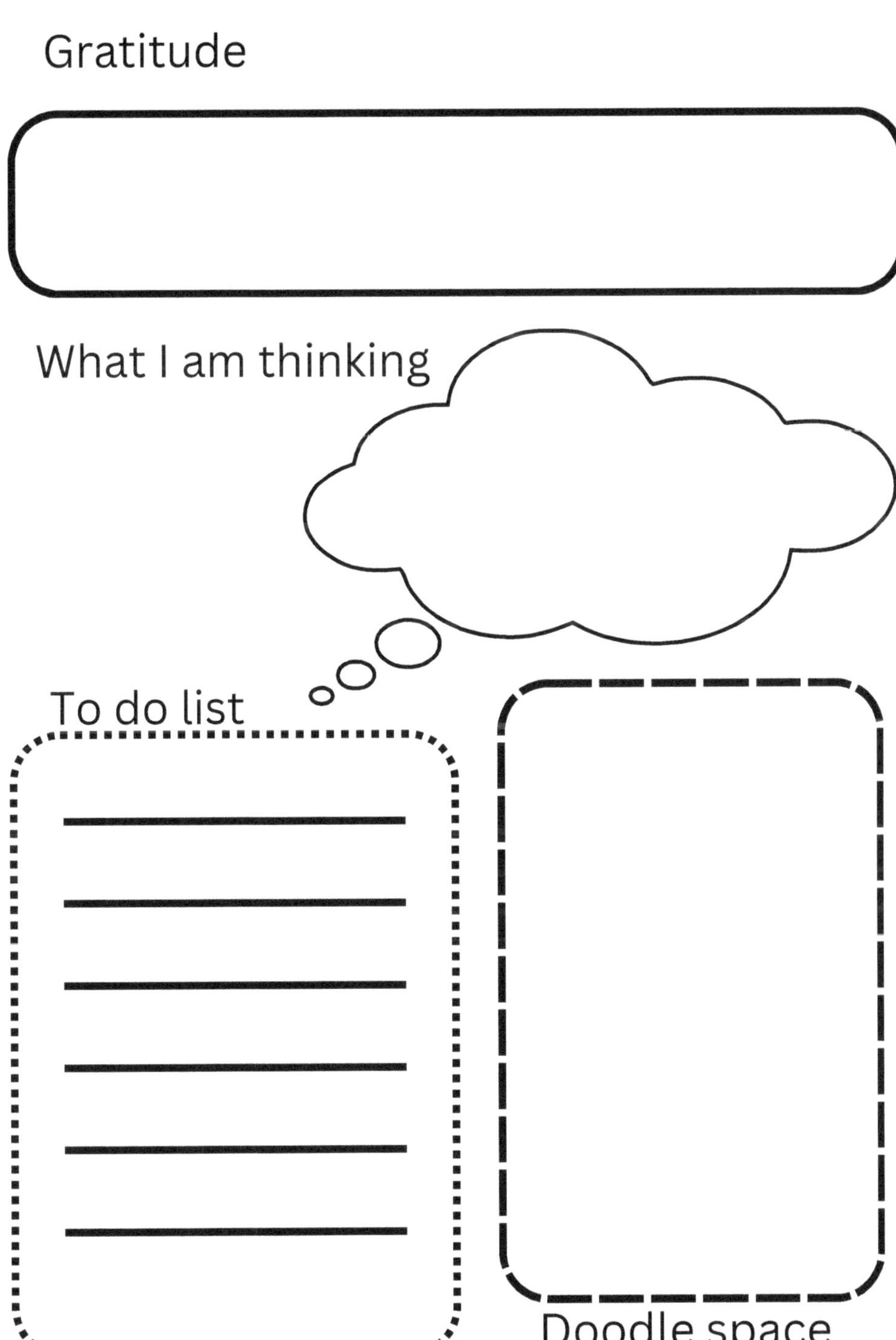

Weekly planner

Date:..../.../.....to..../.../....

MON

TUE

WED

THU

FRI

SAT

SUN

Date:..............

Date:..............

Date:..............

Date:..............

Date:..............

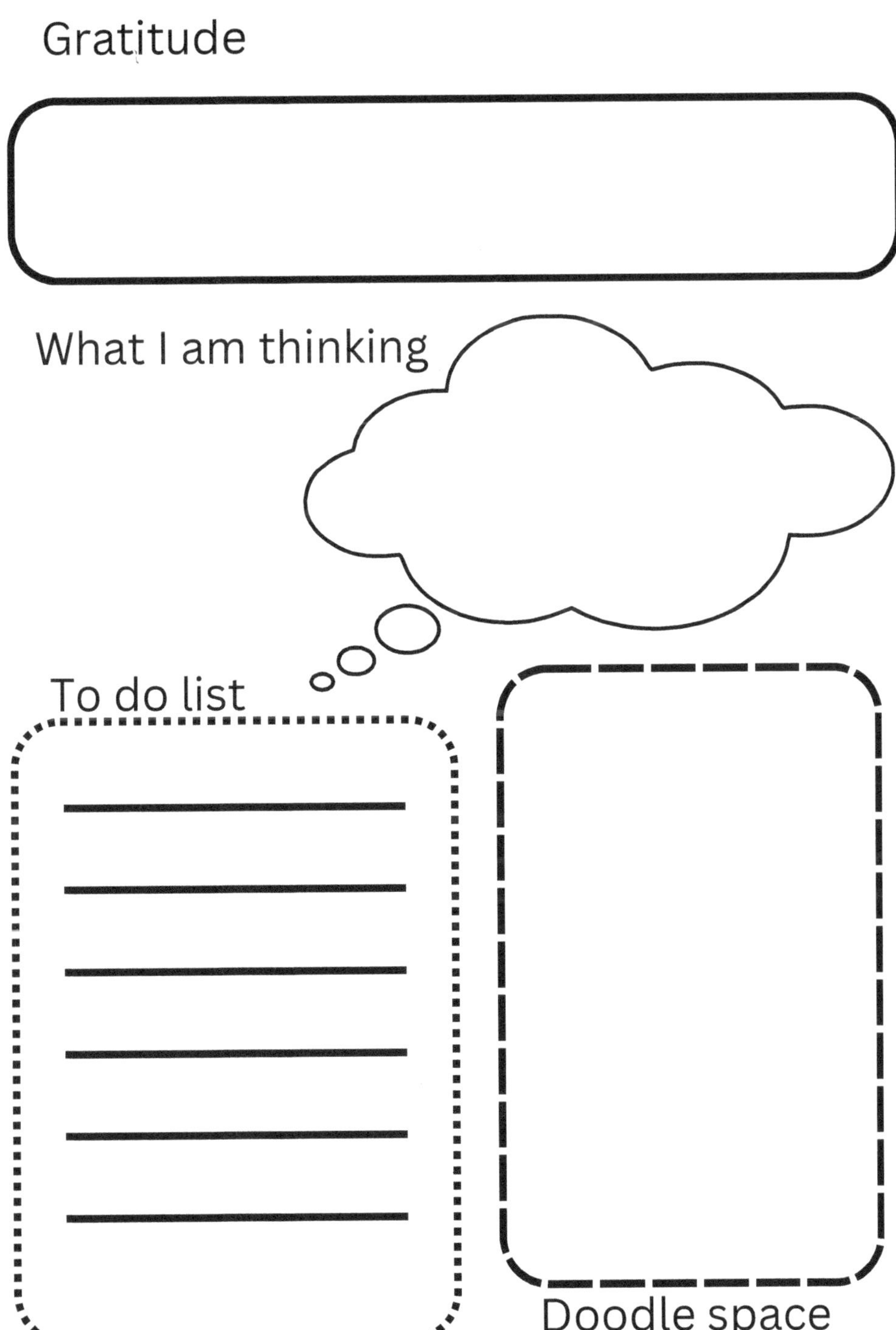

Date:..............
Gratitude
What I am thinking
To do list
Doodle space

Date:..............

Gratitude

What I am thinking

To do list

Doodle space

Weekly planner

Date:..../.../.....to..../.../....

MON

TUE

WED

THU

FRI

SAT

SUN

Date:..............

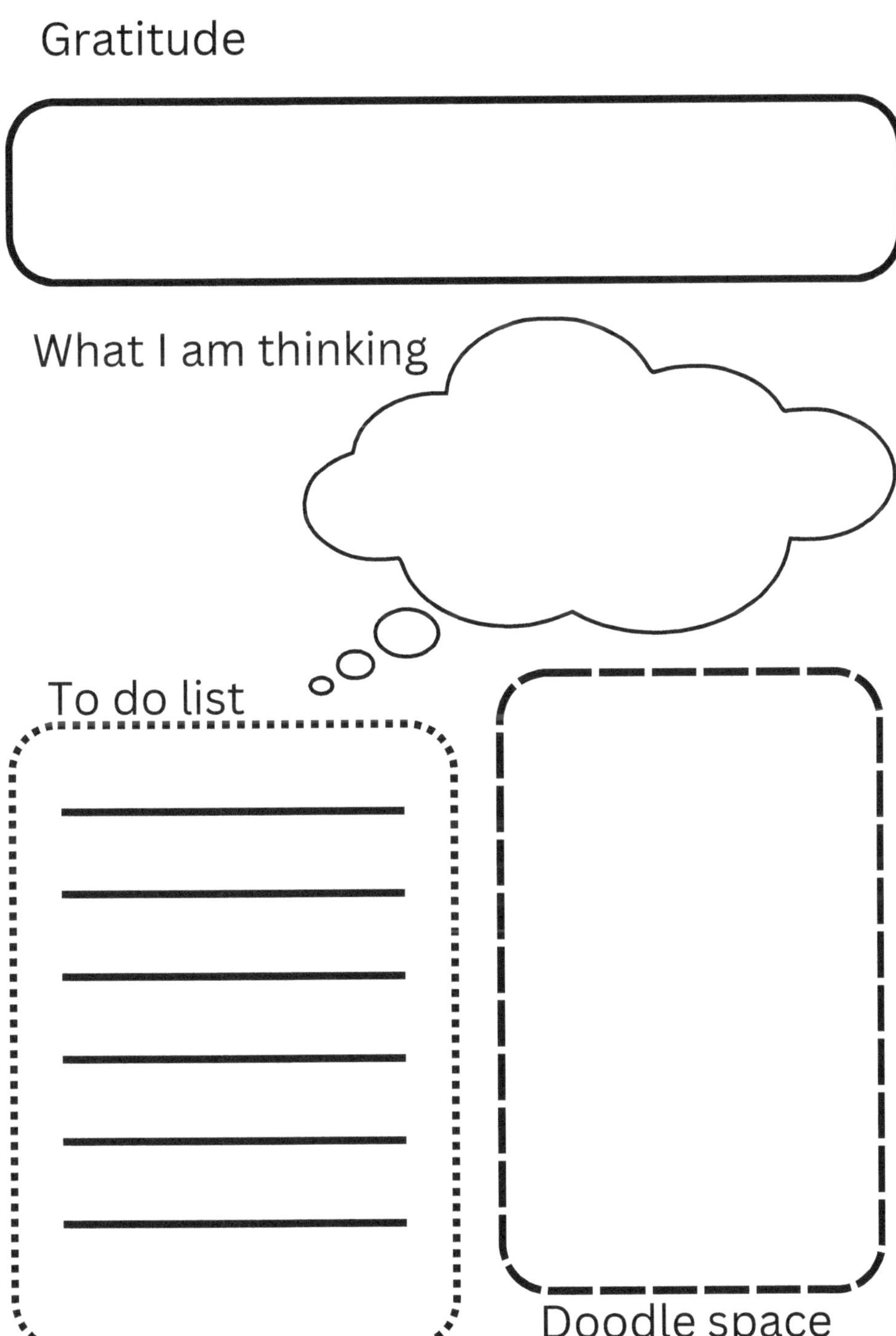

Date:...............

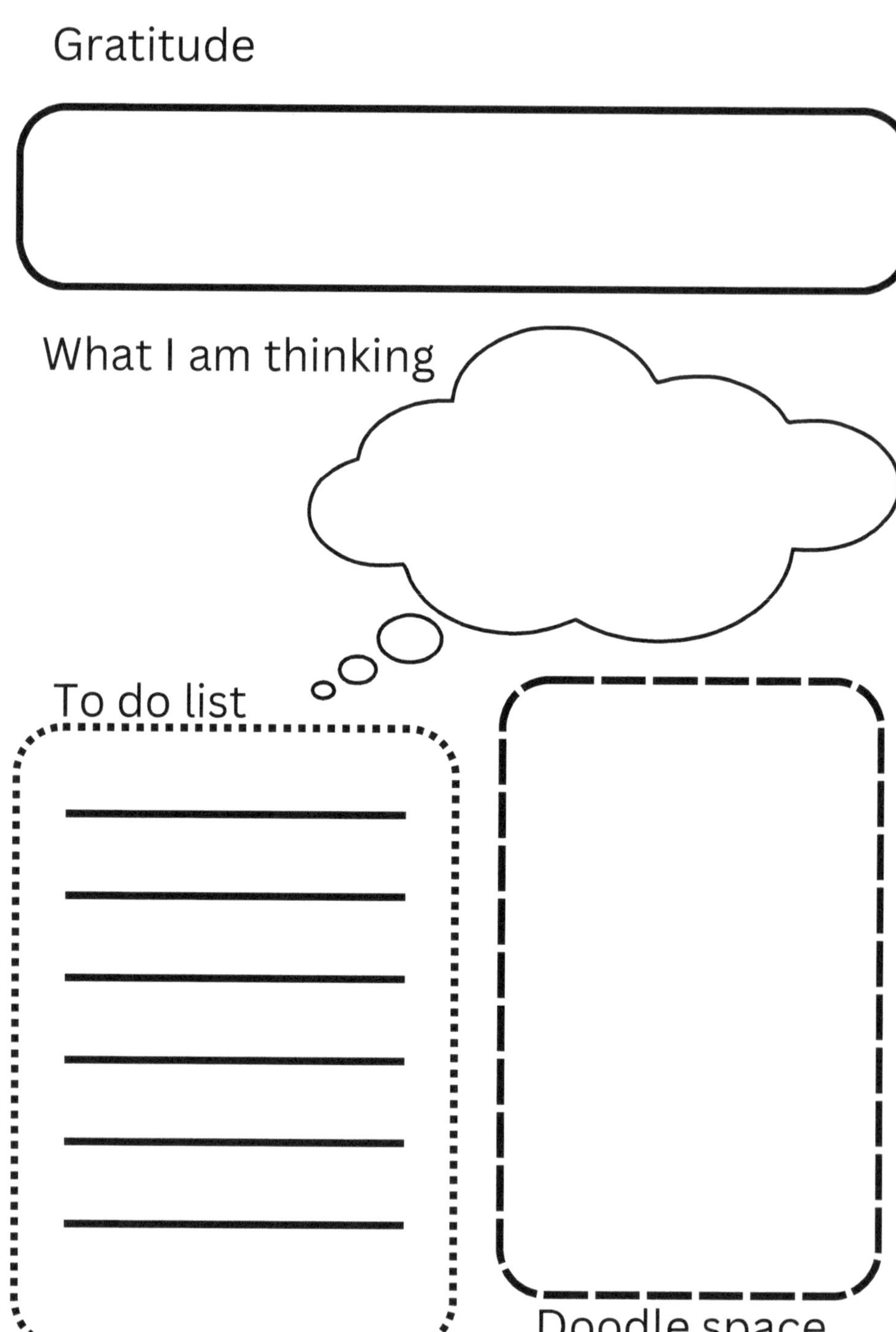

Date:..............

Date:..............

Gratitude

What I am thinking

To do list

Doodle space

Date:..............

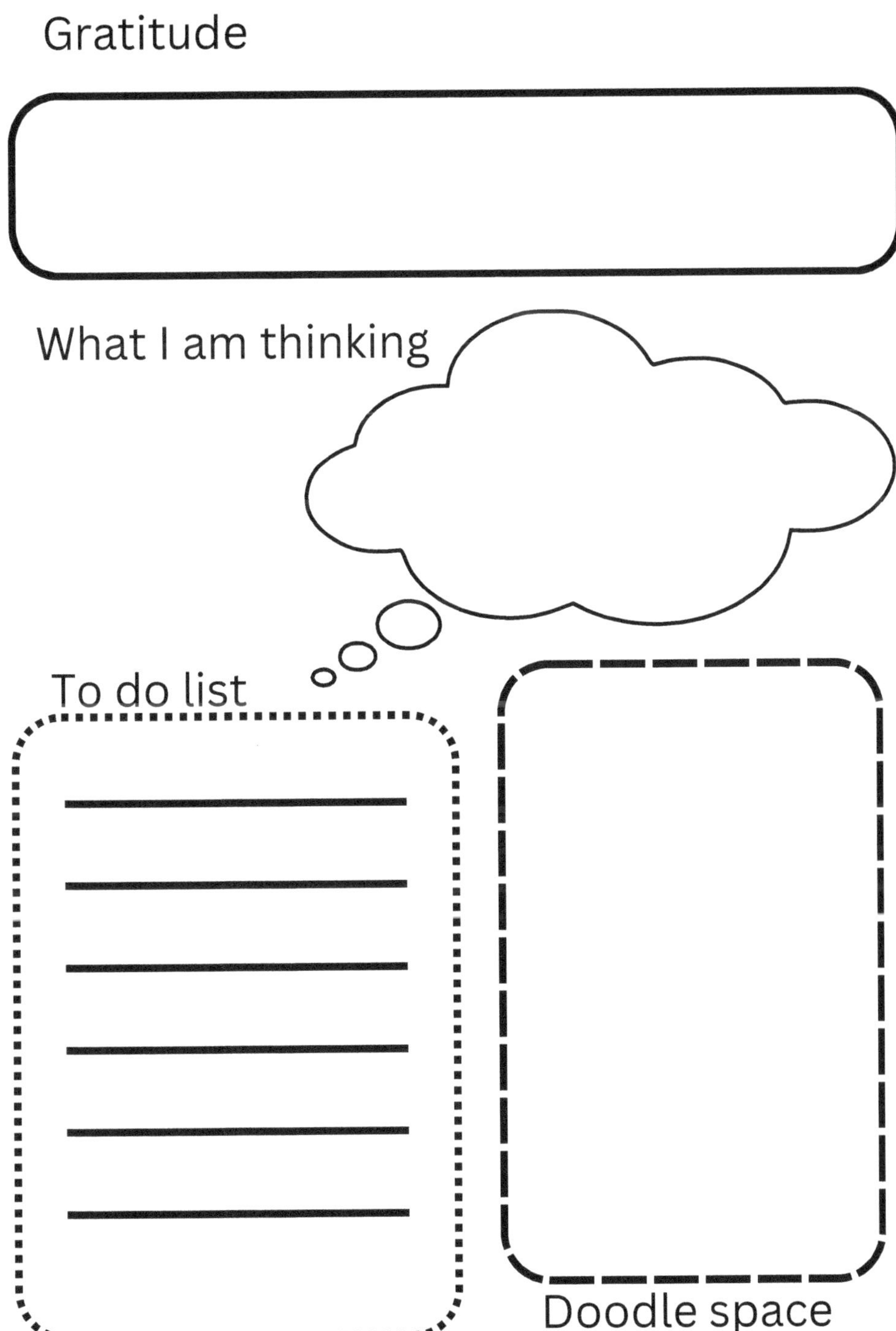

Date:...............

Gratitude

What I am thinking

To do list

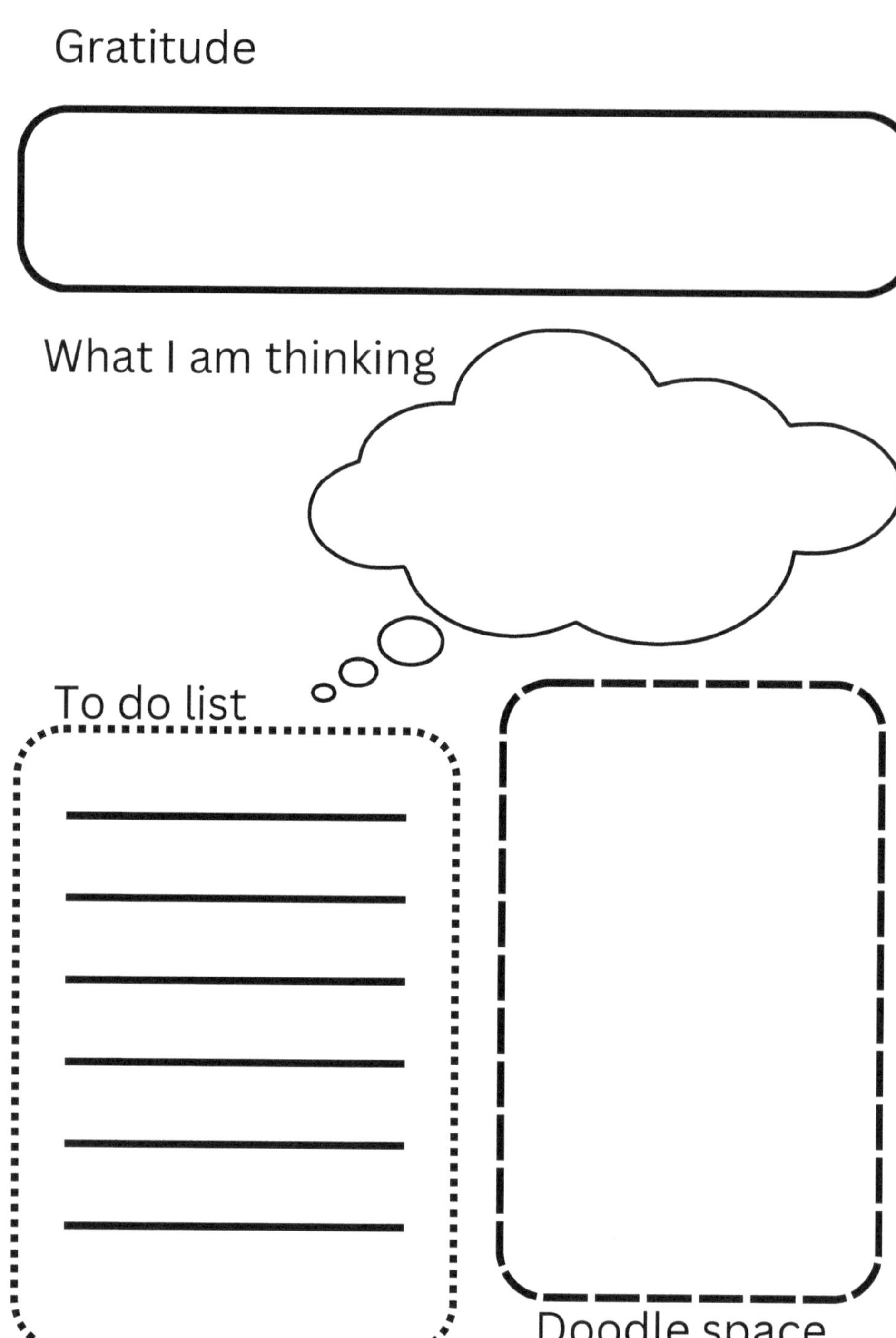

Doodle space

Date:..............

Weekly planner

Date:..../.../.....to..../.../....

MON

TUE

WED

THU

FRI

SAT

SUN

Date:..............

Date:..............

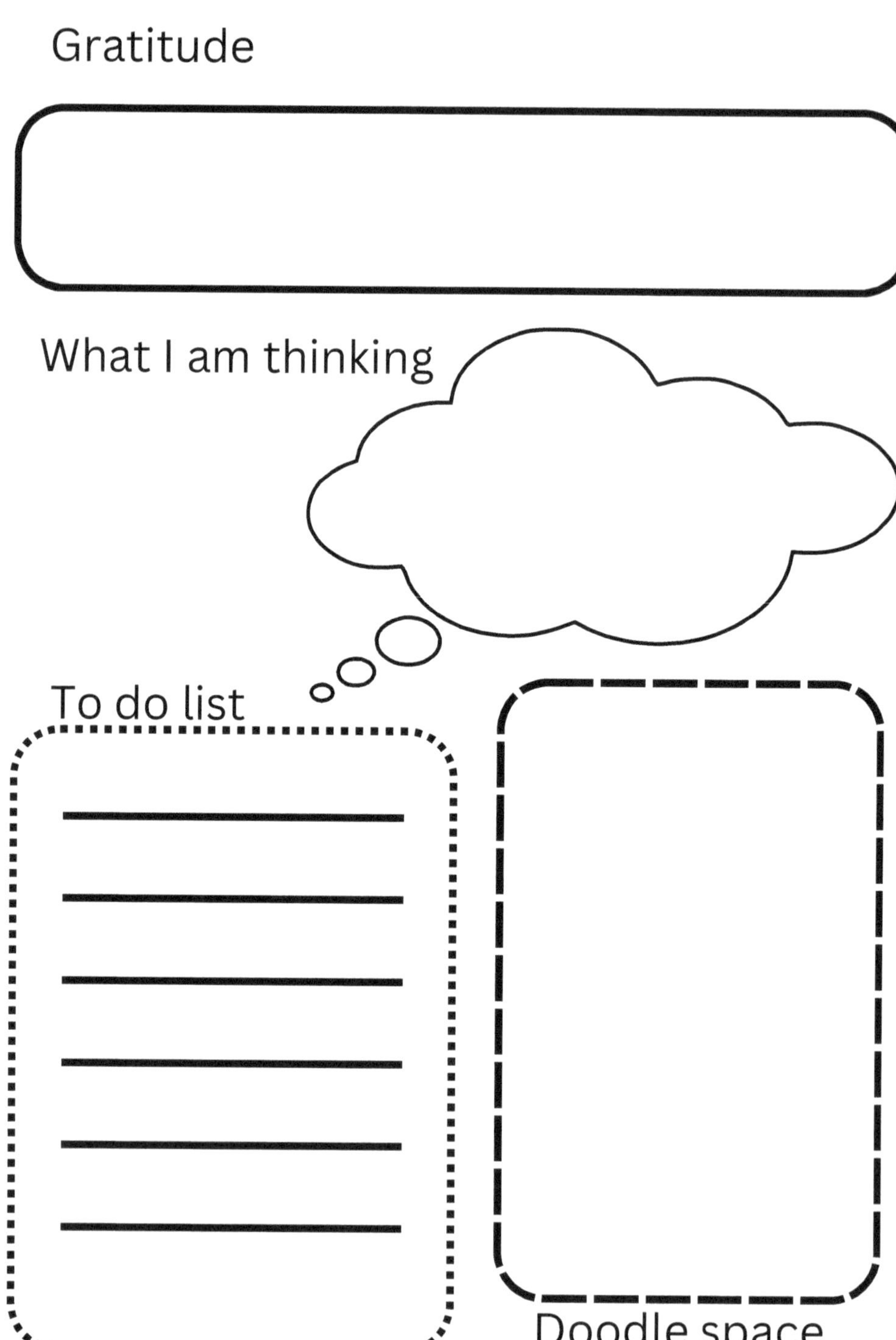

Date:..............

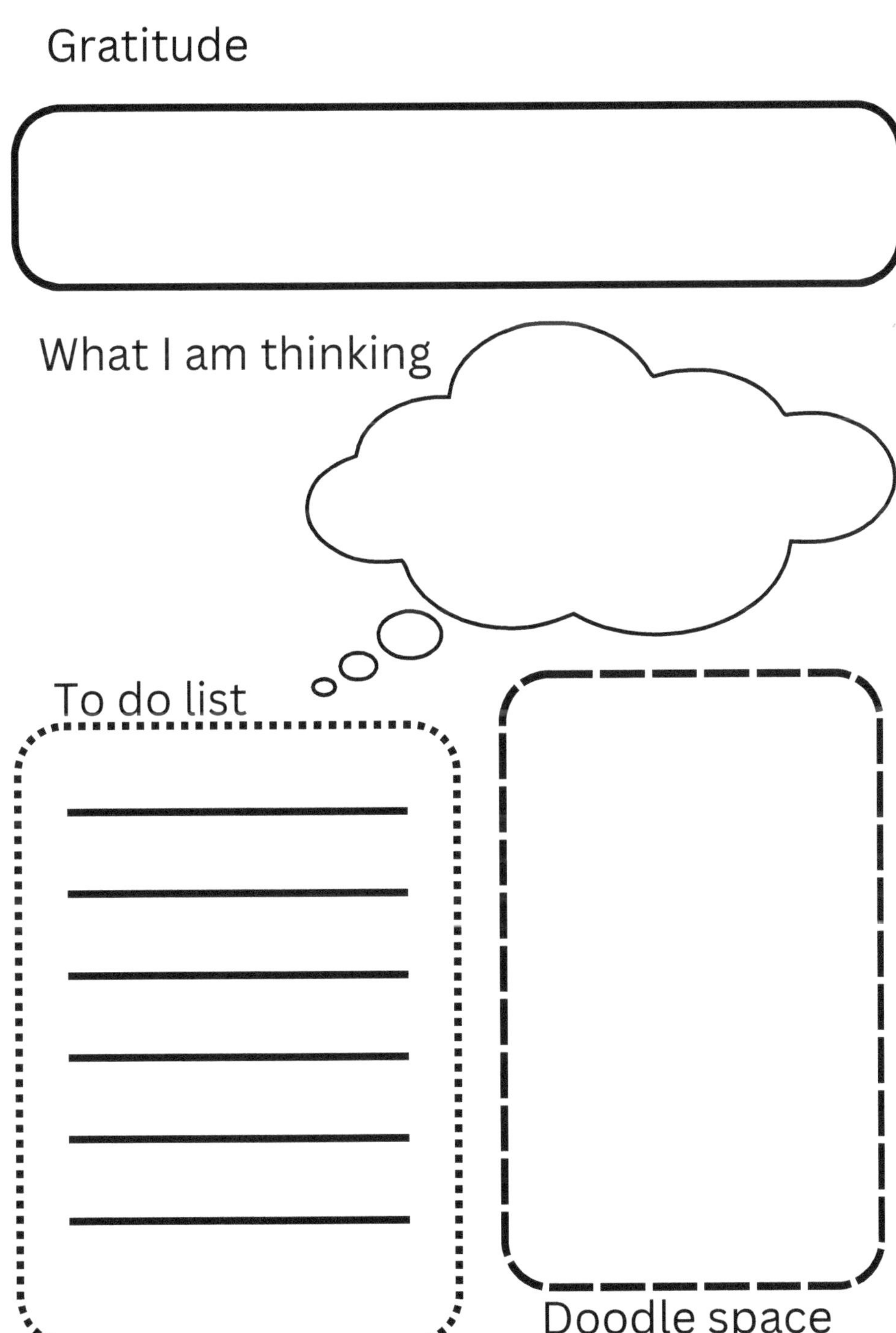

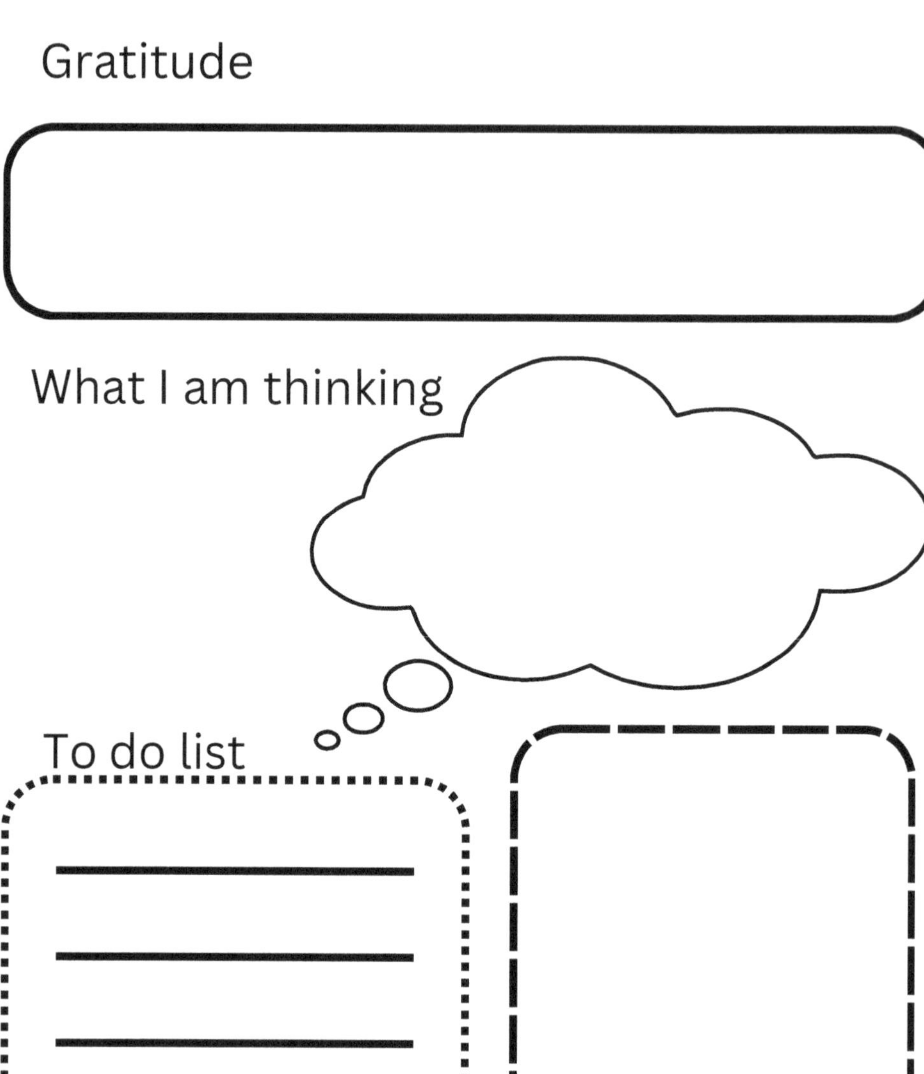

Doodle space

Date:..............

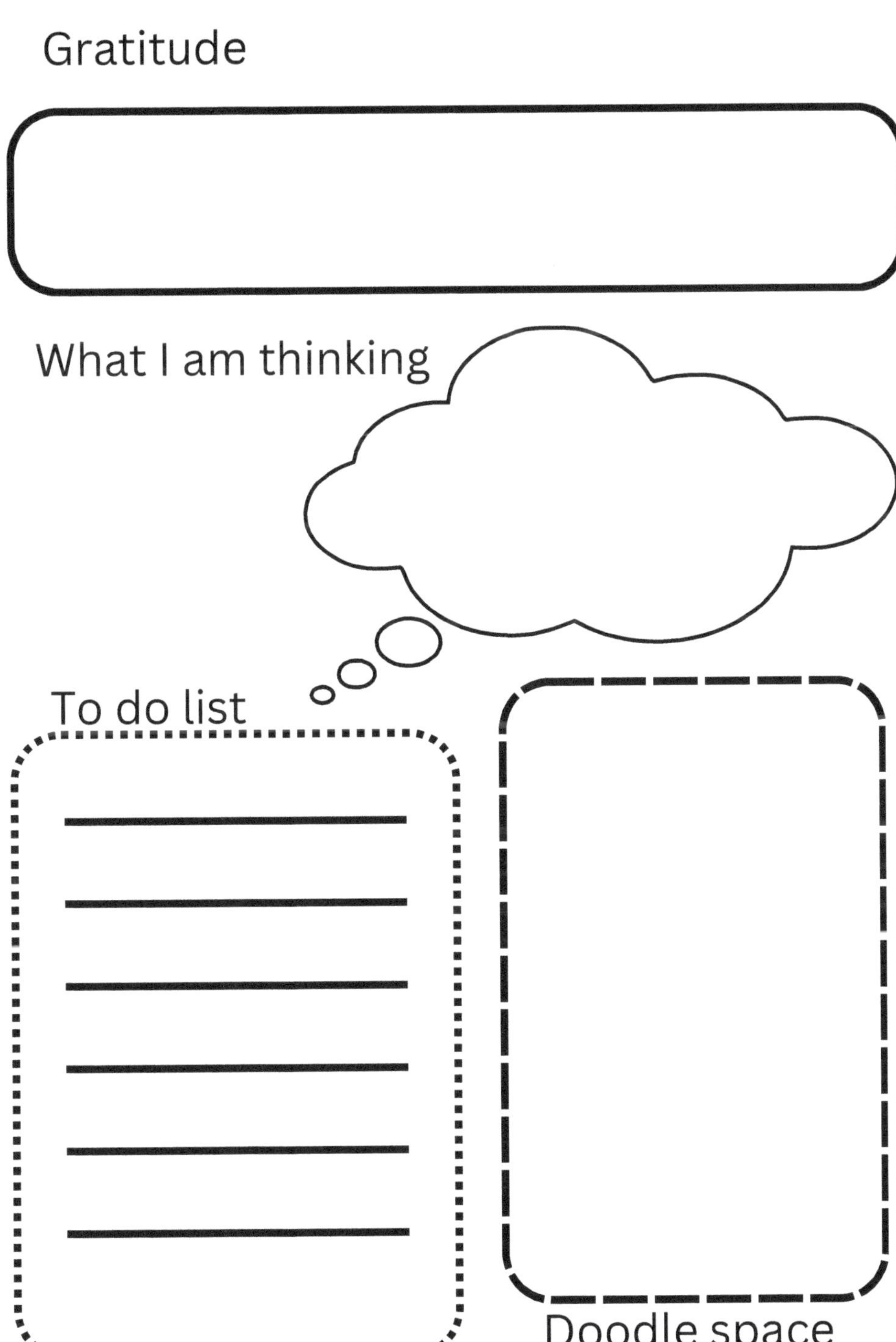

Date:..............

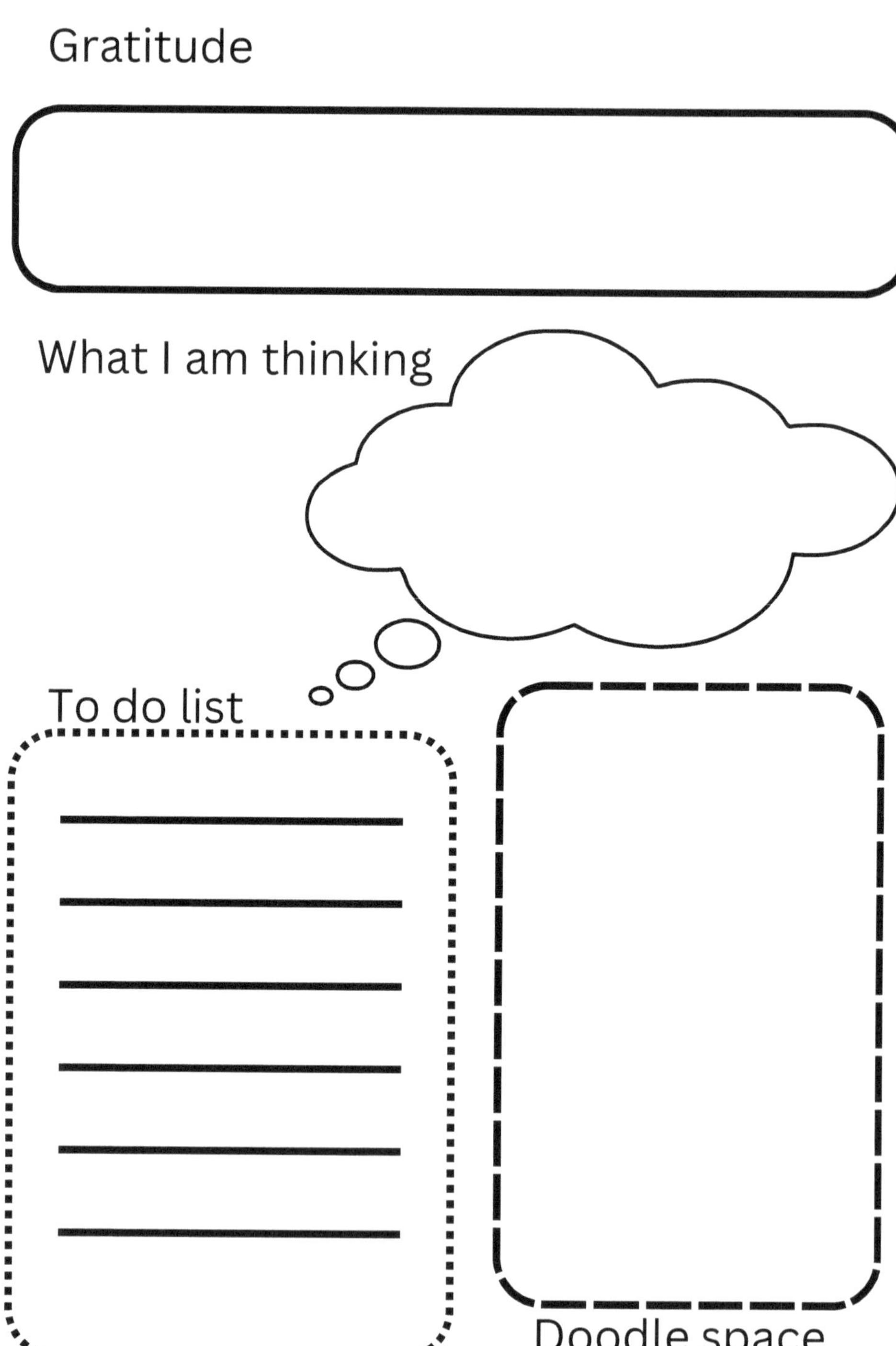

Date:..............

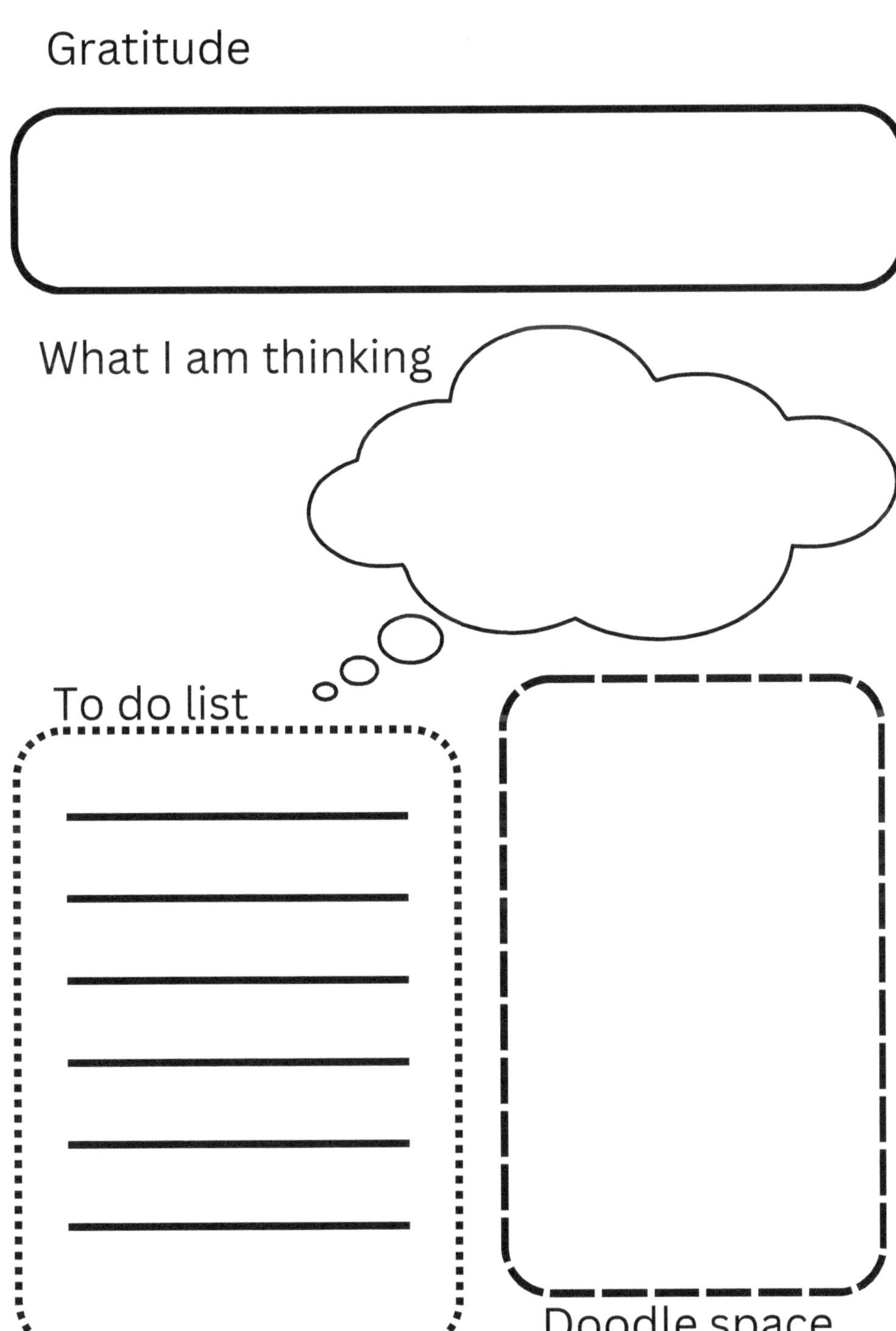

Weekly planner

Date:...../.../.....to..../.../....

MON

TUE

WED

THU

FRI

SAT

SUN

Date:..............

Date:..............

Gratitude

What I am thinking

To do list

Doodle space

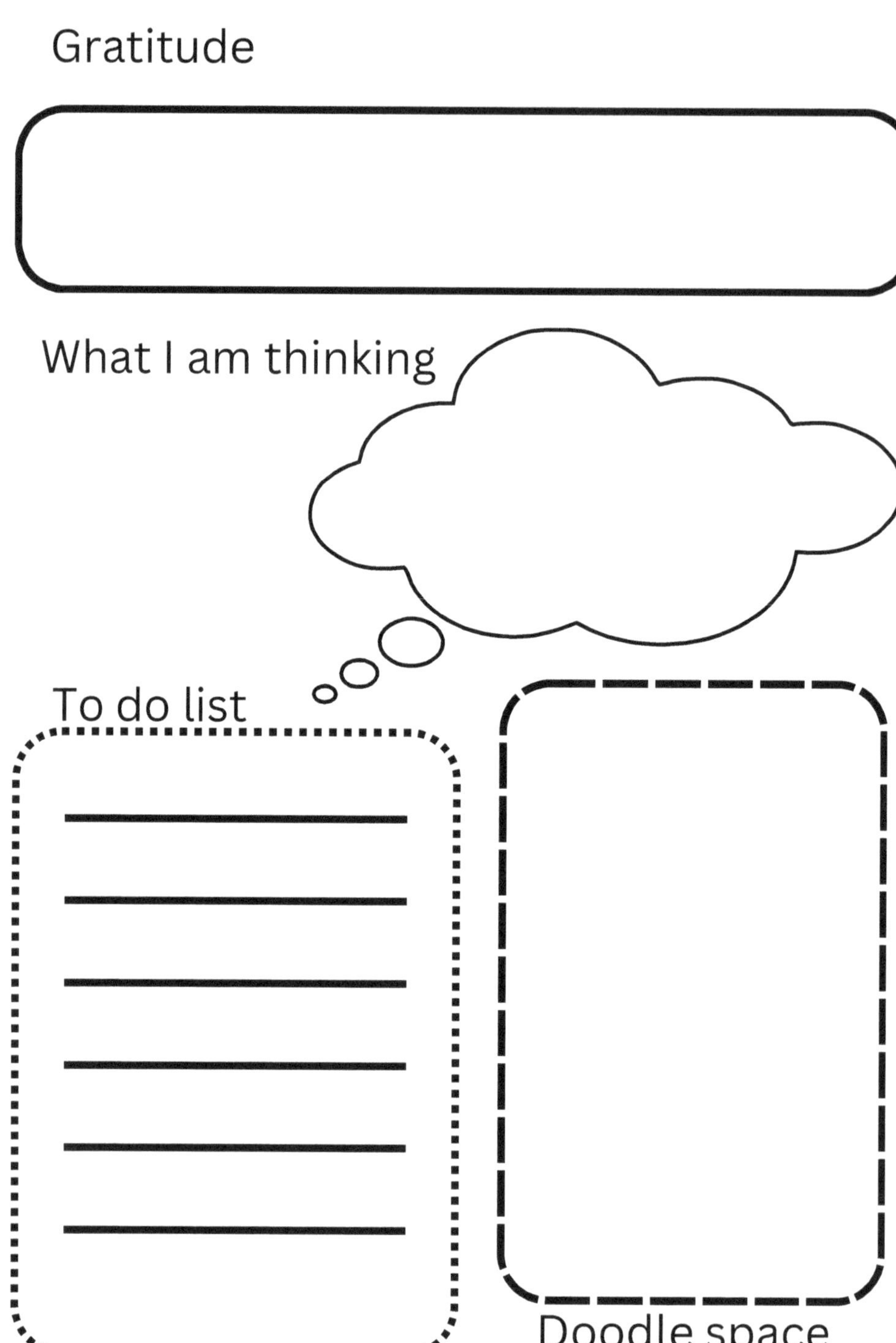

Date:..............

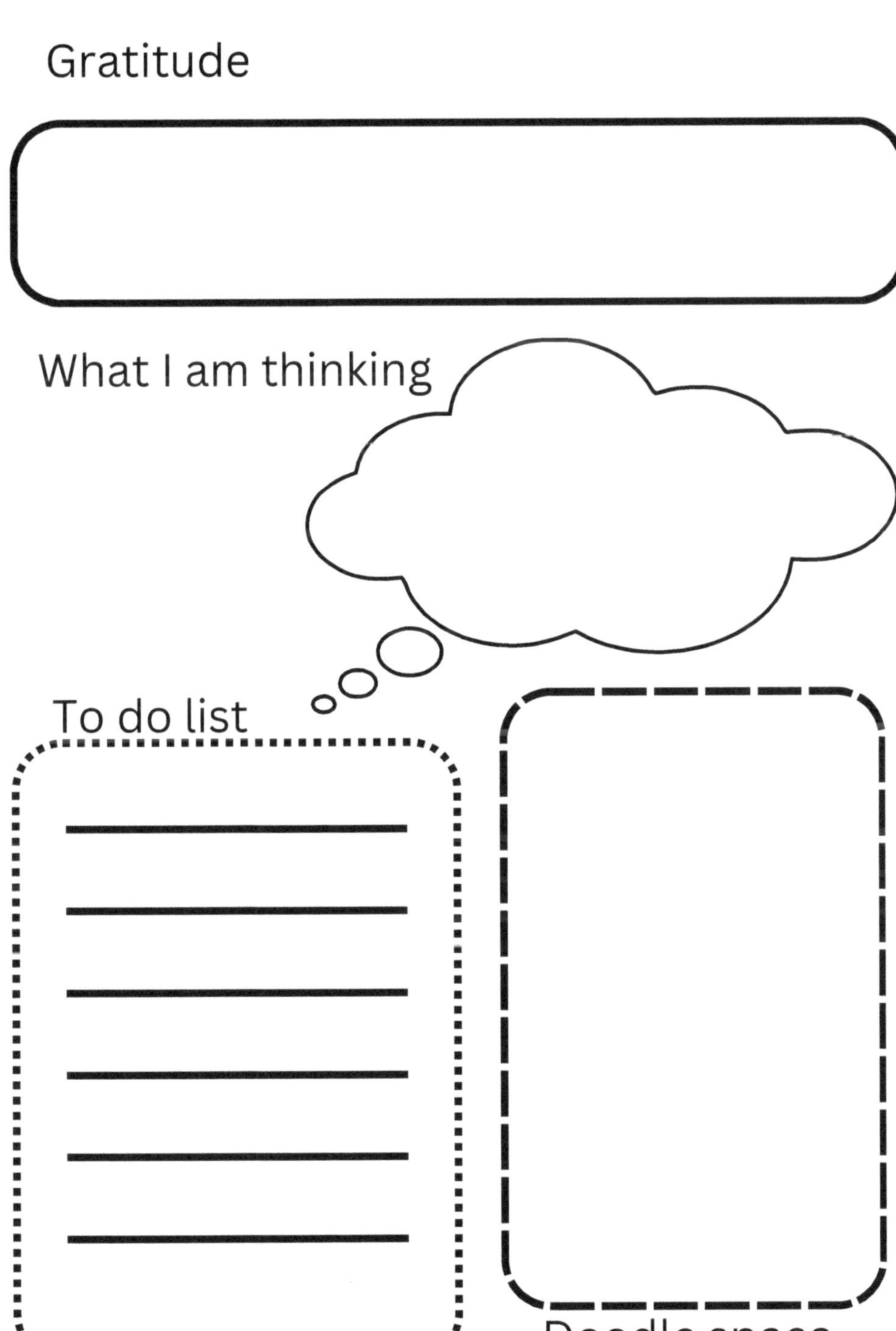
Gratitude

What I am thinking

To do list

Doodle space

Date:..............

Date:..............

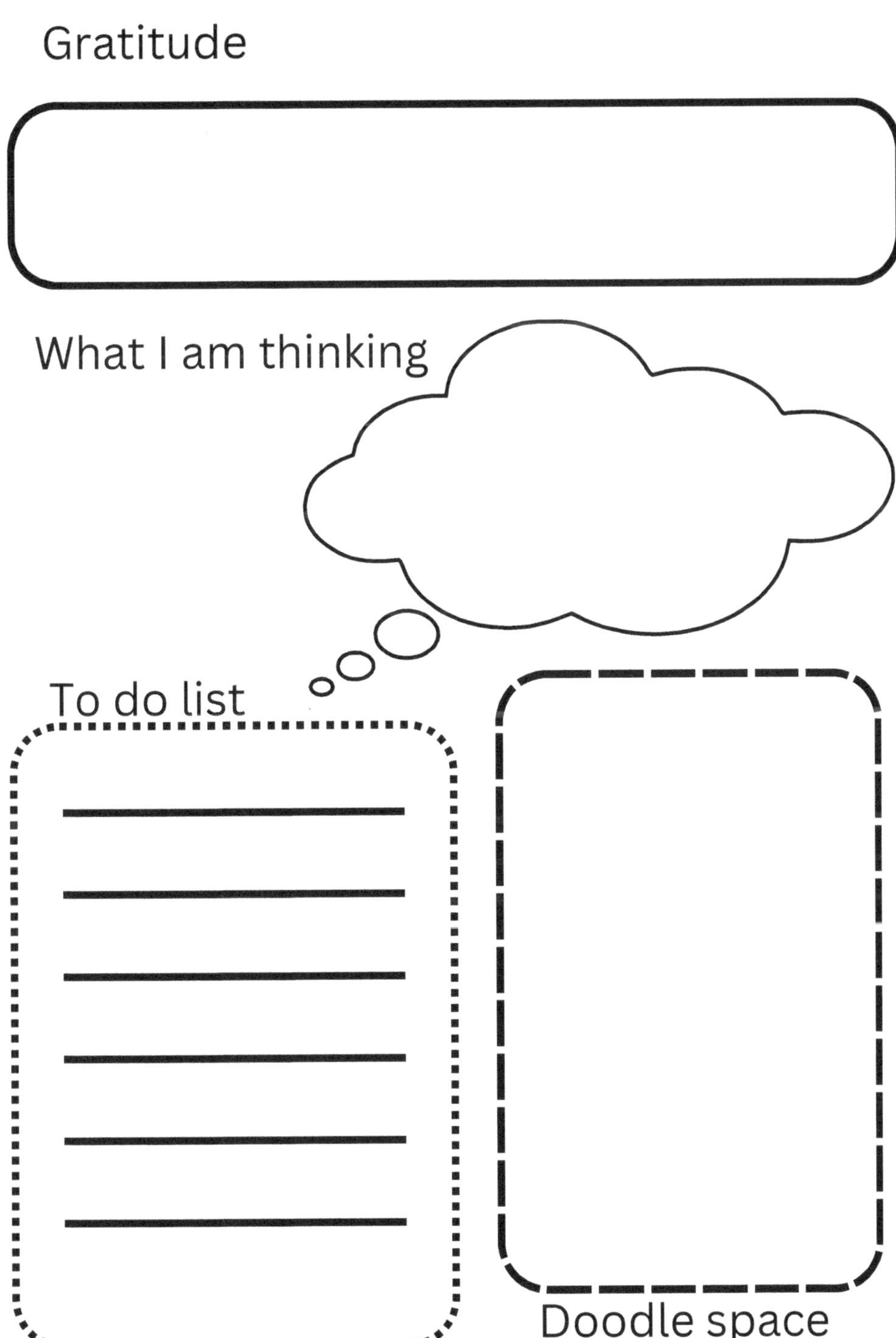

Date:..............

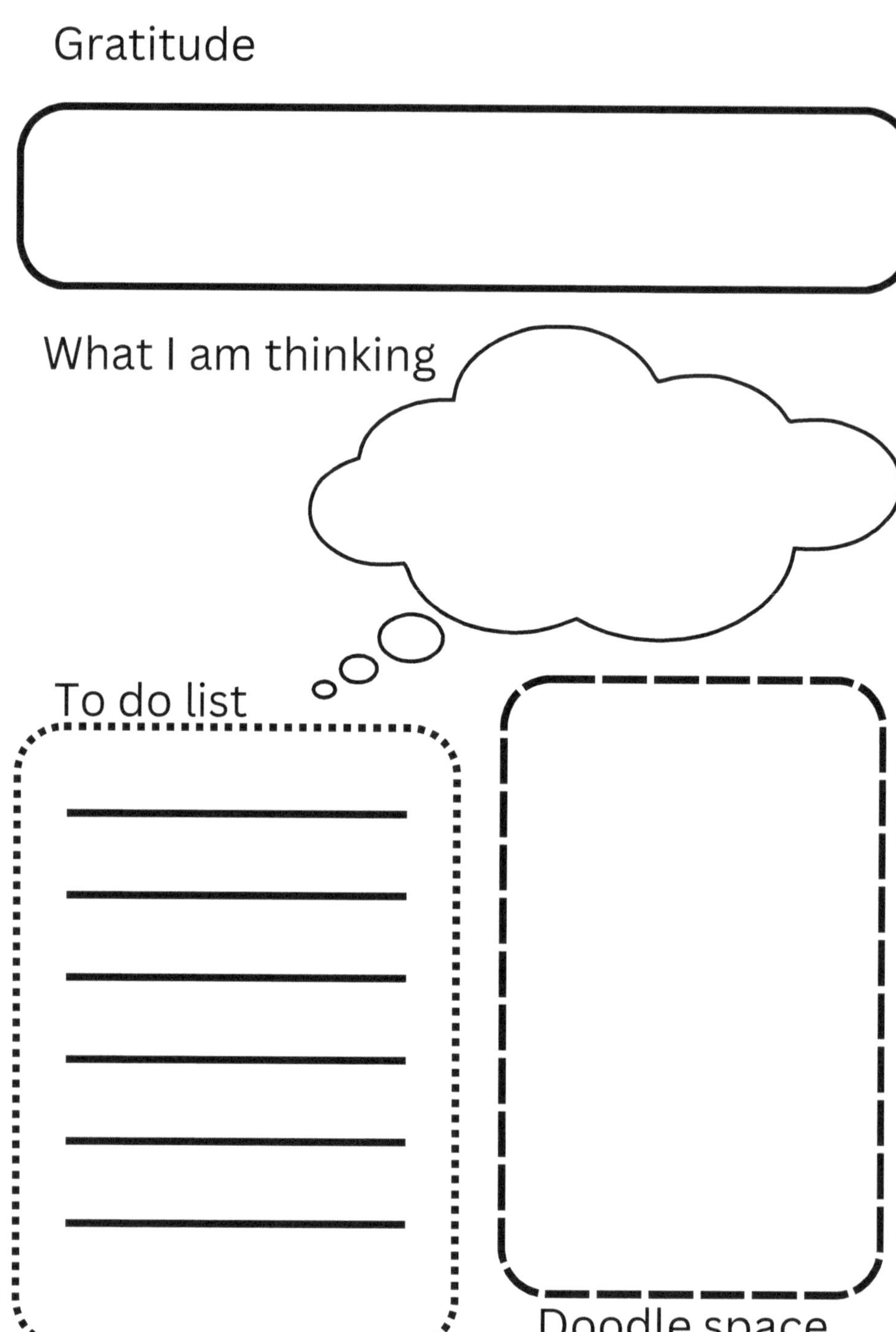

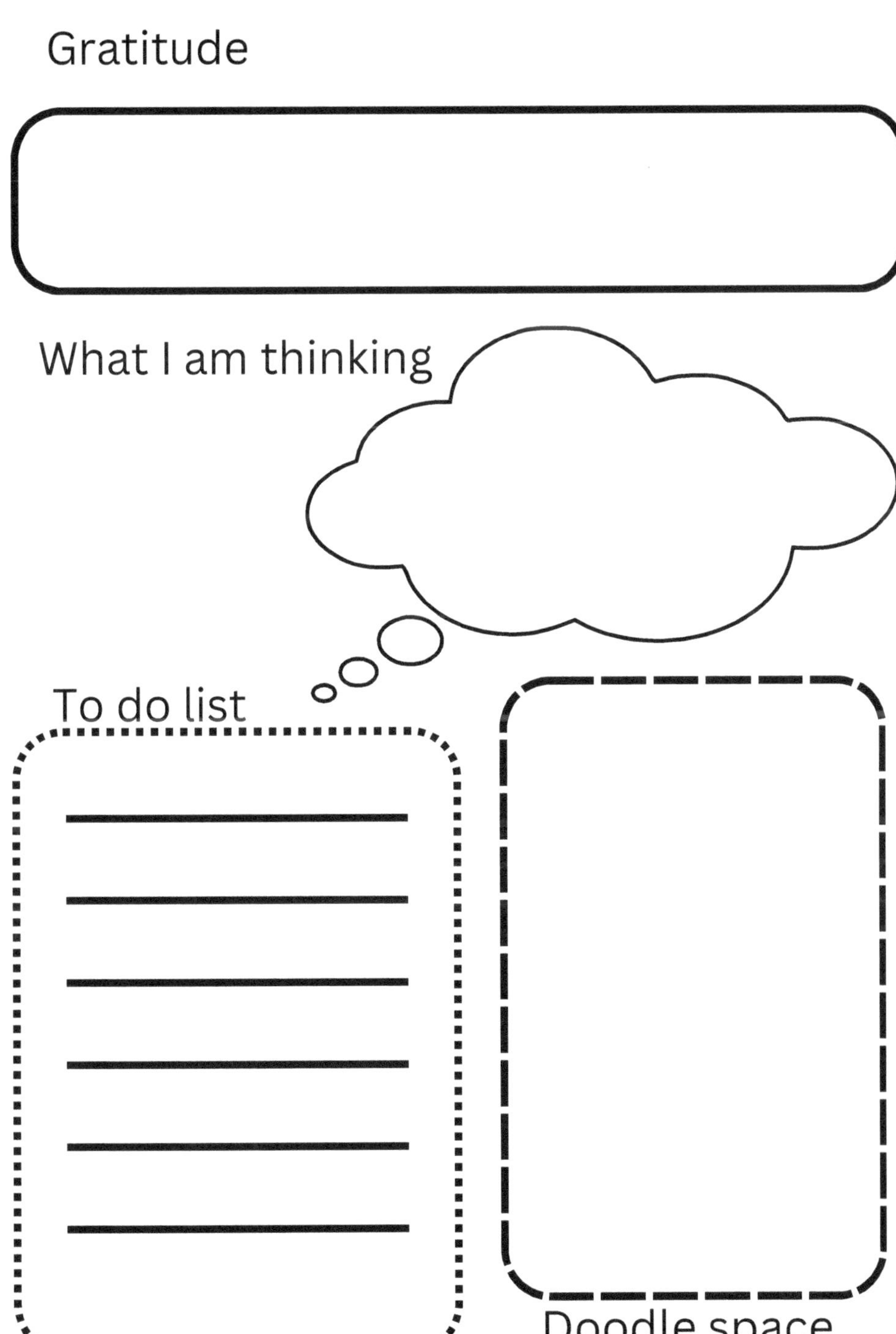
Date:..............
Gratitude
What I am thinking
To do list
Doodle space

Weekly planner

Date:..../.../.....to..../.../....

MON

TUE

WED

THU

FRI

SAT

SUN

Date:..............

Date:..............

Date:..............

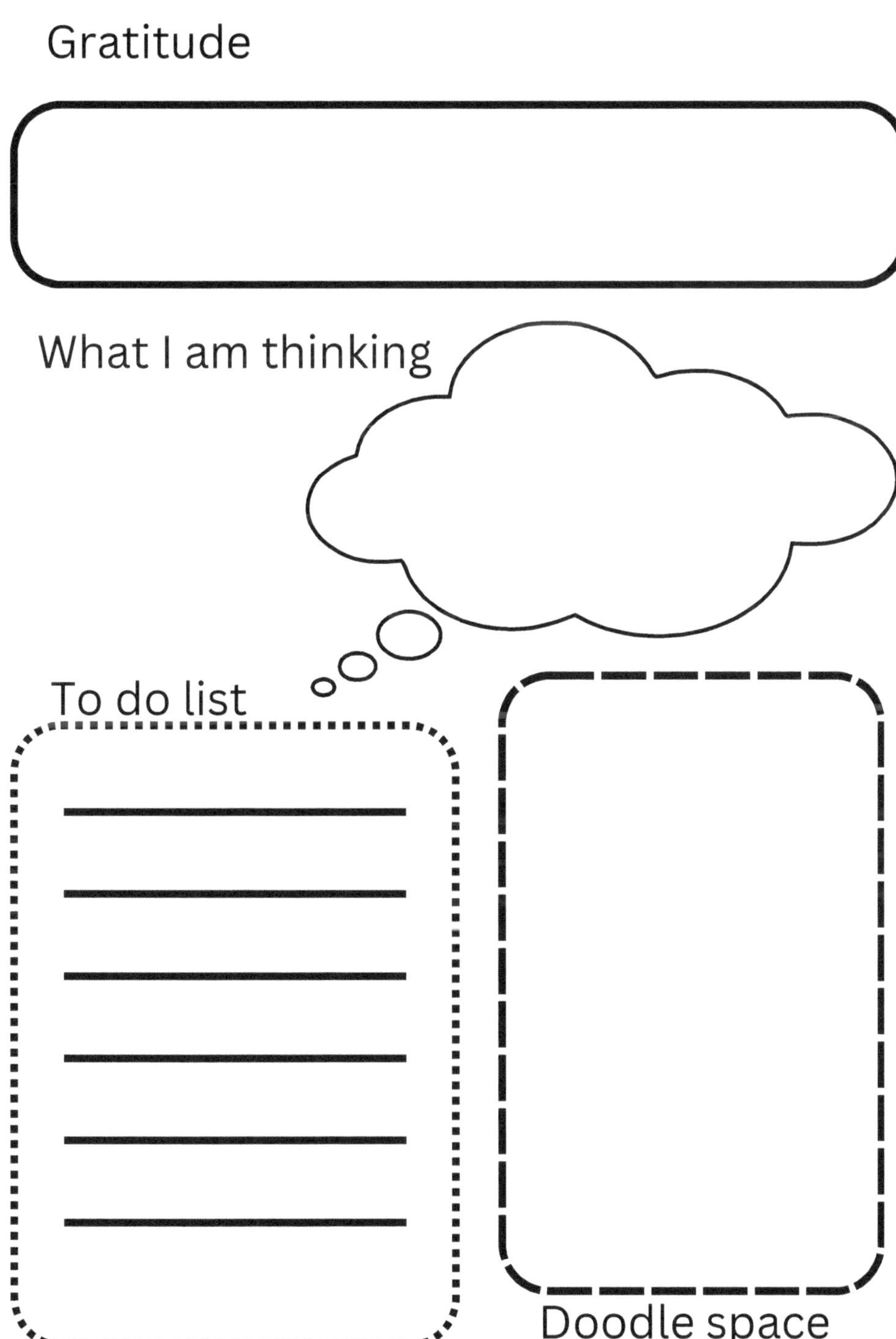

Date:..............

Date:..............

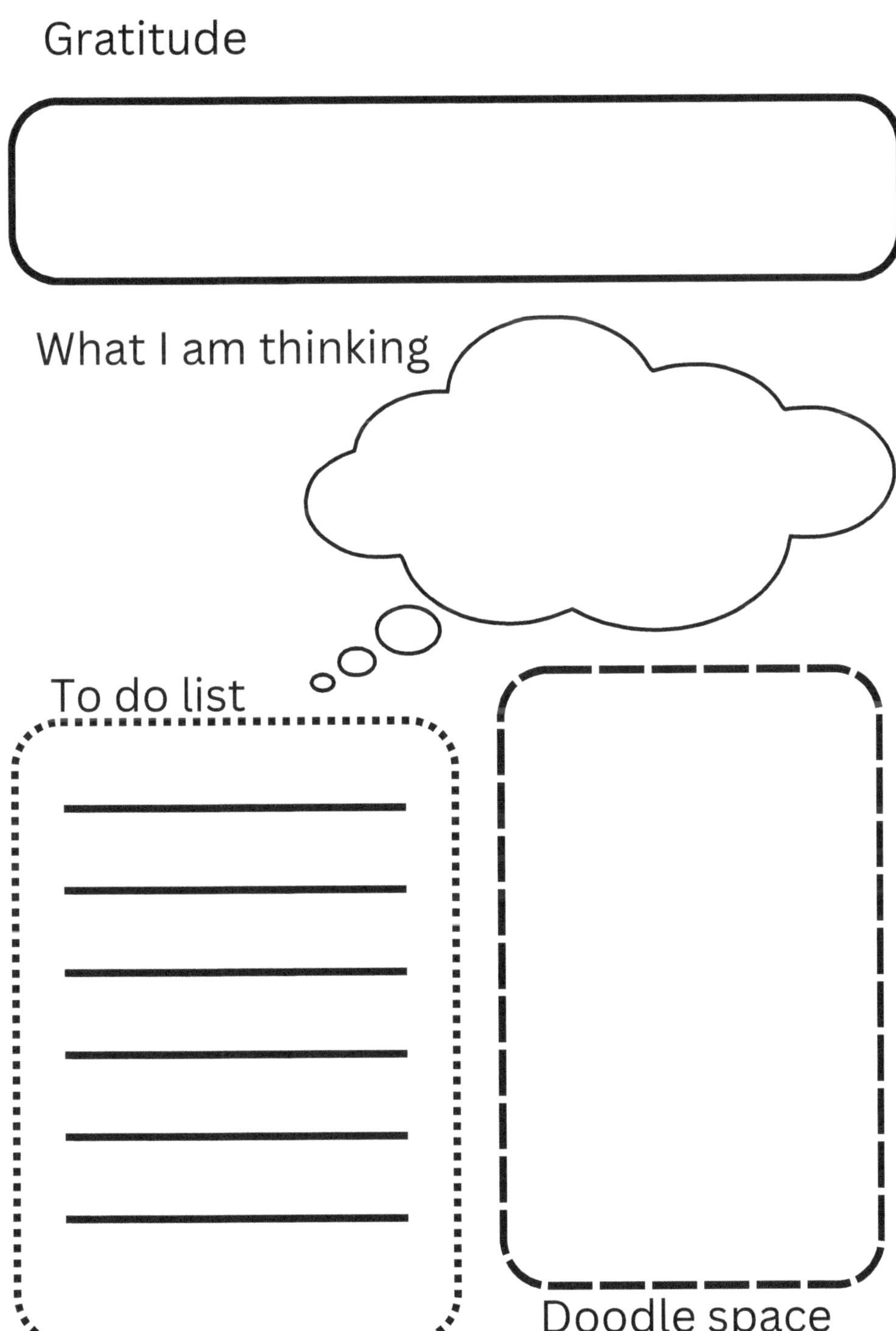

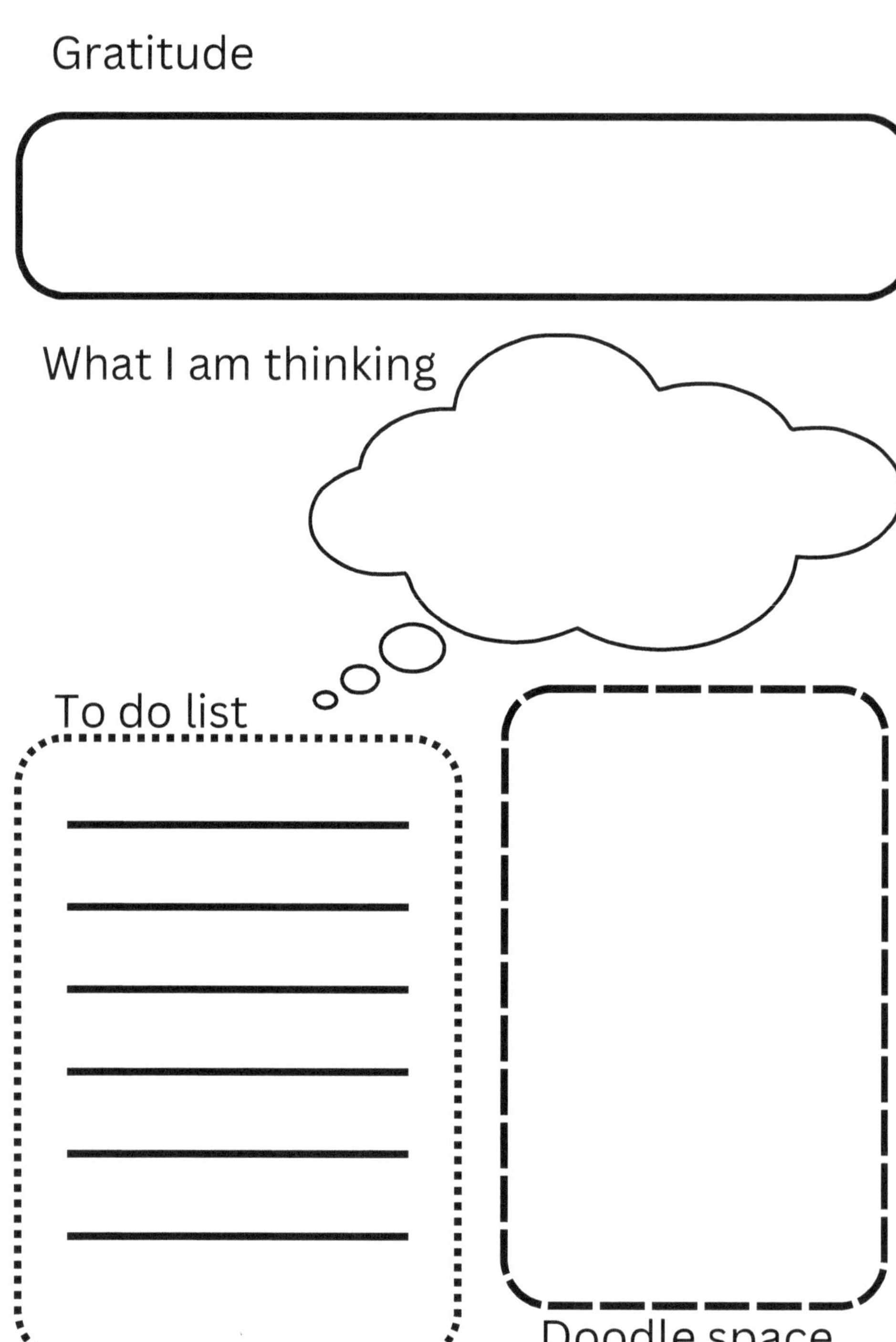
Date:..............
Gratitude
What I am thinking
To do list
Doodle space

Date:..............

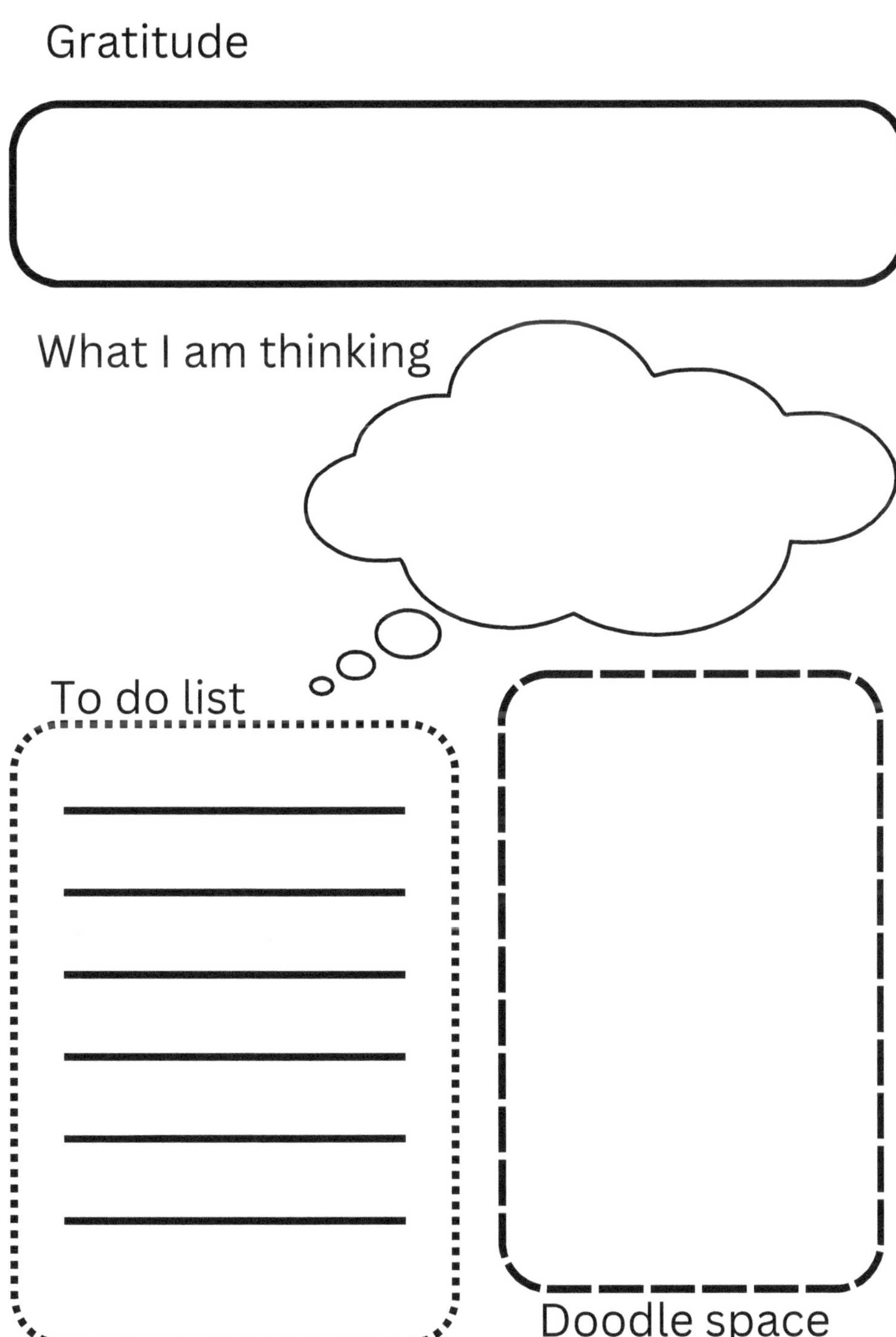

Weekly planner

Date:..../.../.....to..../.../....

MON

TUE

WED

THU

FRI

SAT

SUN

Date:...............

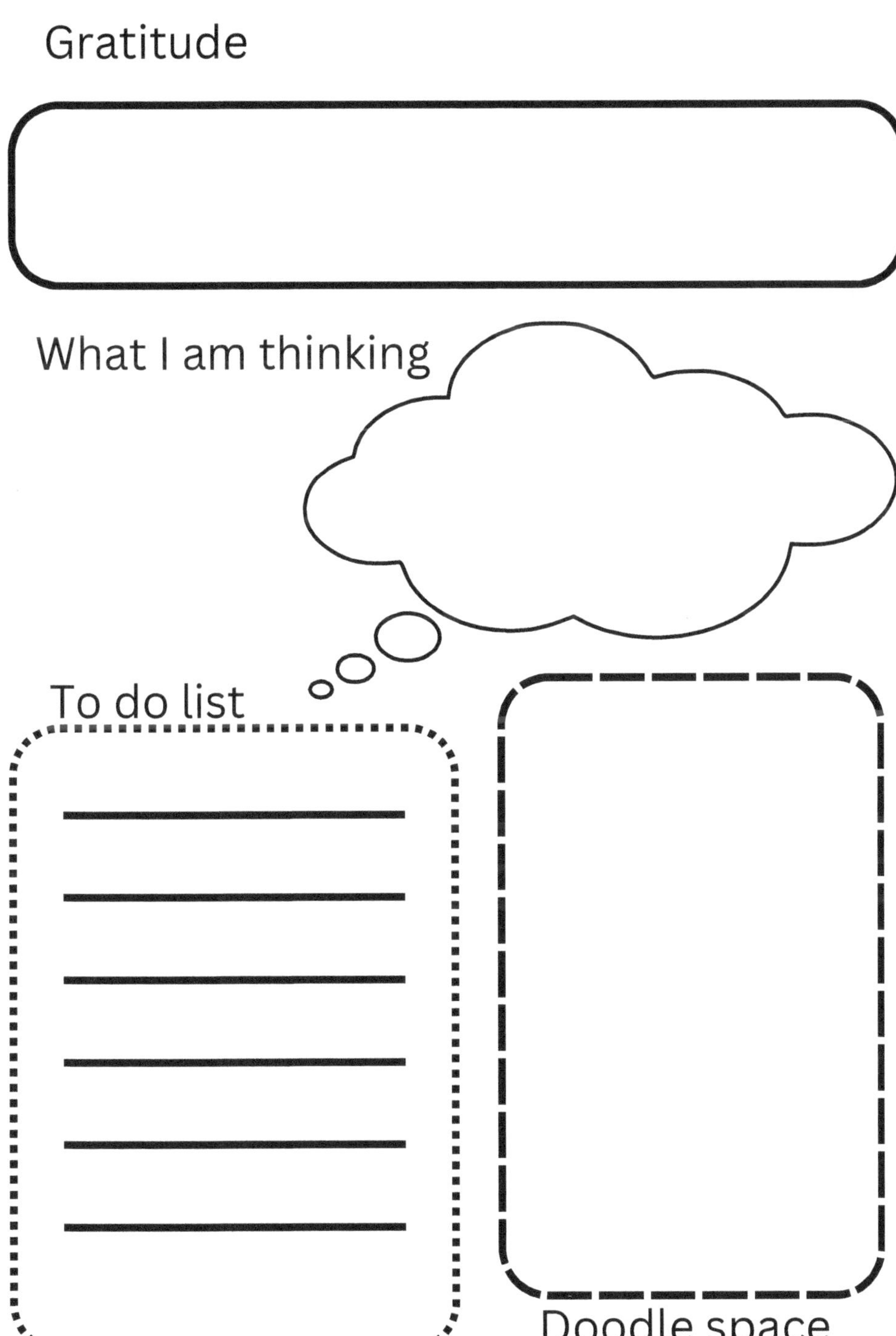

Date:...............

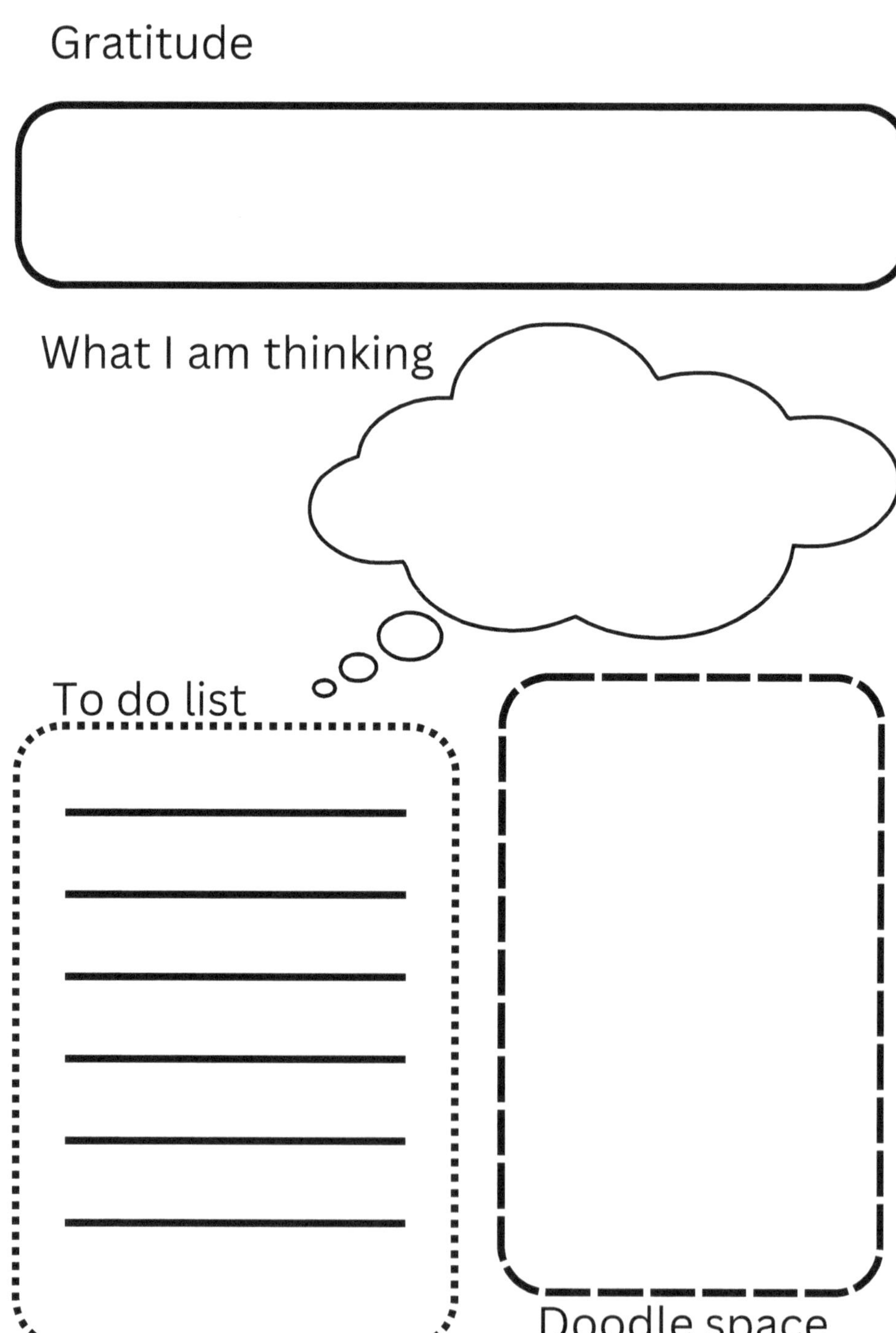

Date:..............

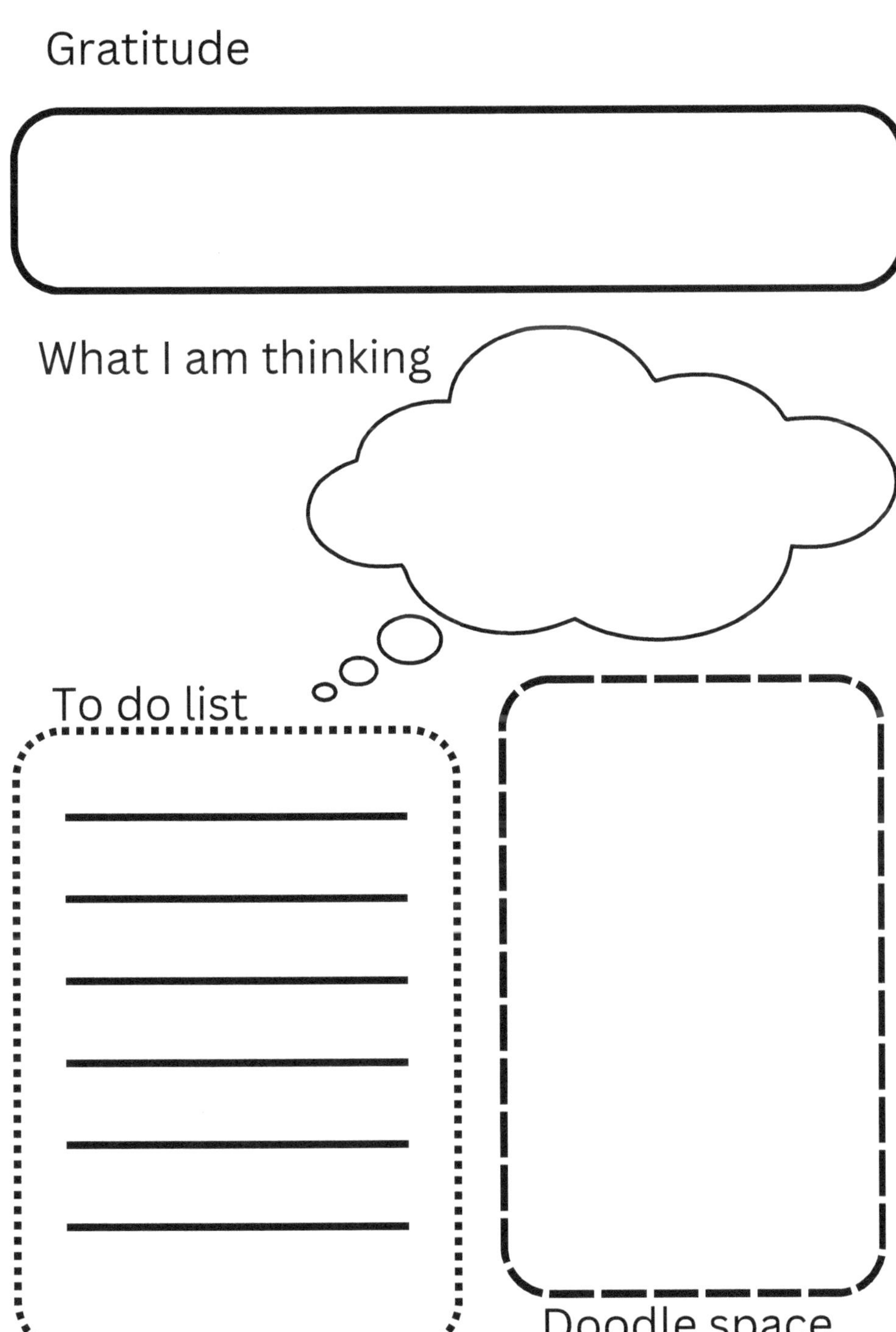

Date:..............

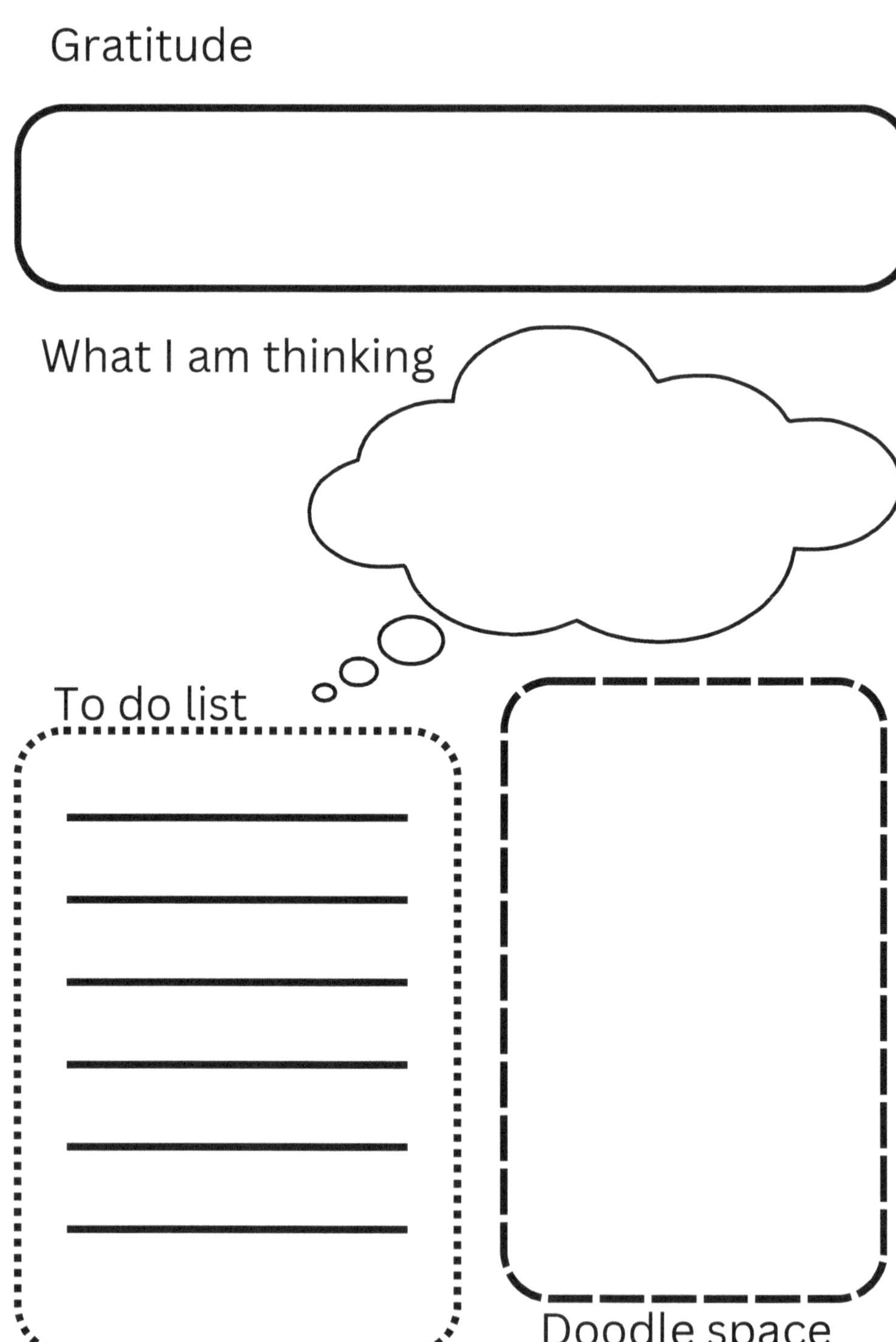

Date:..............

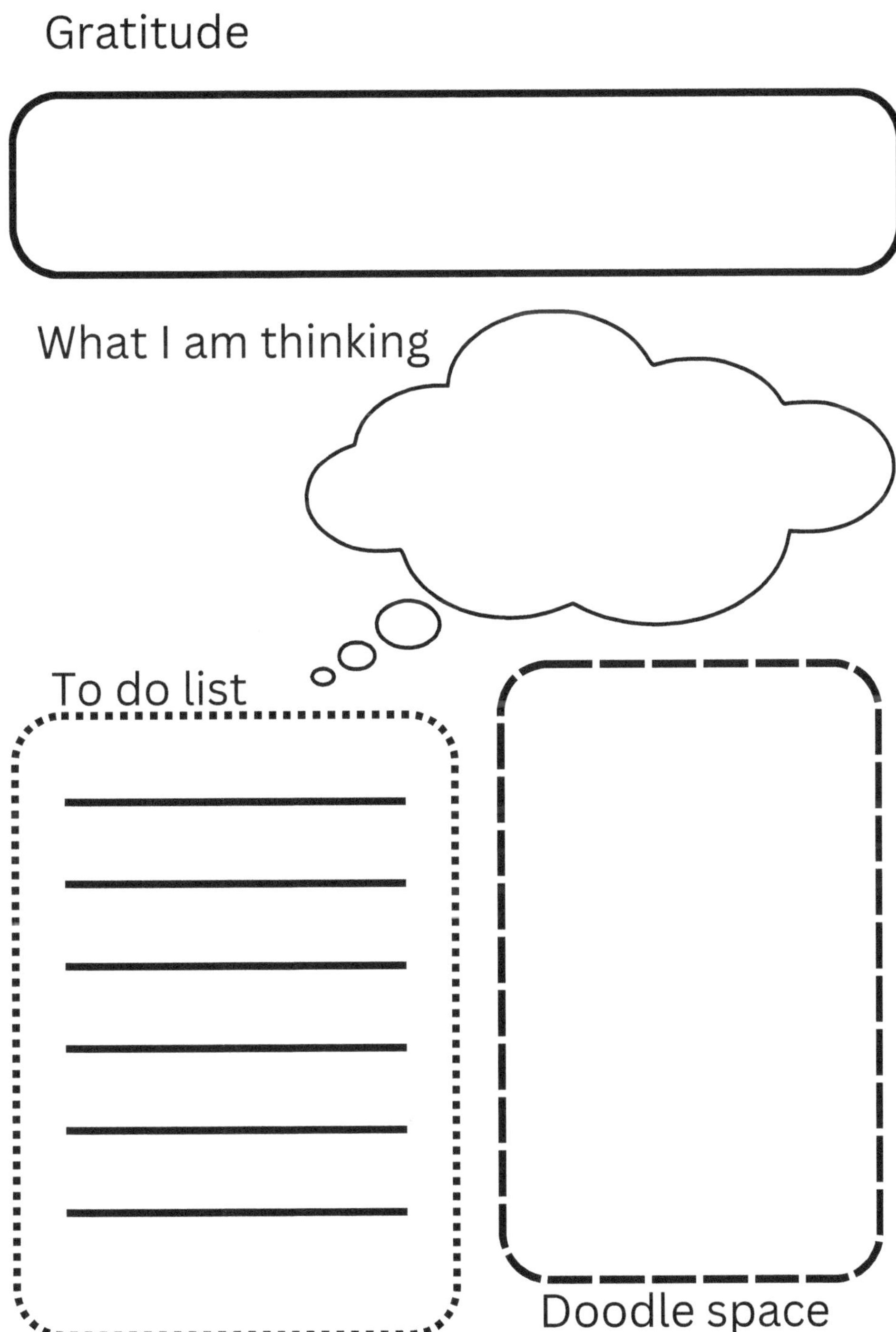

Date:..............

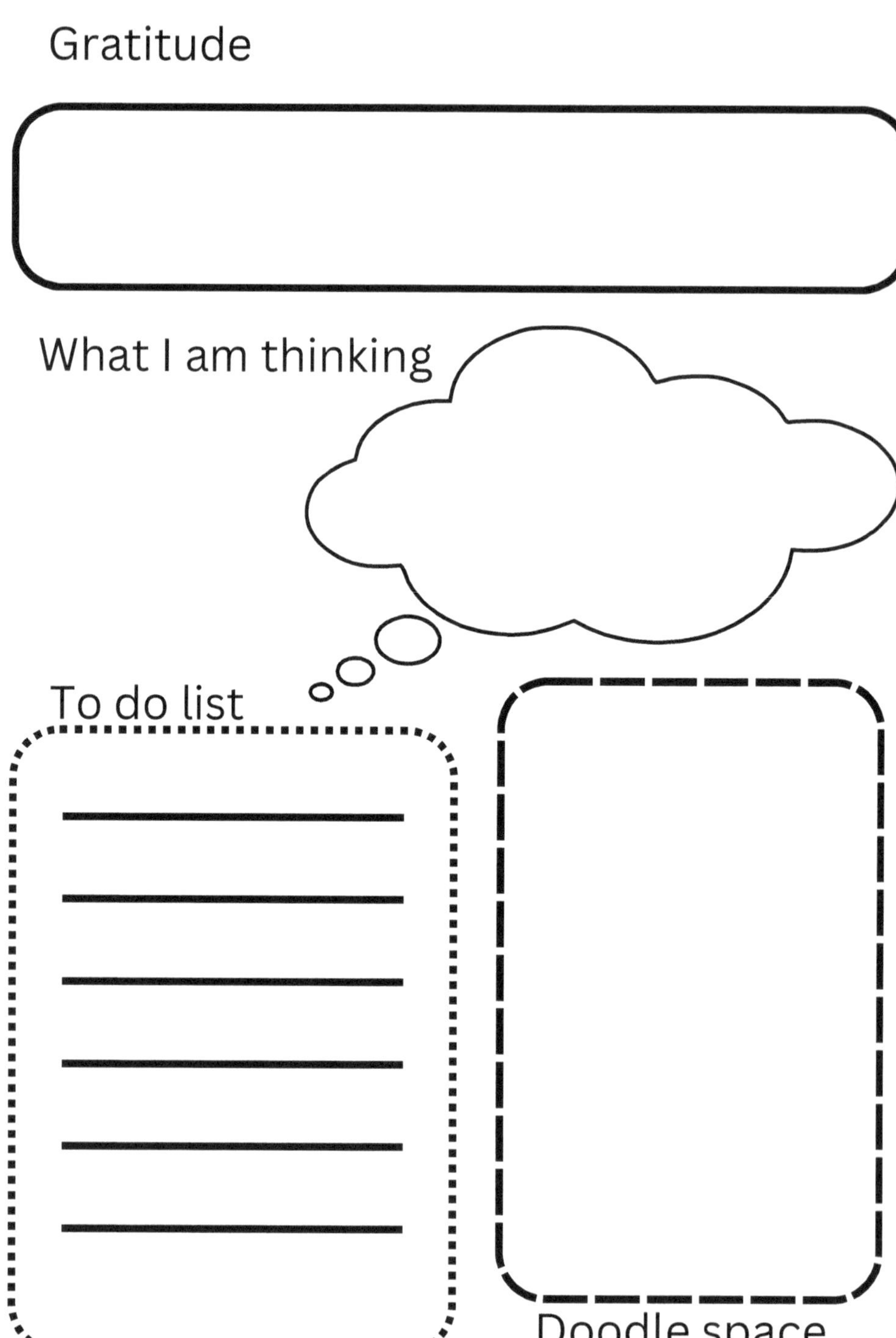

Date:..............

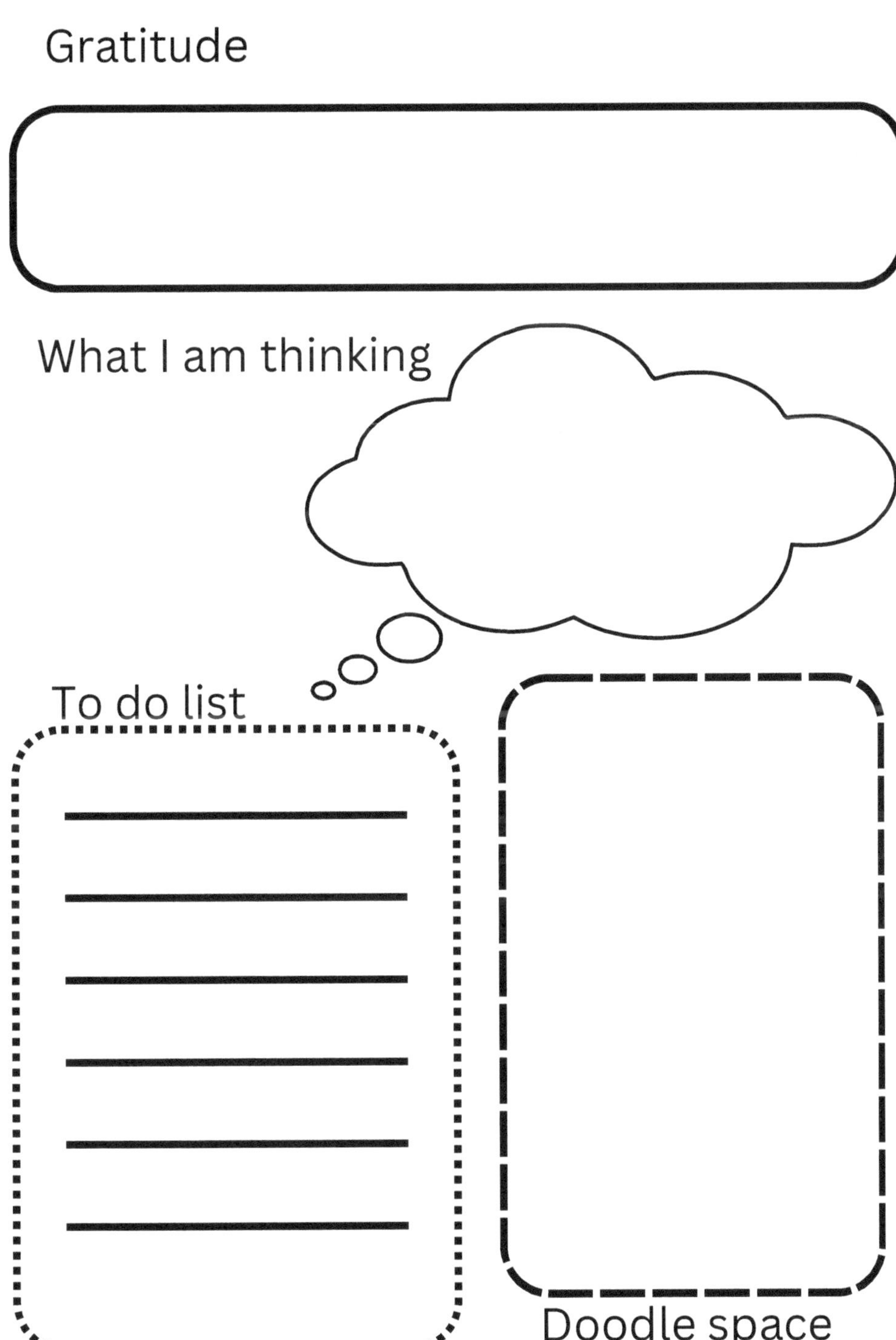

Weekly planner

Date:..../.../.....to..../.../....

MON

TUE

WED

THU

FRI

SAT

SUN

Date:..............

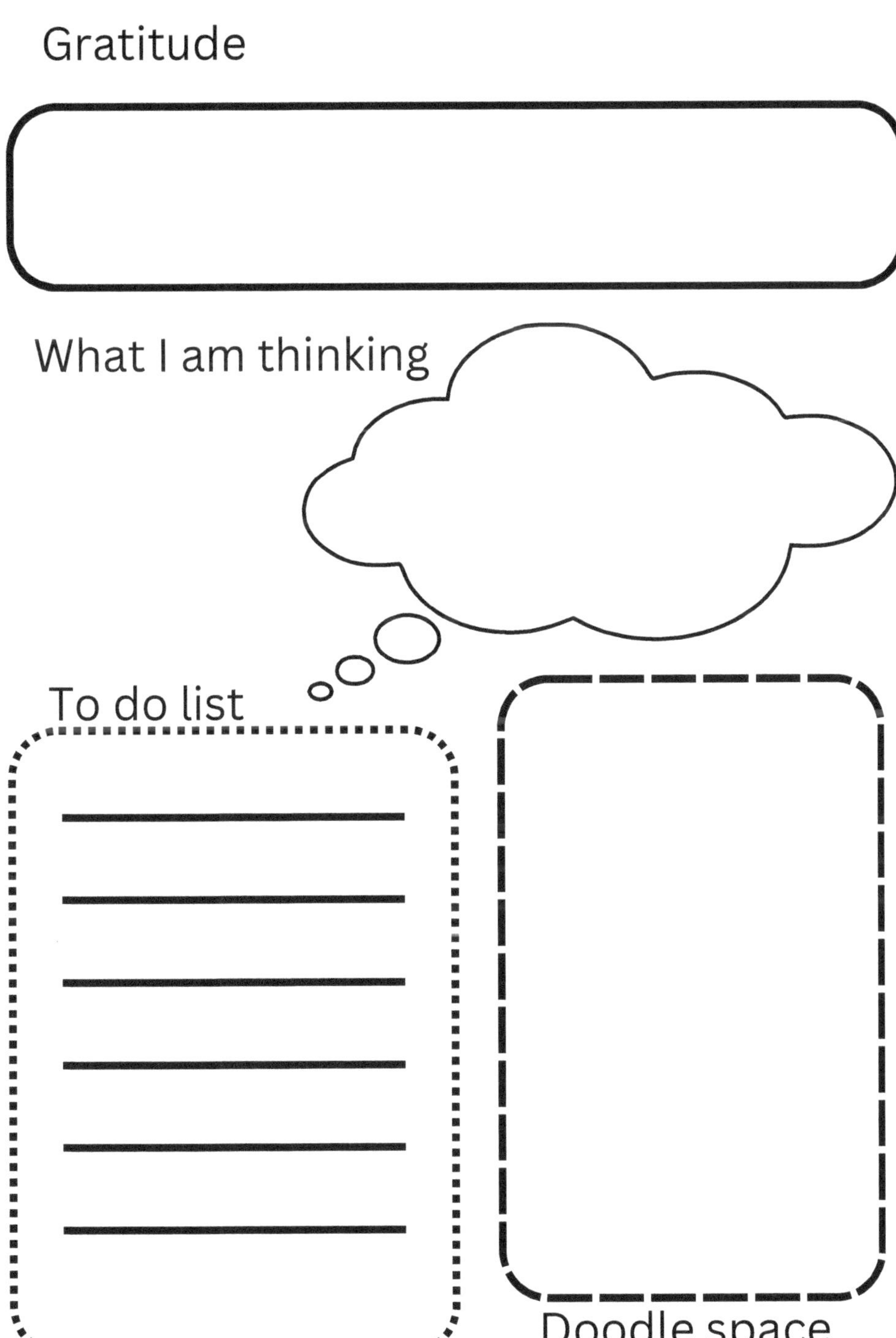

Date:..............

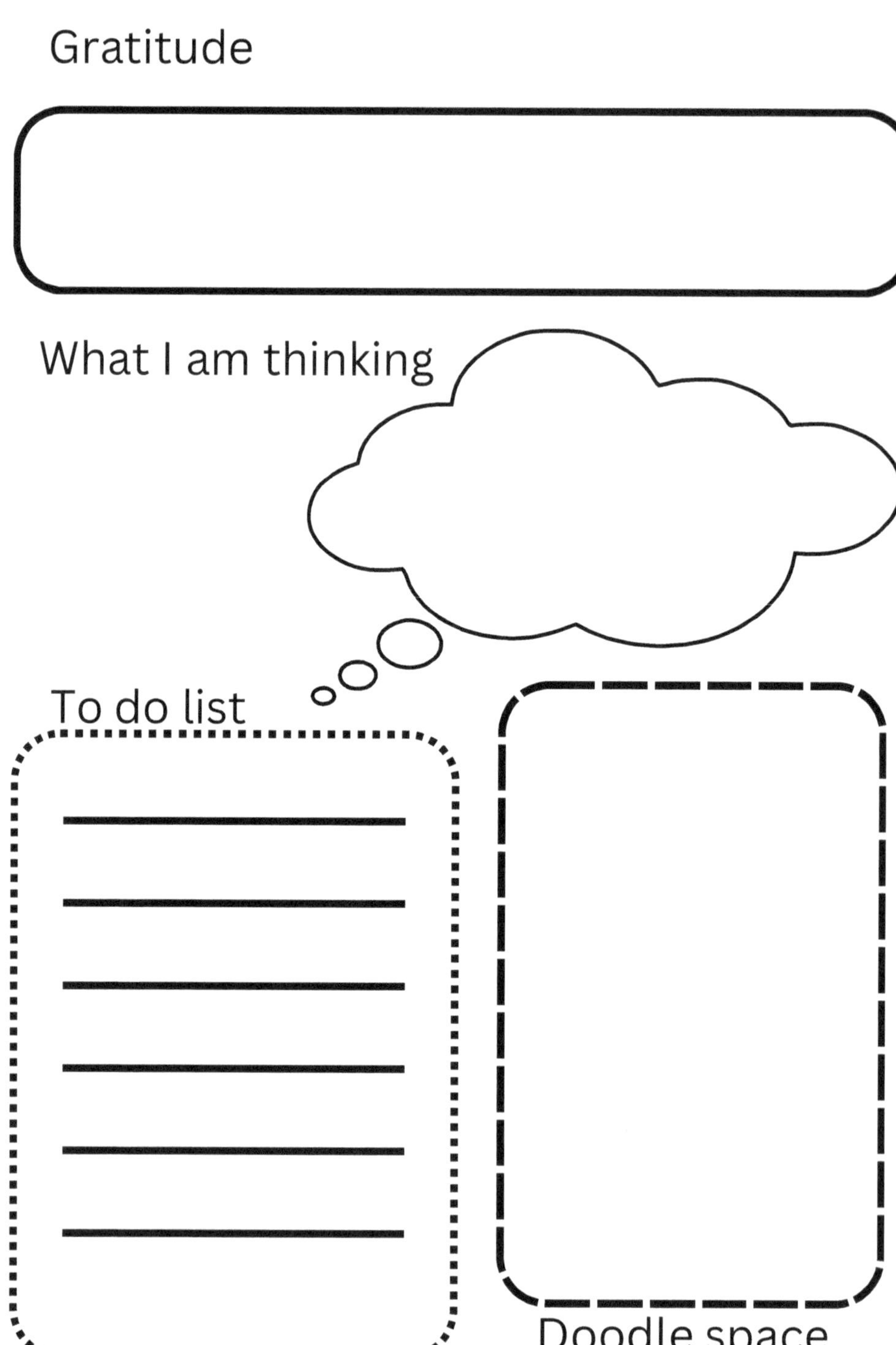

Date:..............

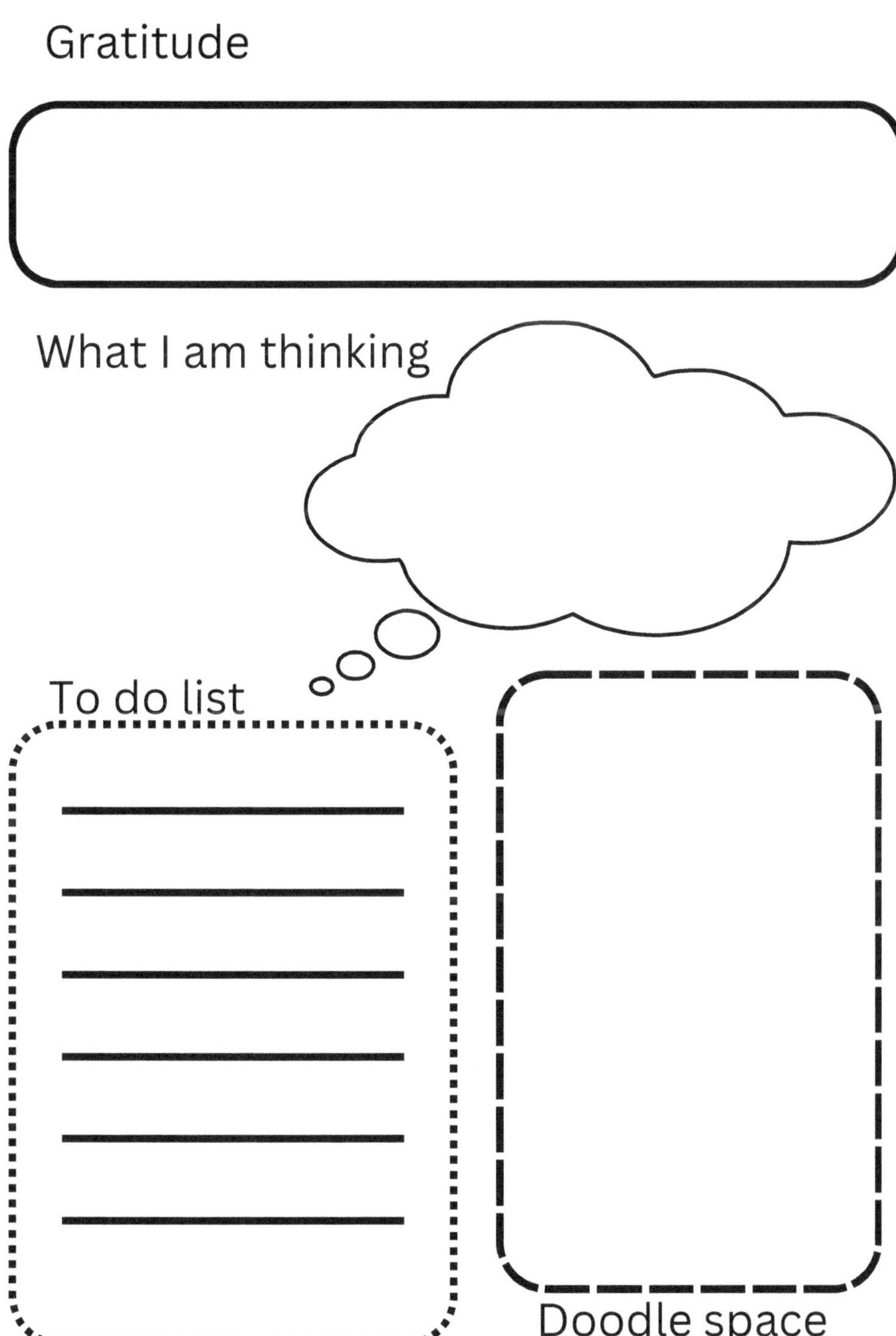

Date:..............

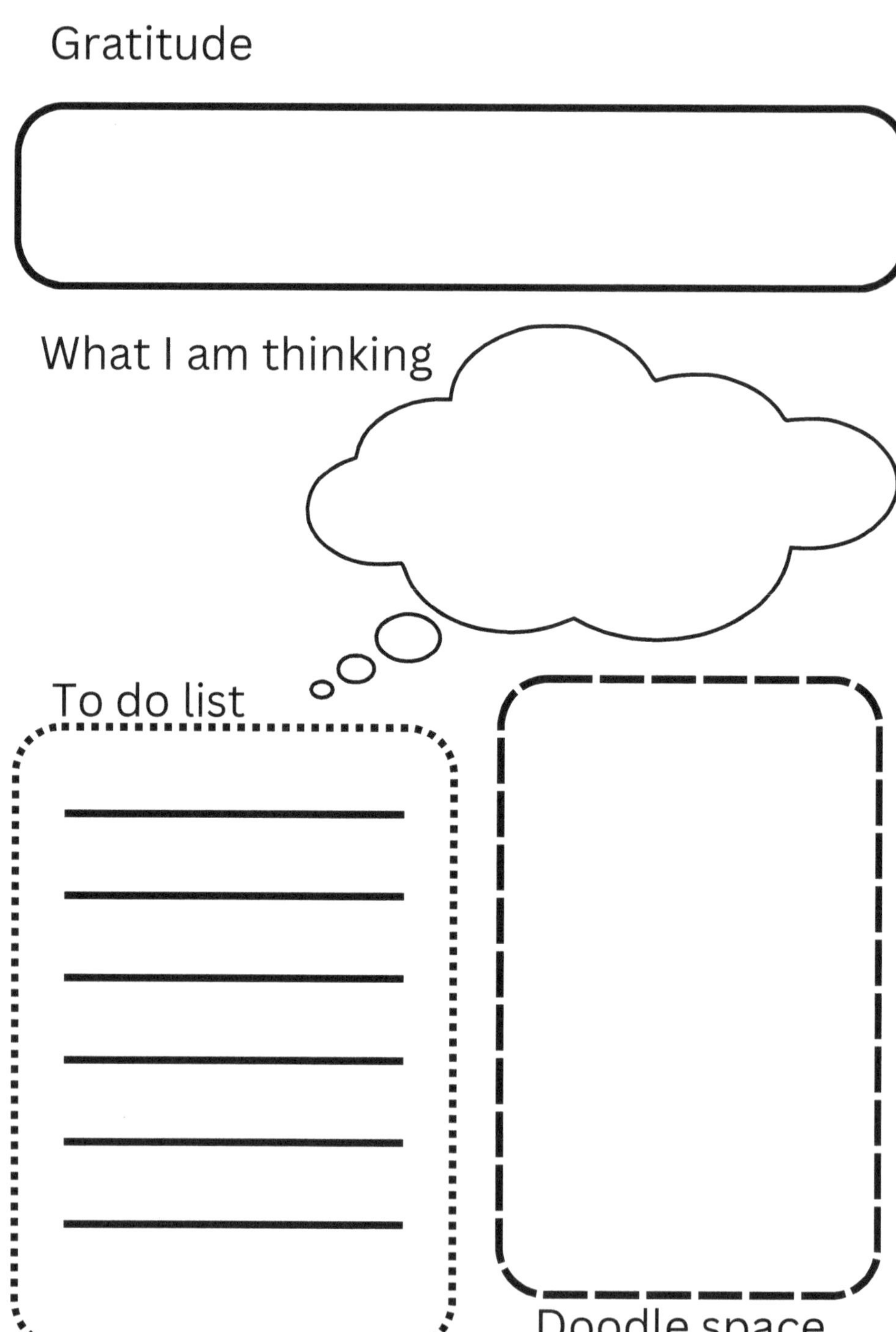

Date:..............

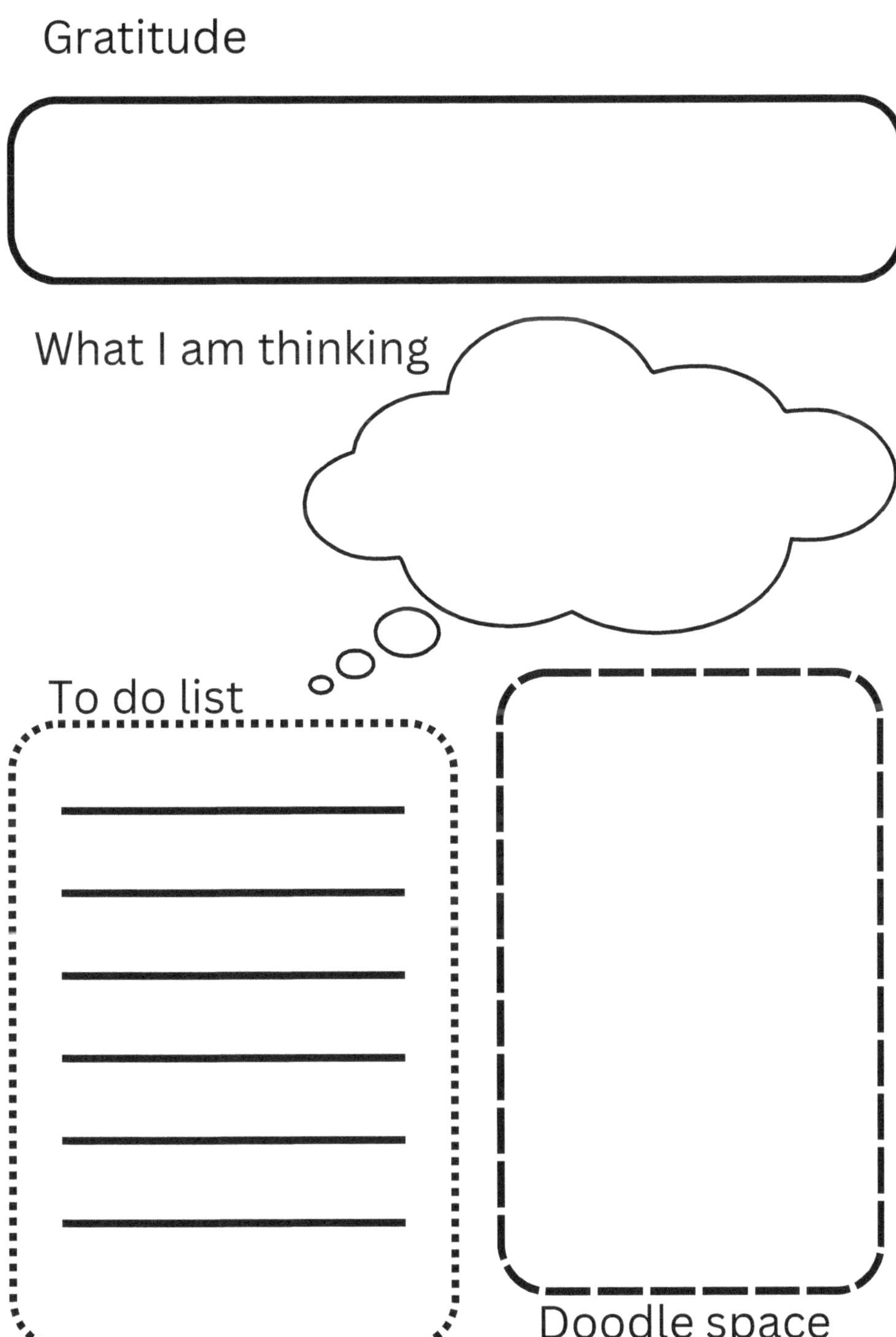

Date:..............

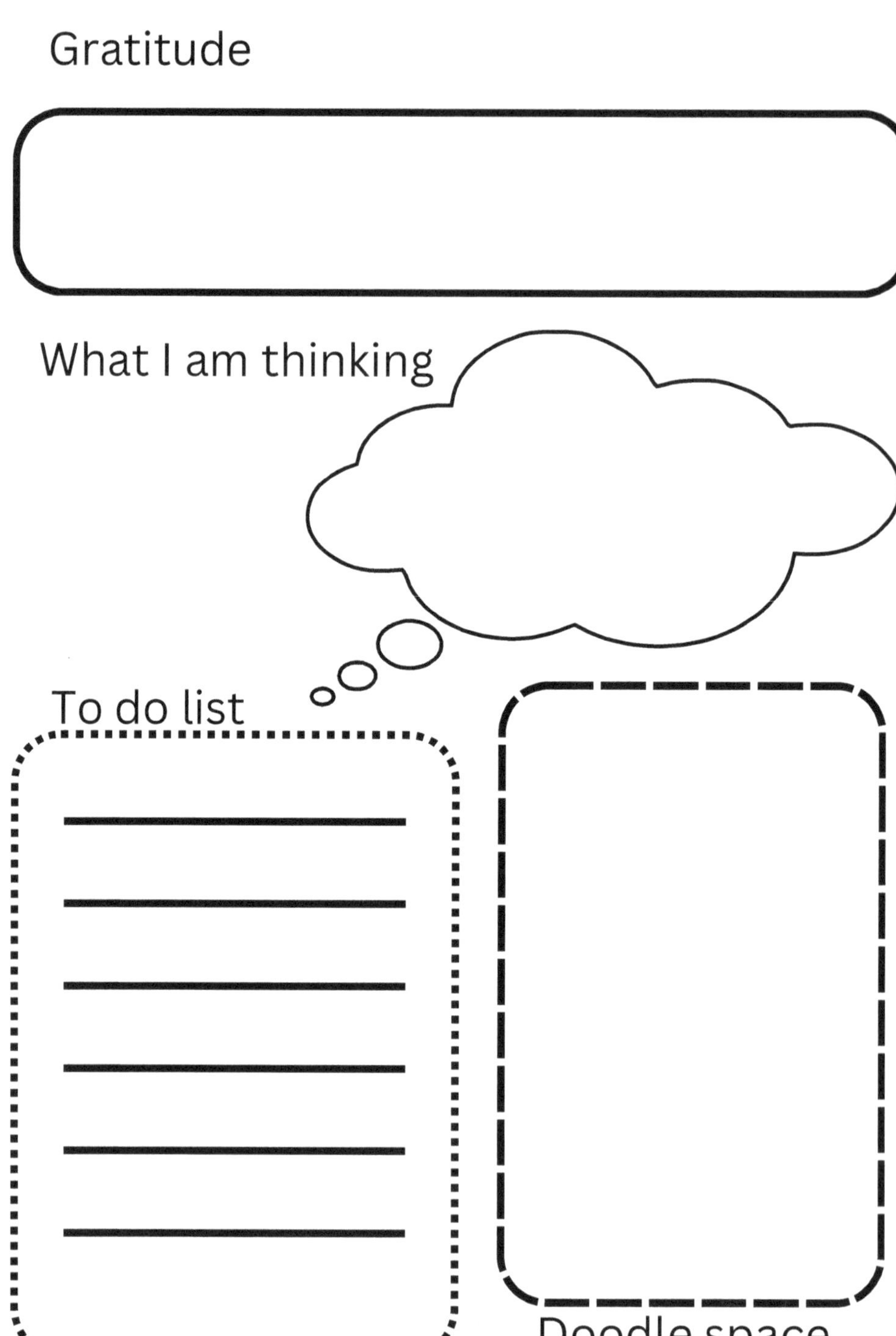

Date:..............

Weekly planner

Date:..../.../.....to..../.../....

MON

TUE

WED

THU

FRI

SAT

SUN

Date:..............

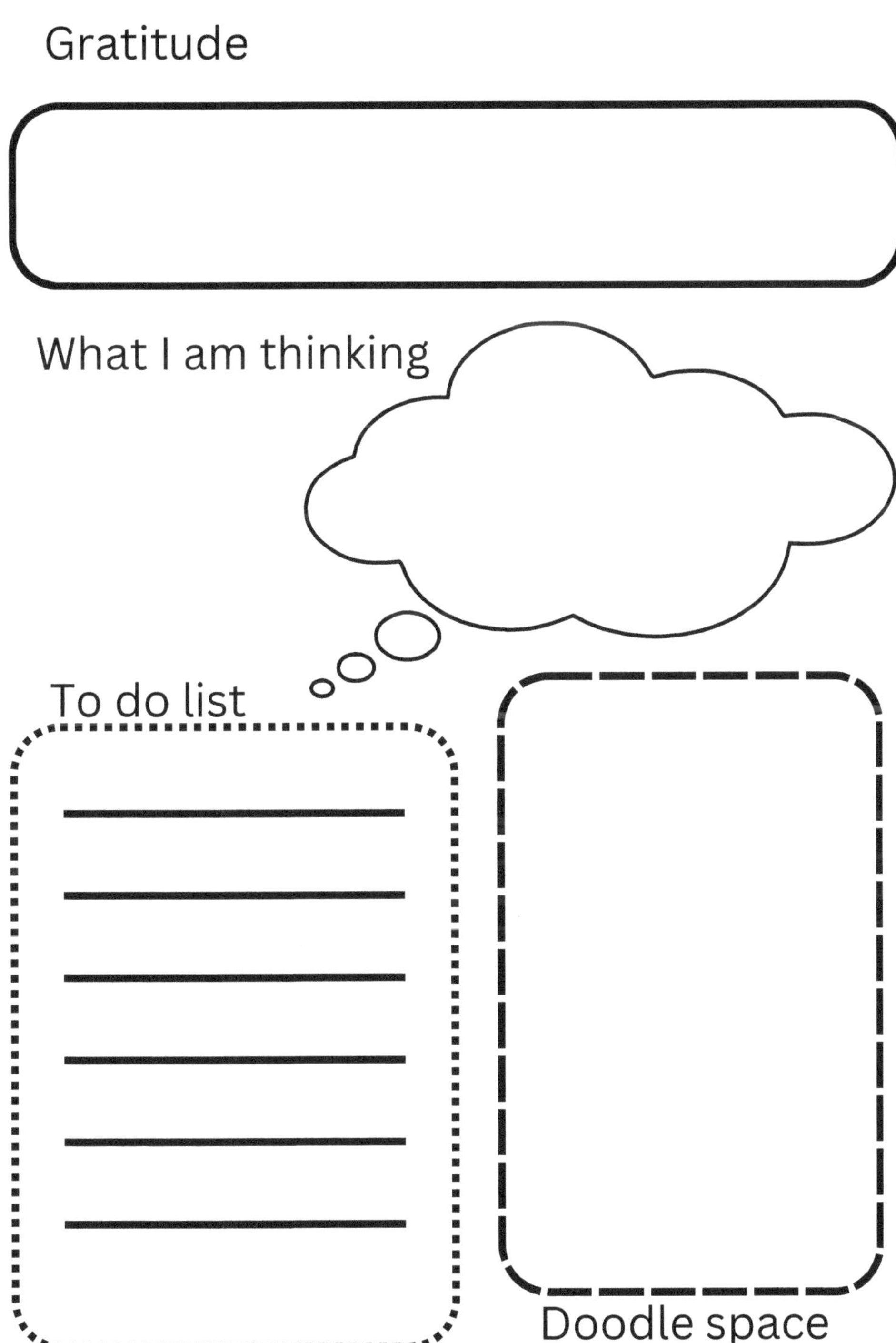
Gratitude

What I am thinking

To do list

Doodle space

Date:..............

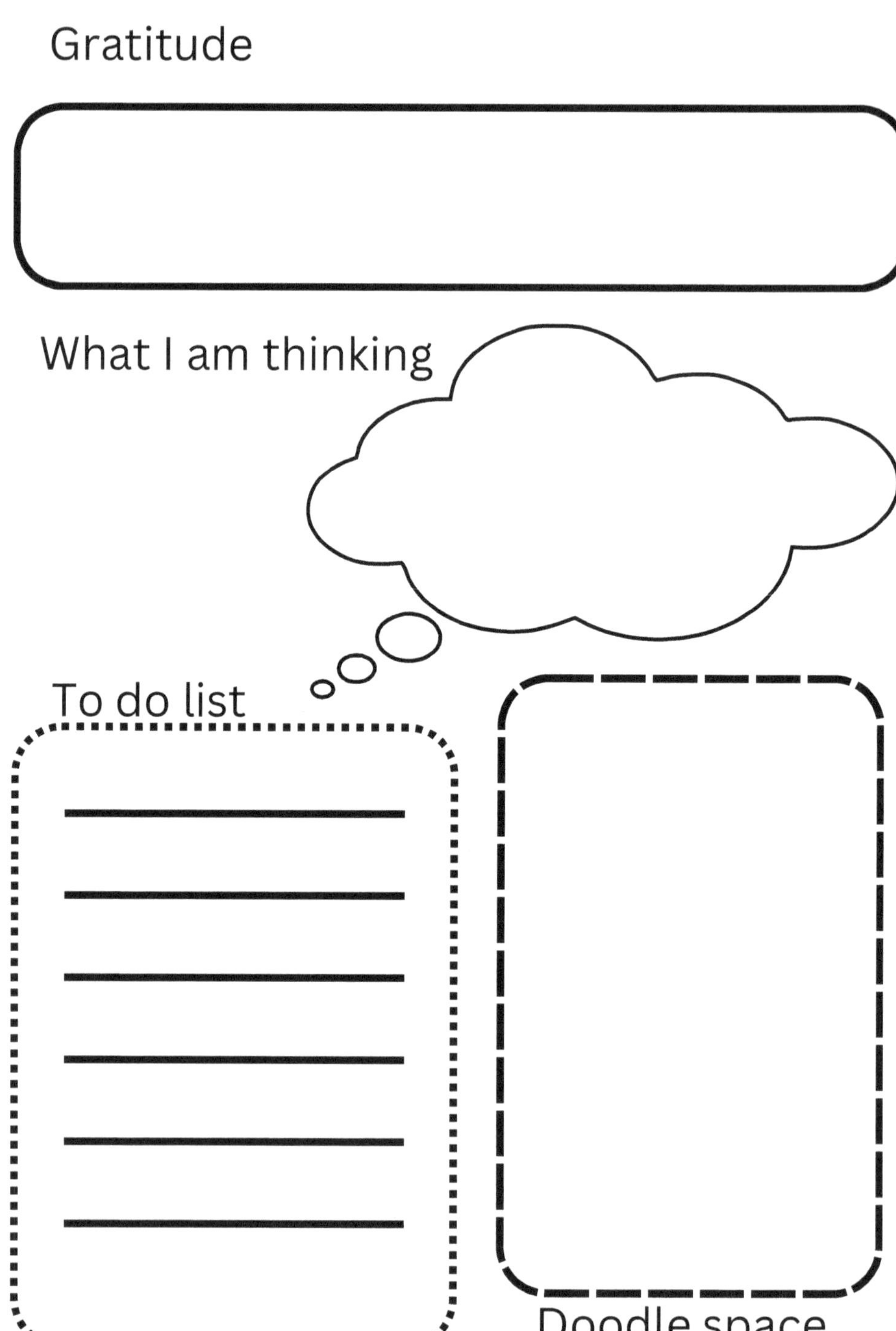

Date:..............

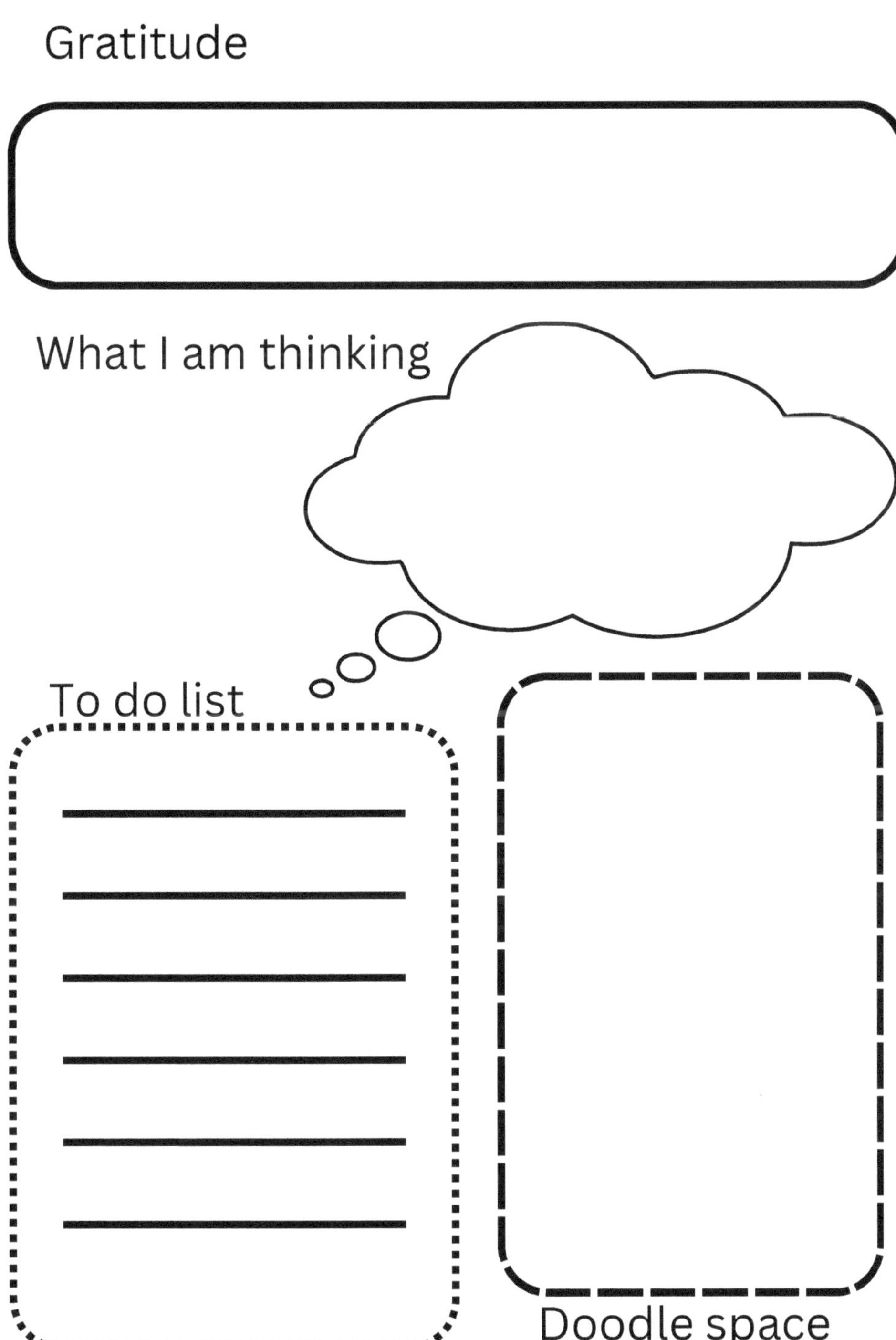

Date:..............

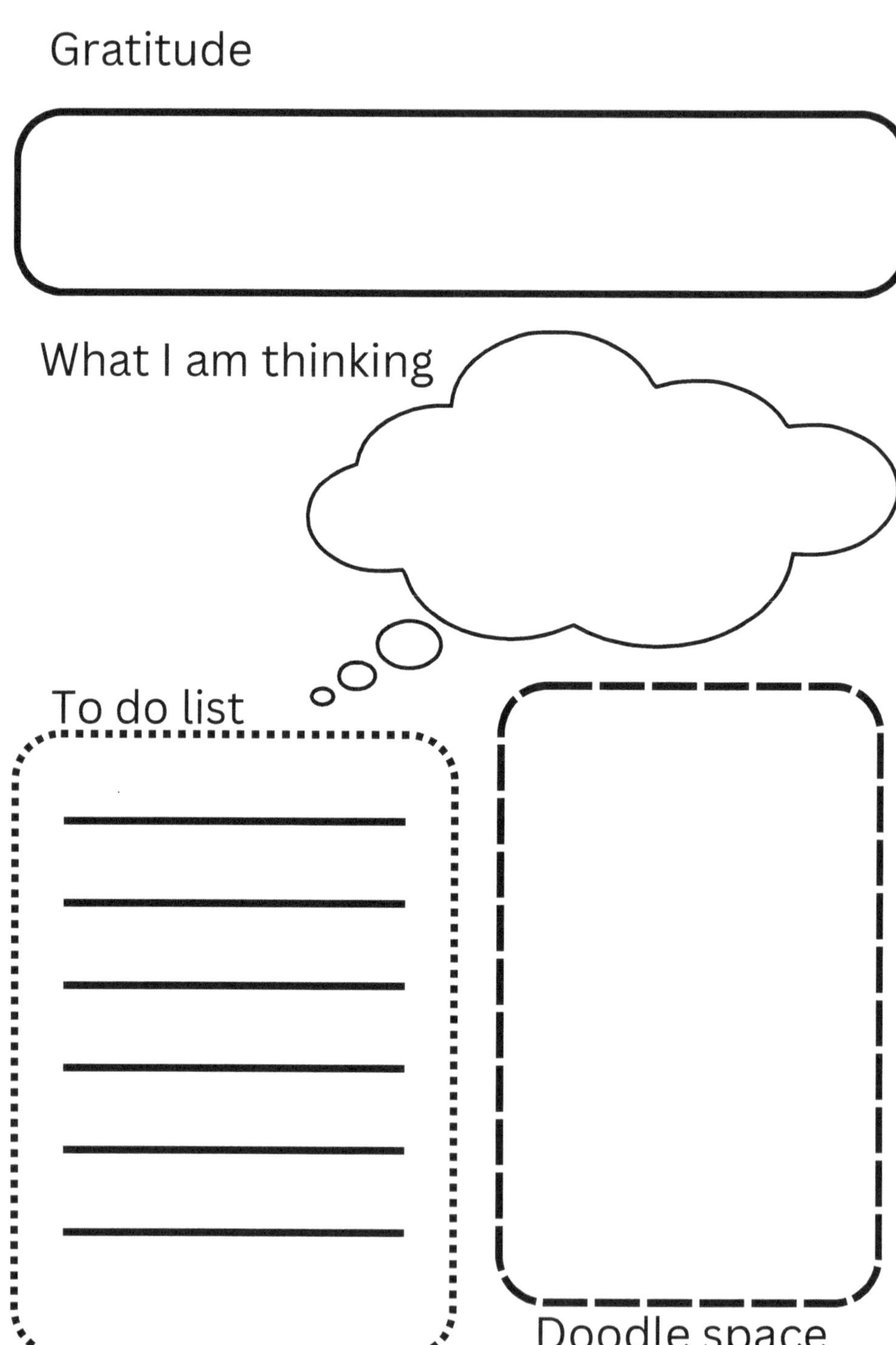

Date:..............

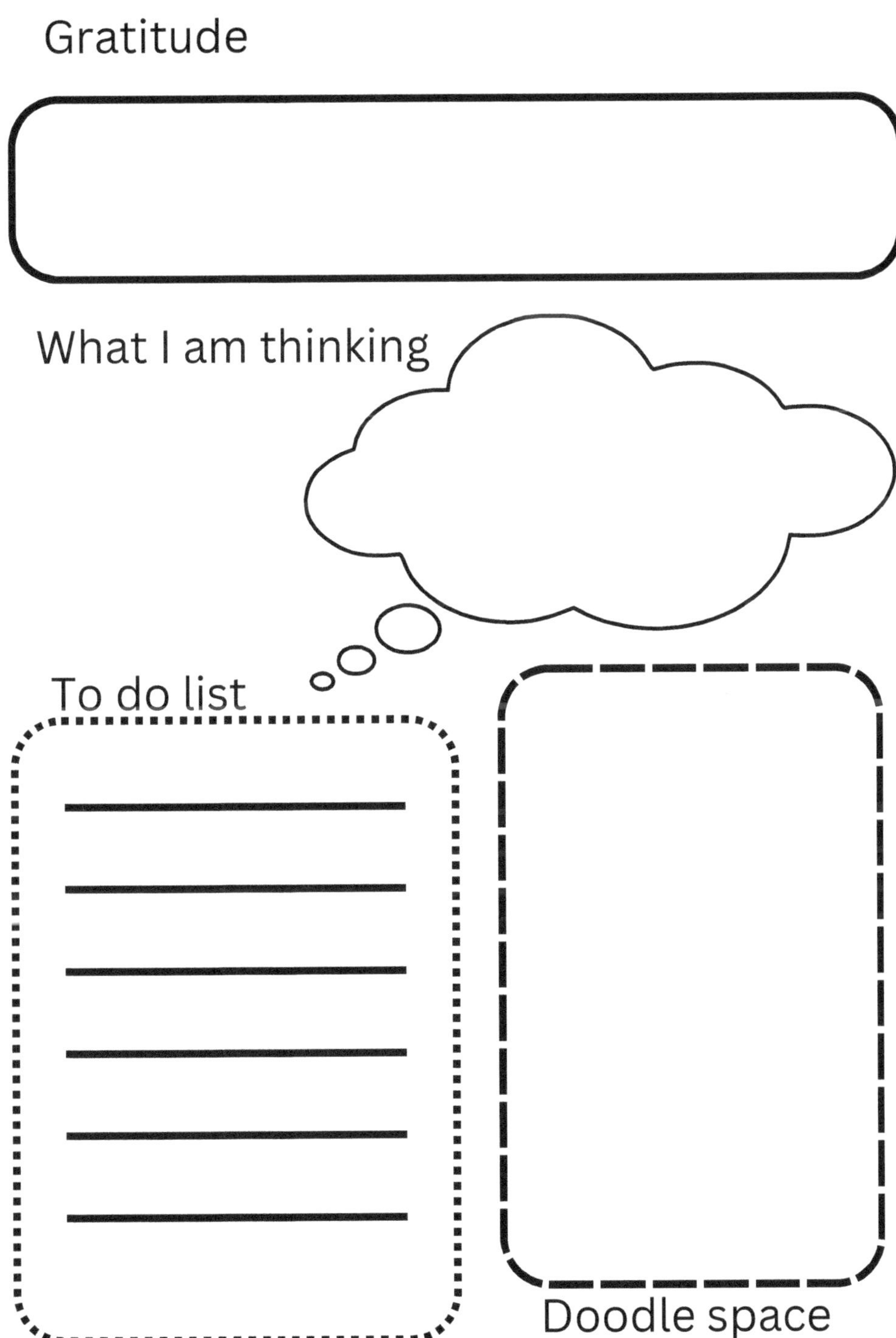

Date:..............

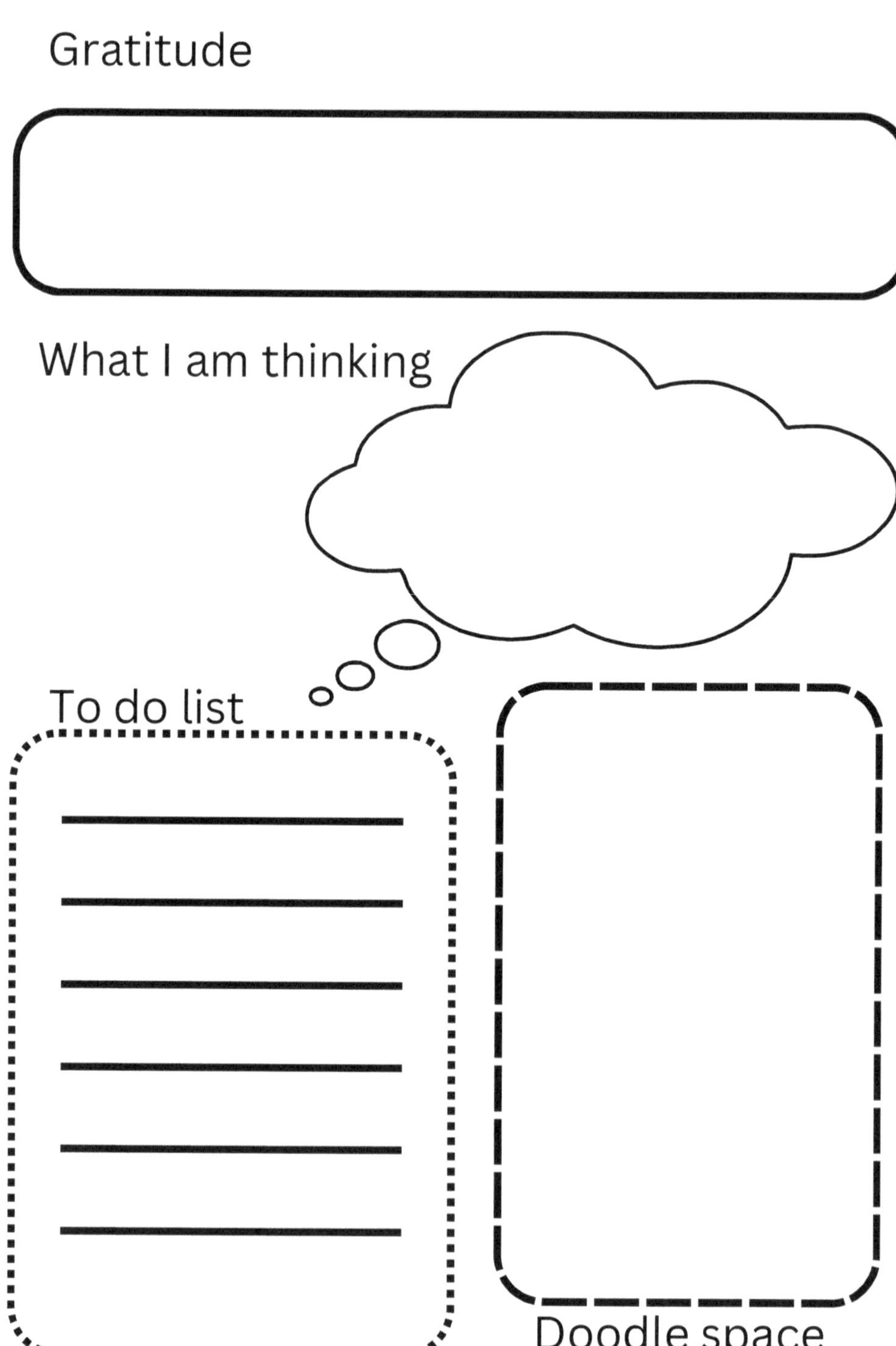

Date:..............

Gratitude

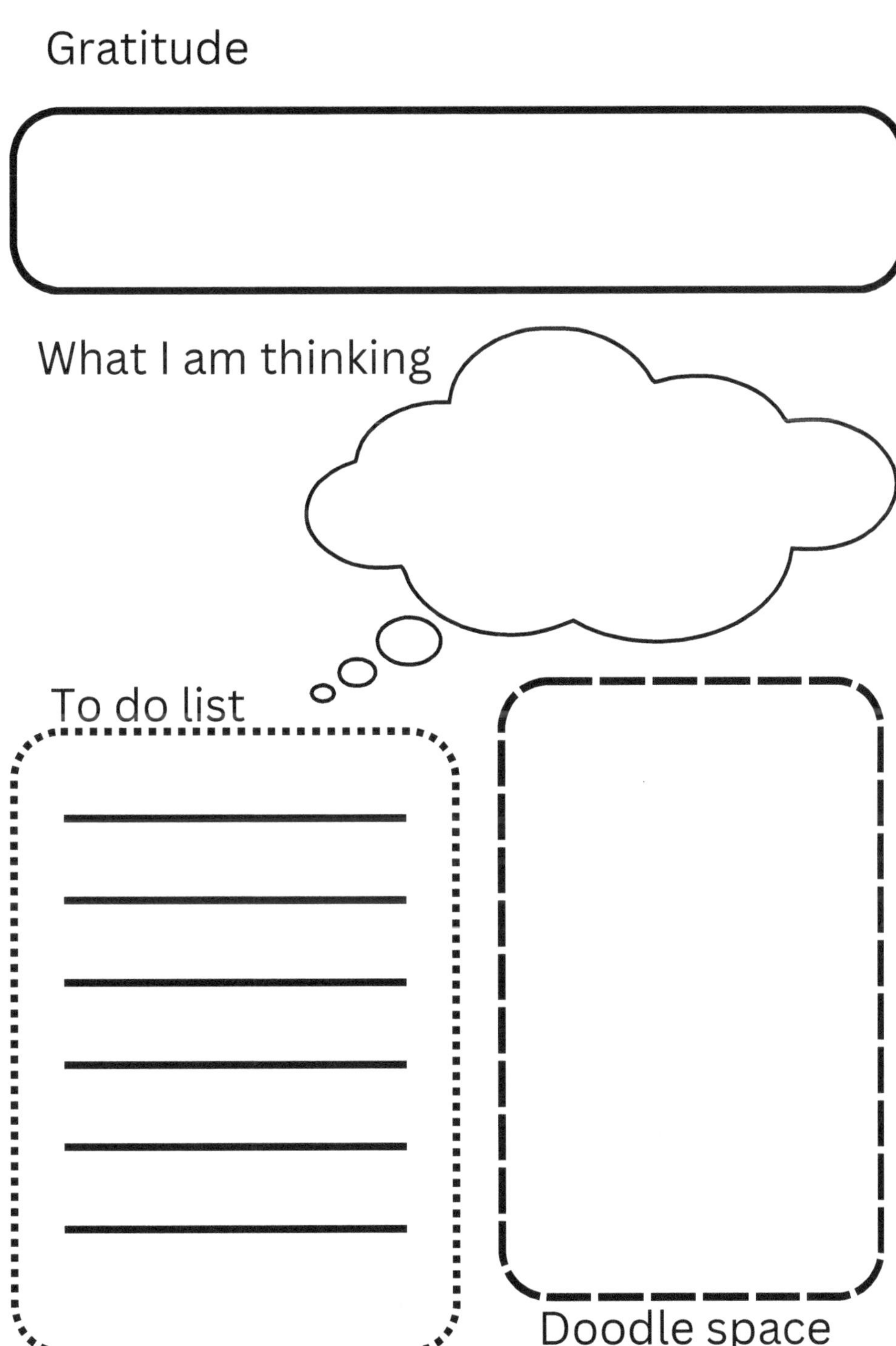

Weekly planner

Date:..../.../.....to..../.../....

MON

TUE

WED

THU

FRI

SAT

SUN

Date:..............

Date:..............

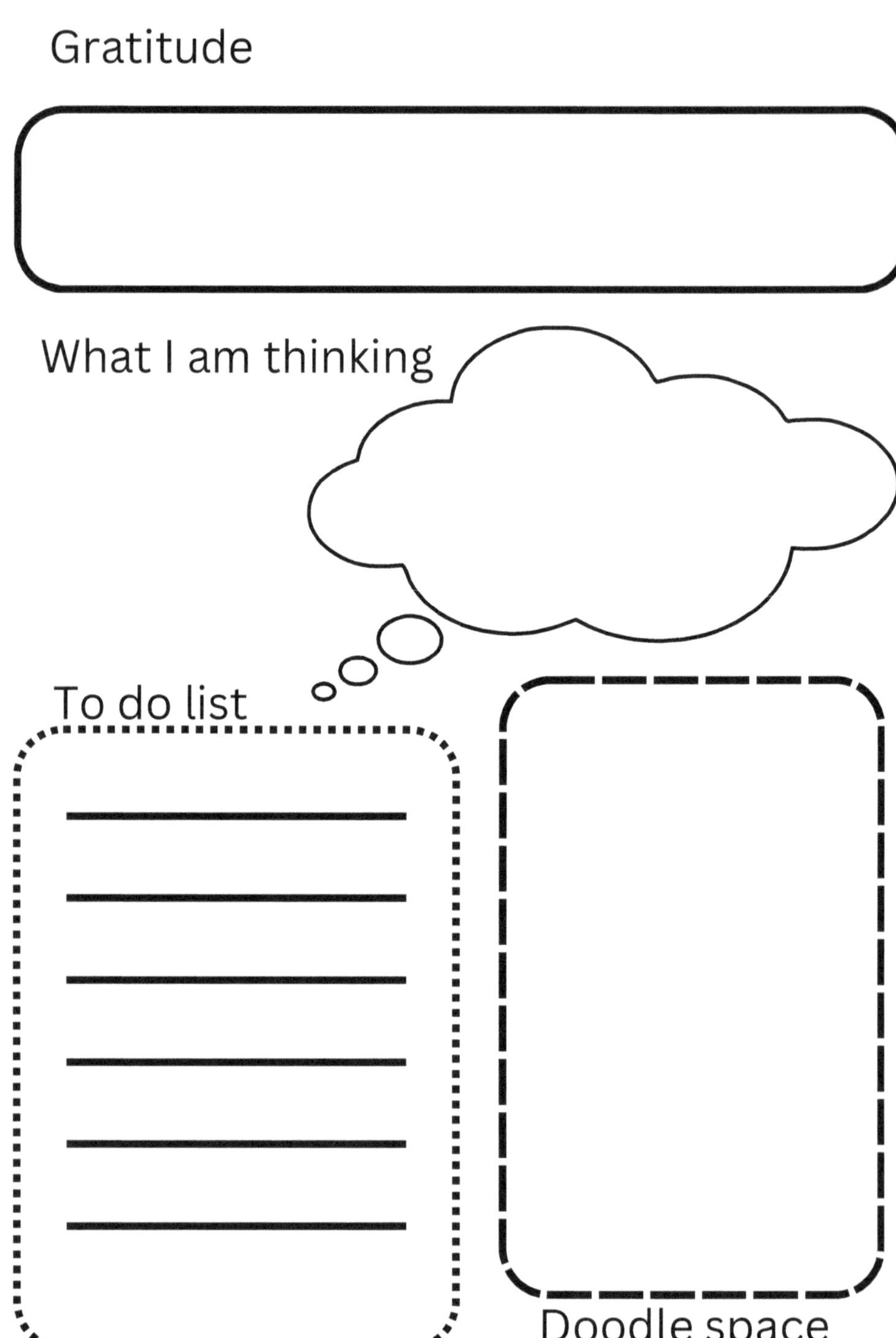

Date:..............

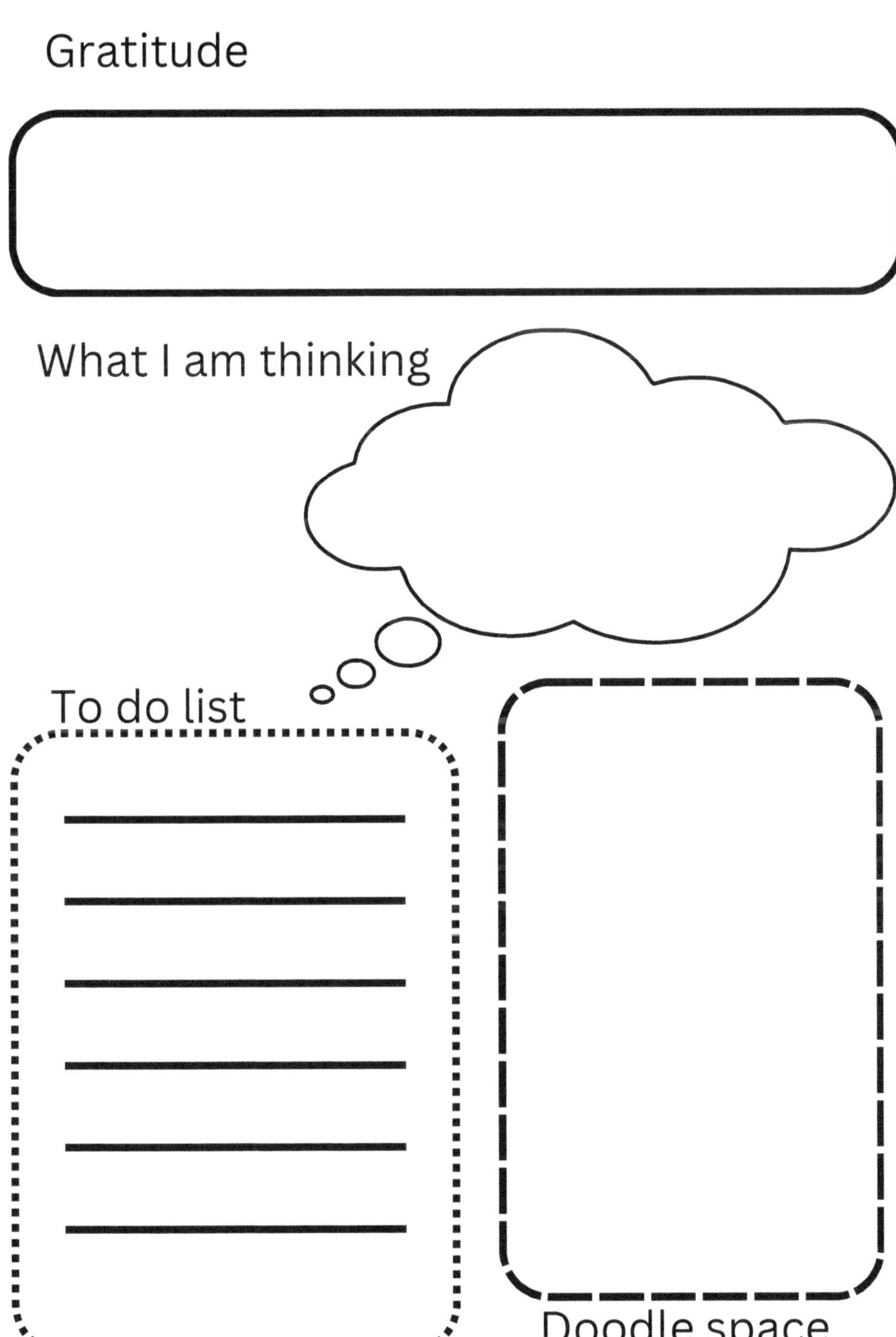

Date:..............

Date:...............

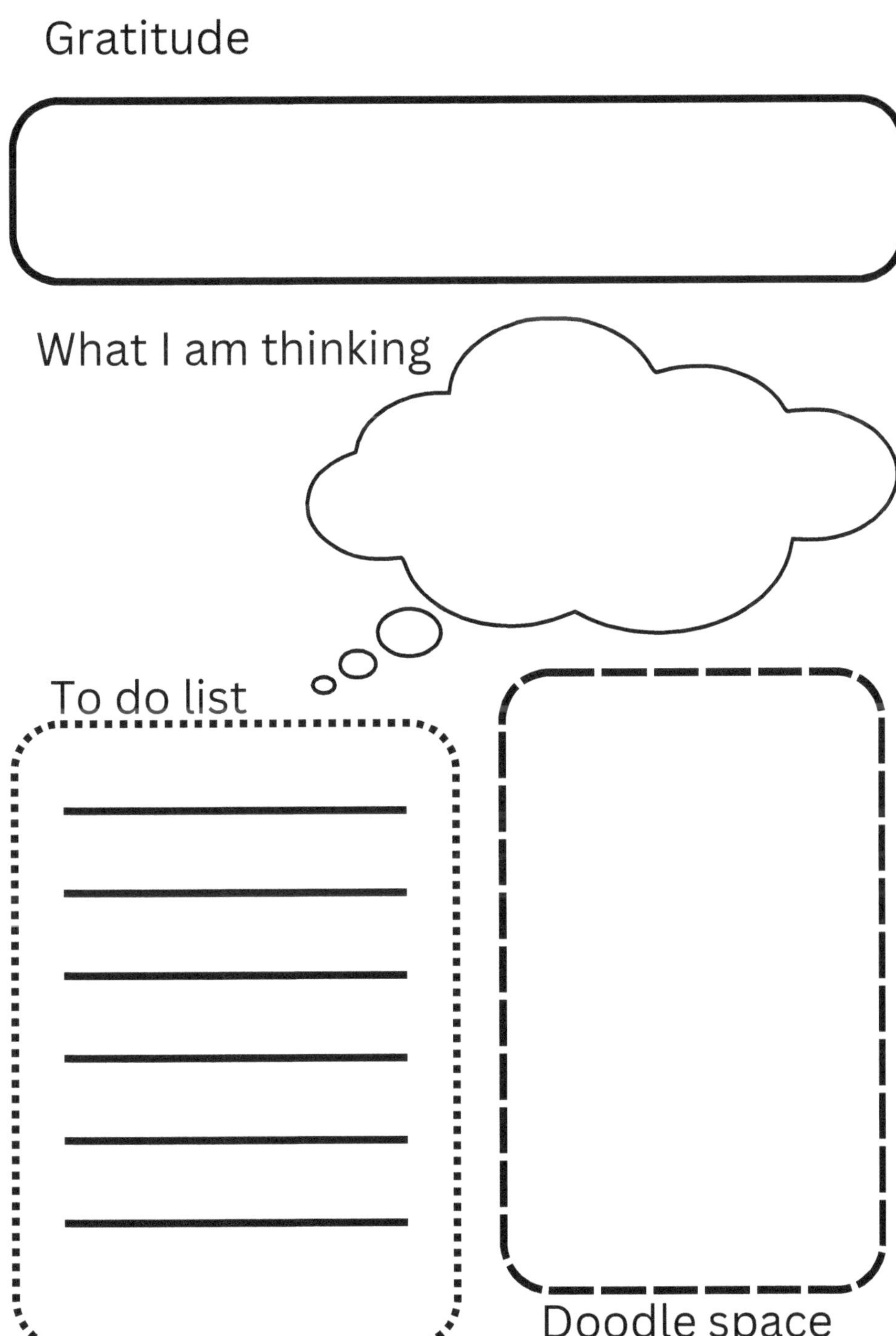

Date:..............

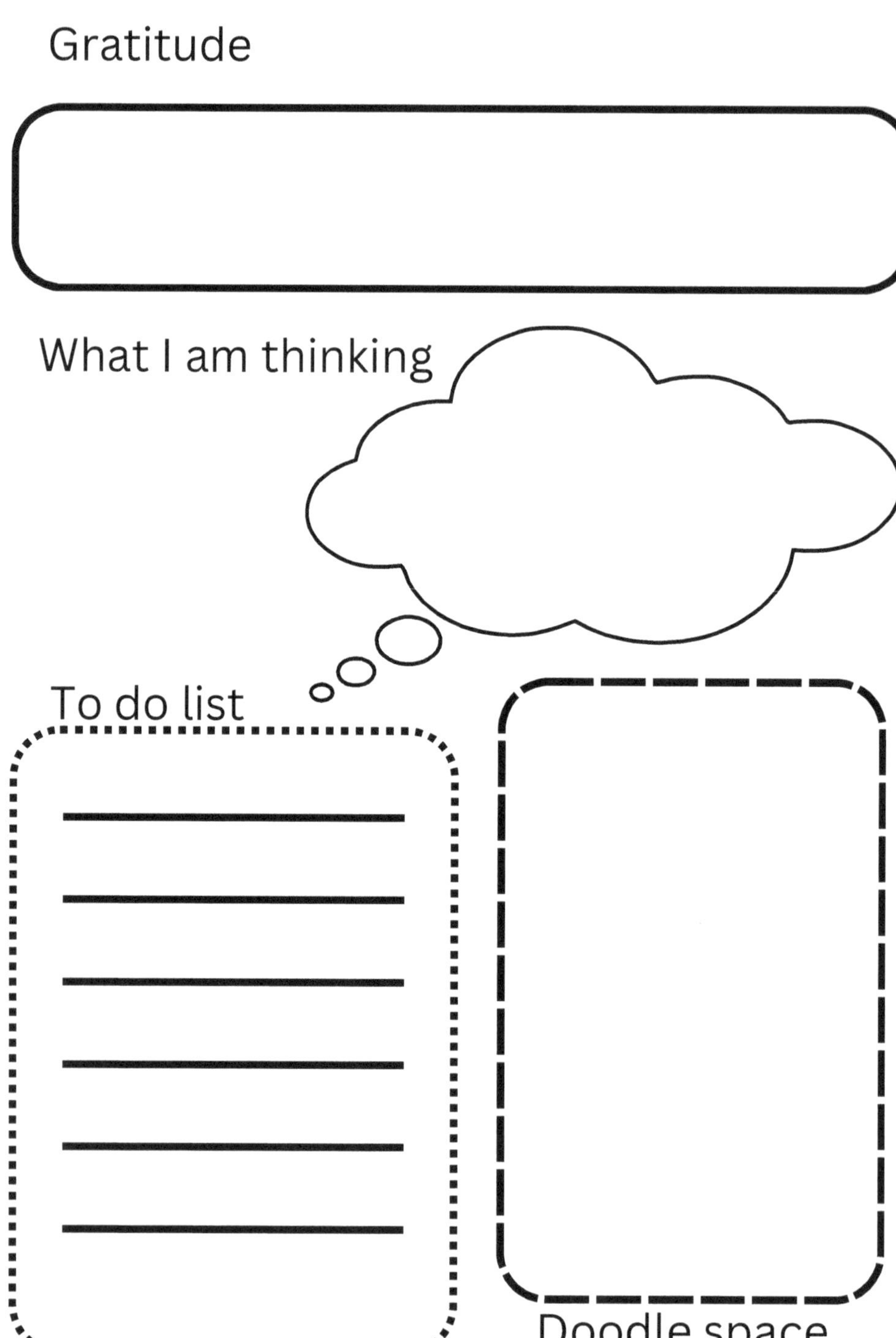

Date:..............

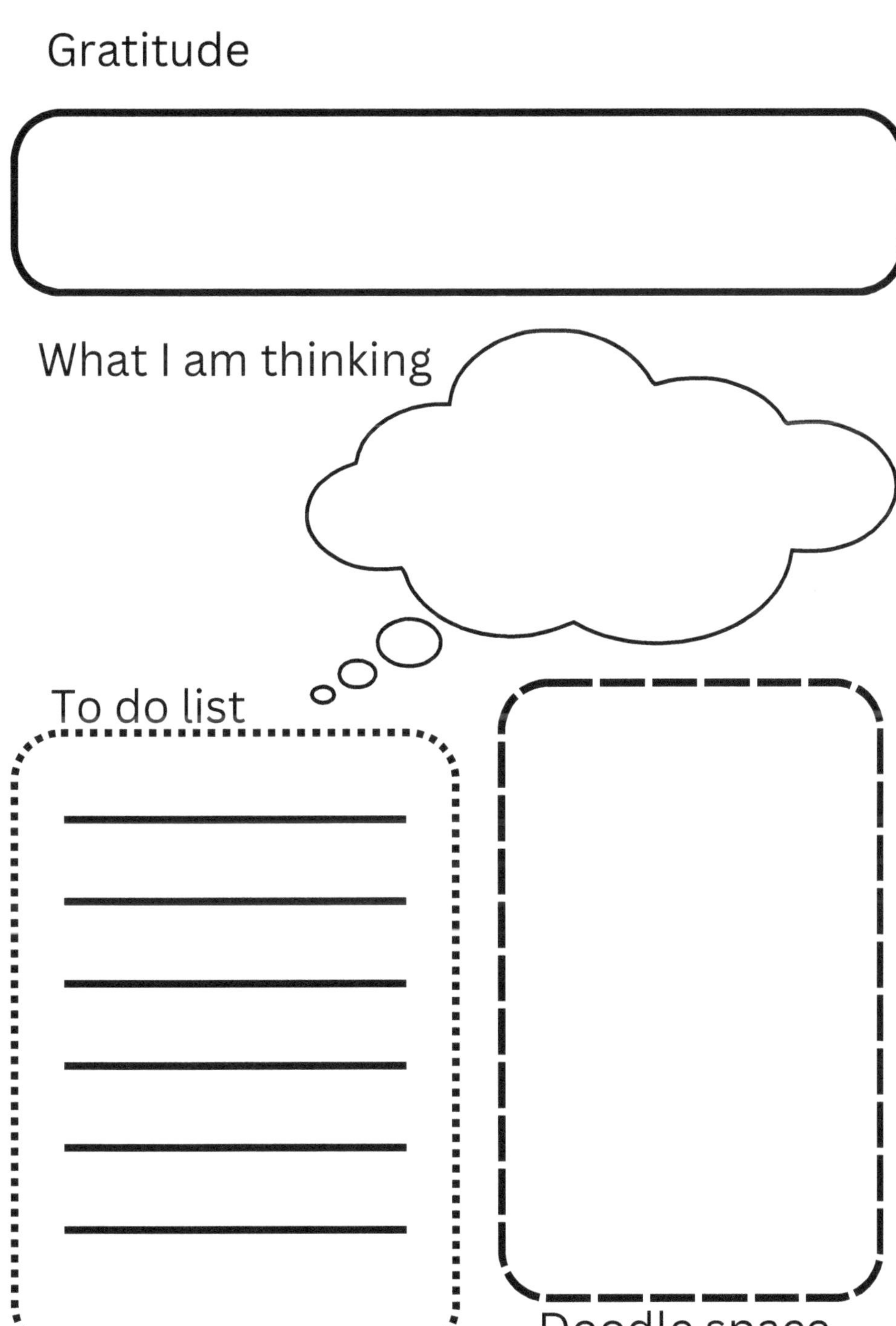

Weekly planner

Date:...../..../......to...../..../.....

MON

TUE

WED

THU

FRI

SAT

SUN

Date:..............

Gratitude

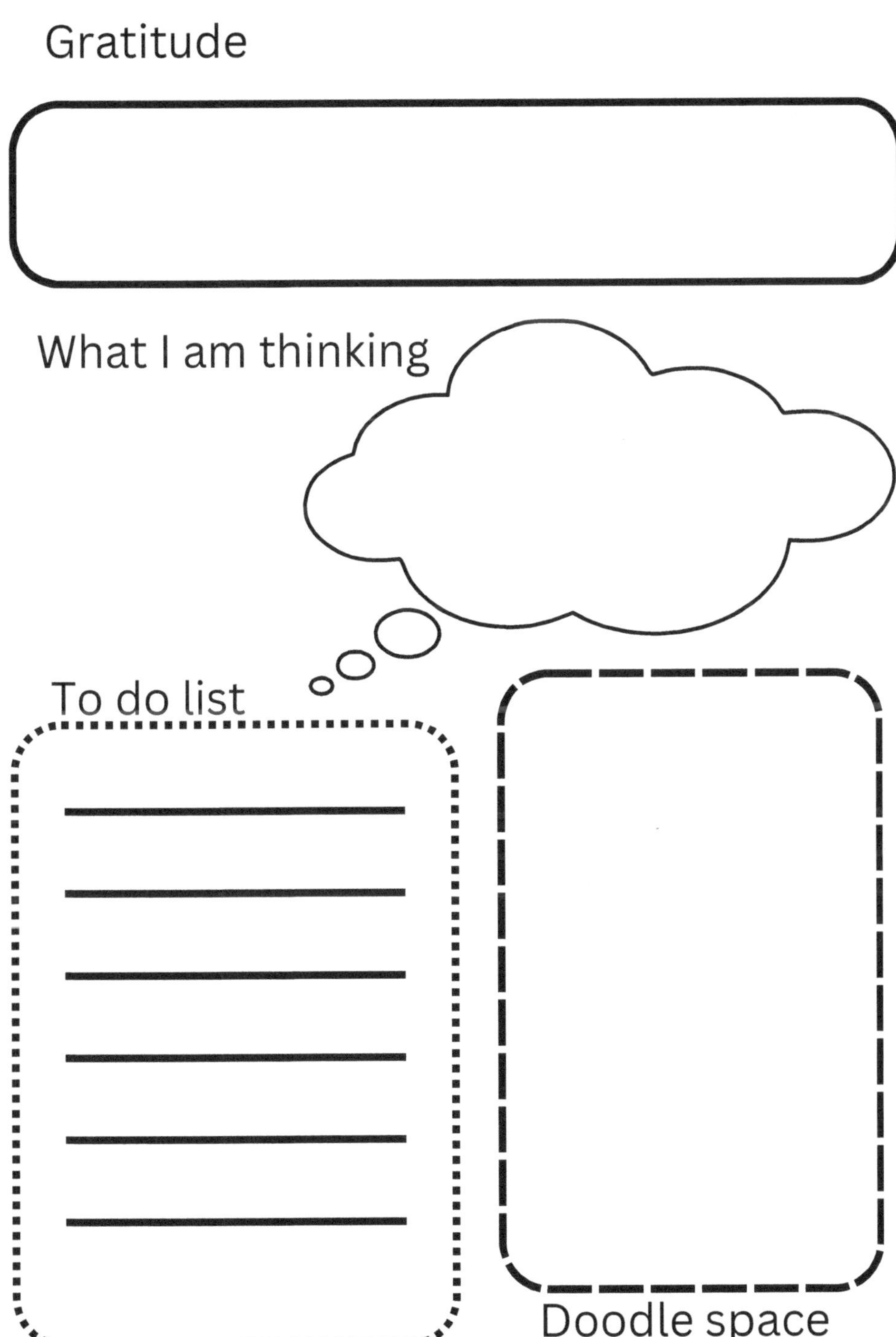

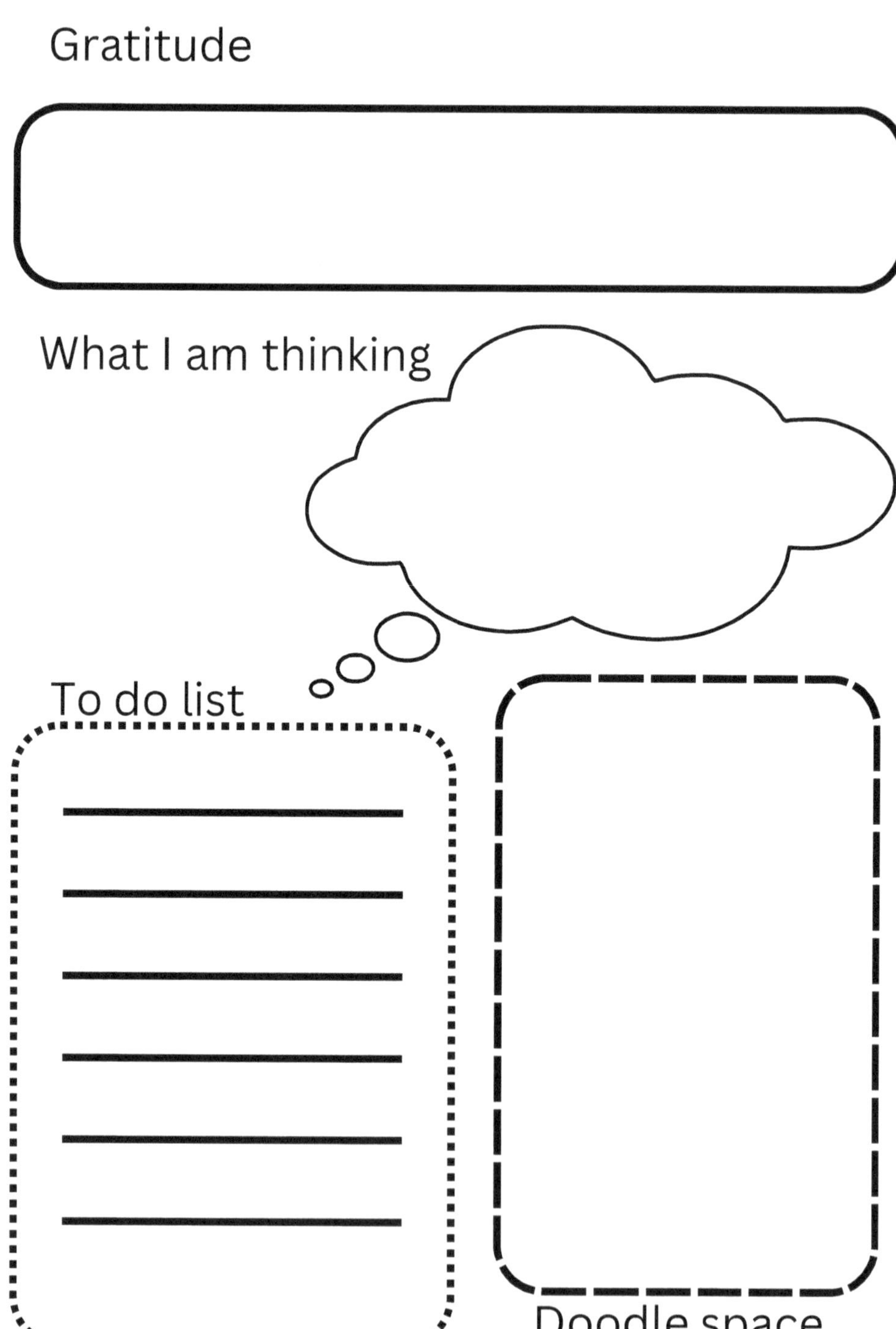
Date:..............
Gratitude
What I am thinking
To do list
Doodle space

Date:..............

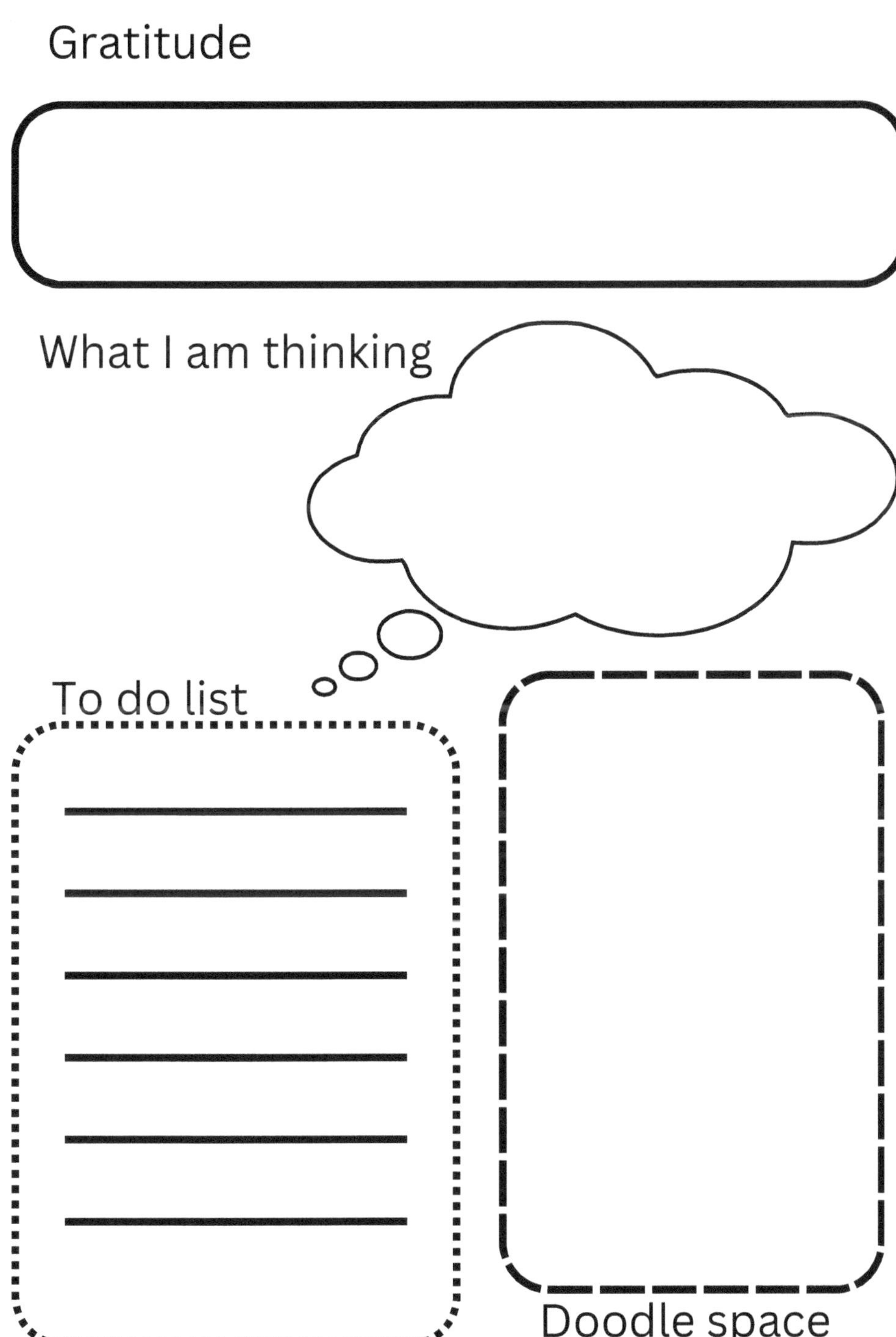

Date:..............

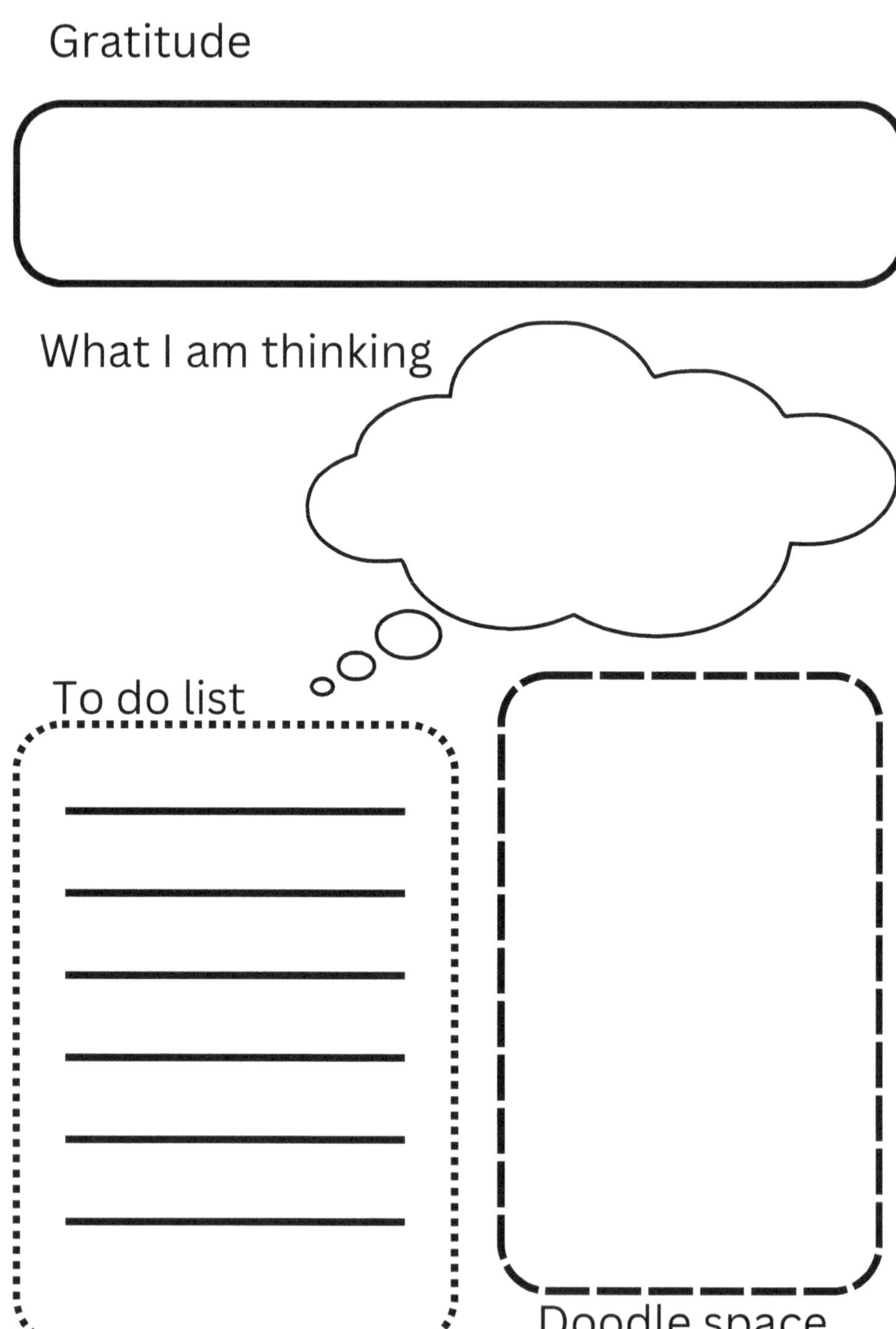

Date:..............

Date:..............

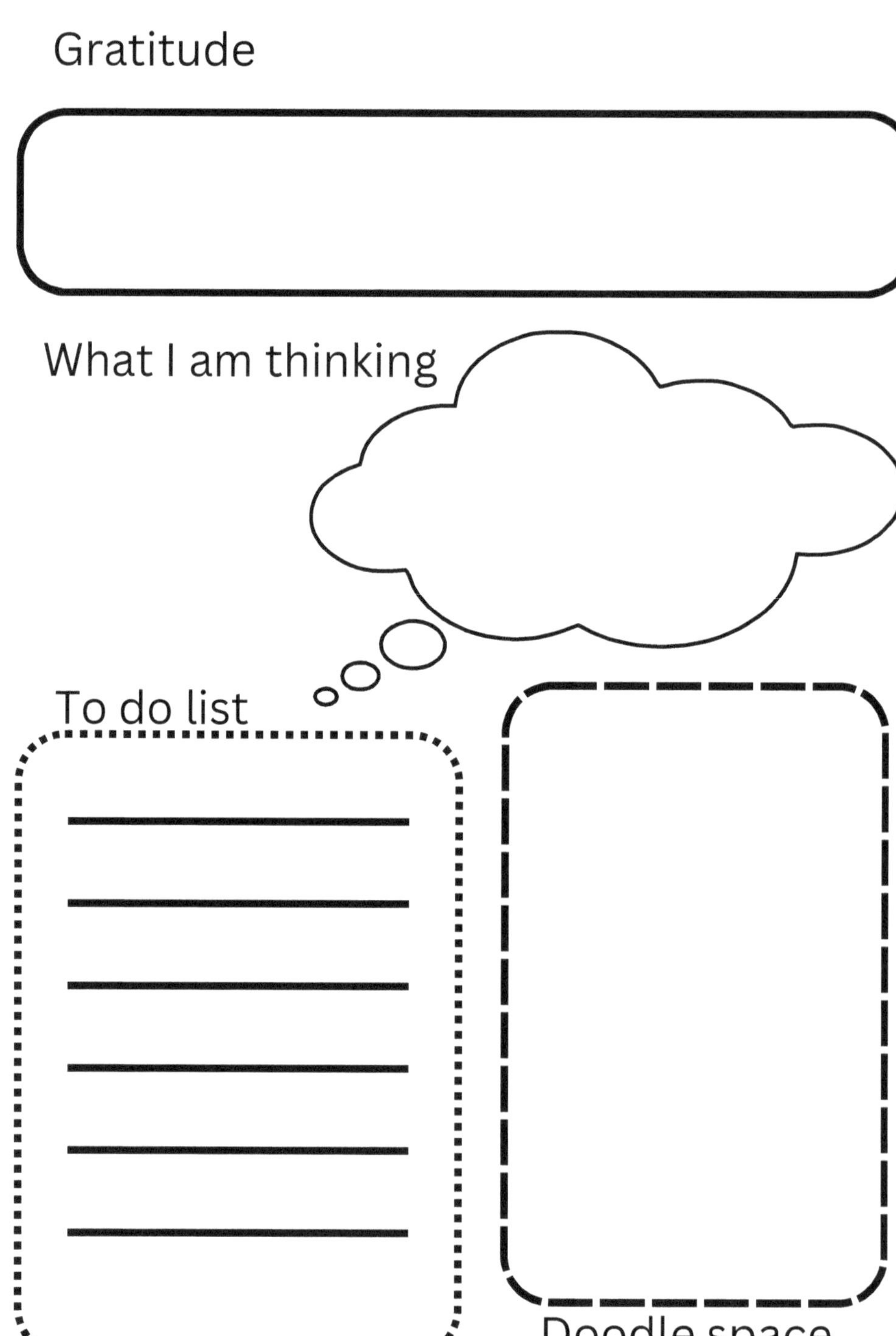

Date:..............

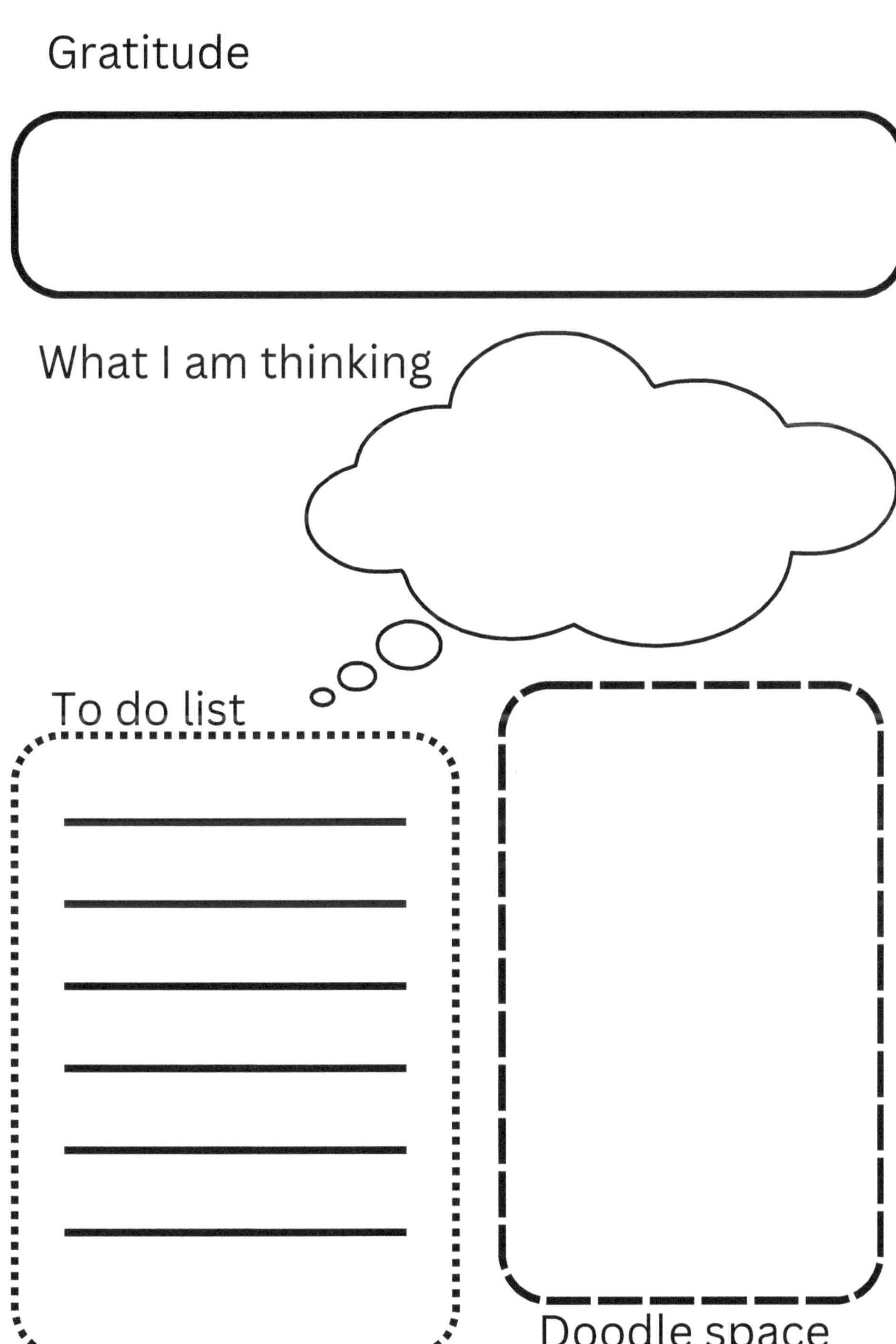

Weekly planner

Date:..../.../.....to..../.../....

MON

TUE

WED

THU

FRI

SAT

SUN

Date:..............

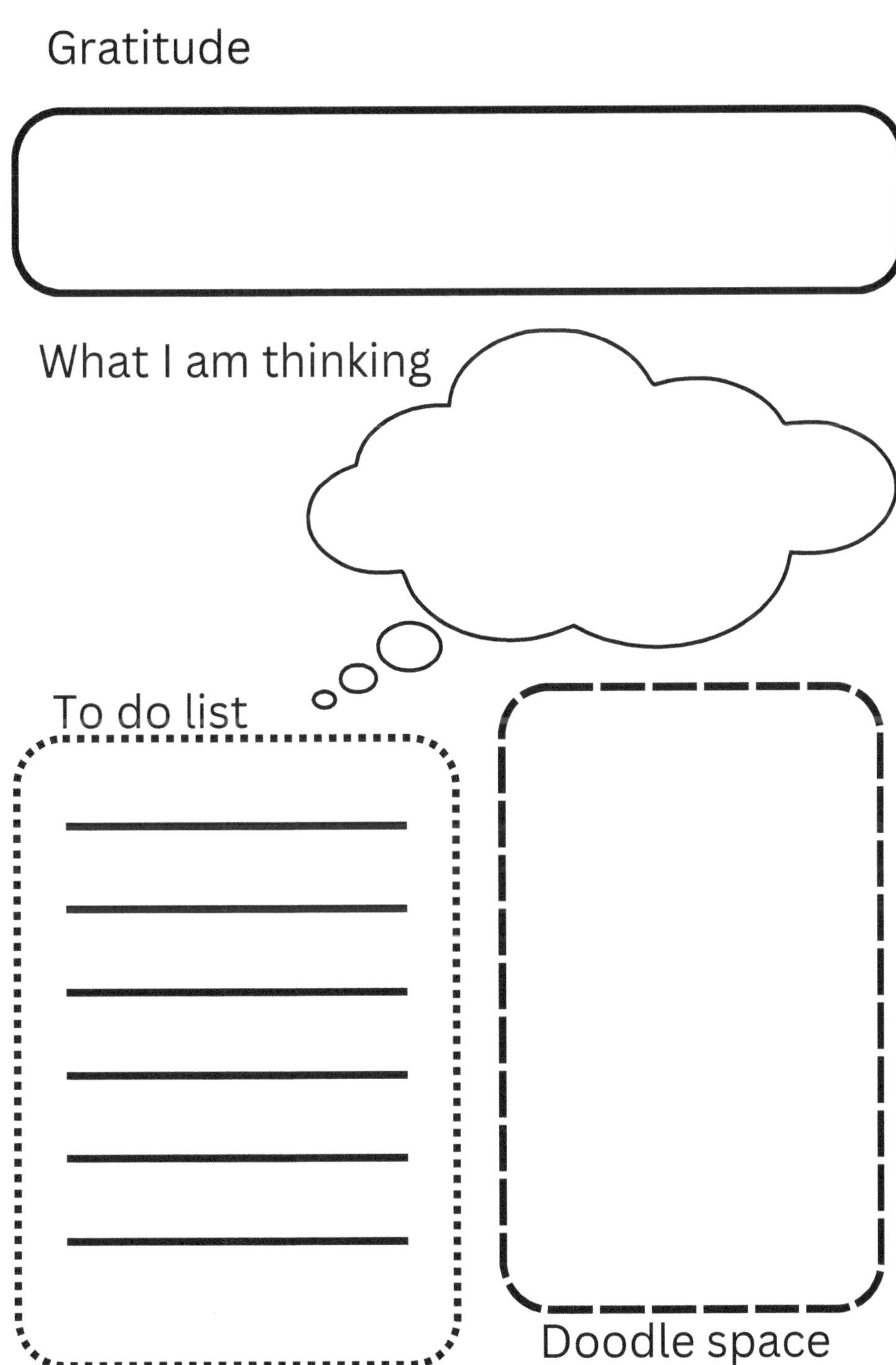

Gratitude

What I am thinking

To do list

Doodle space

Date:..............

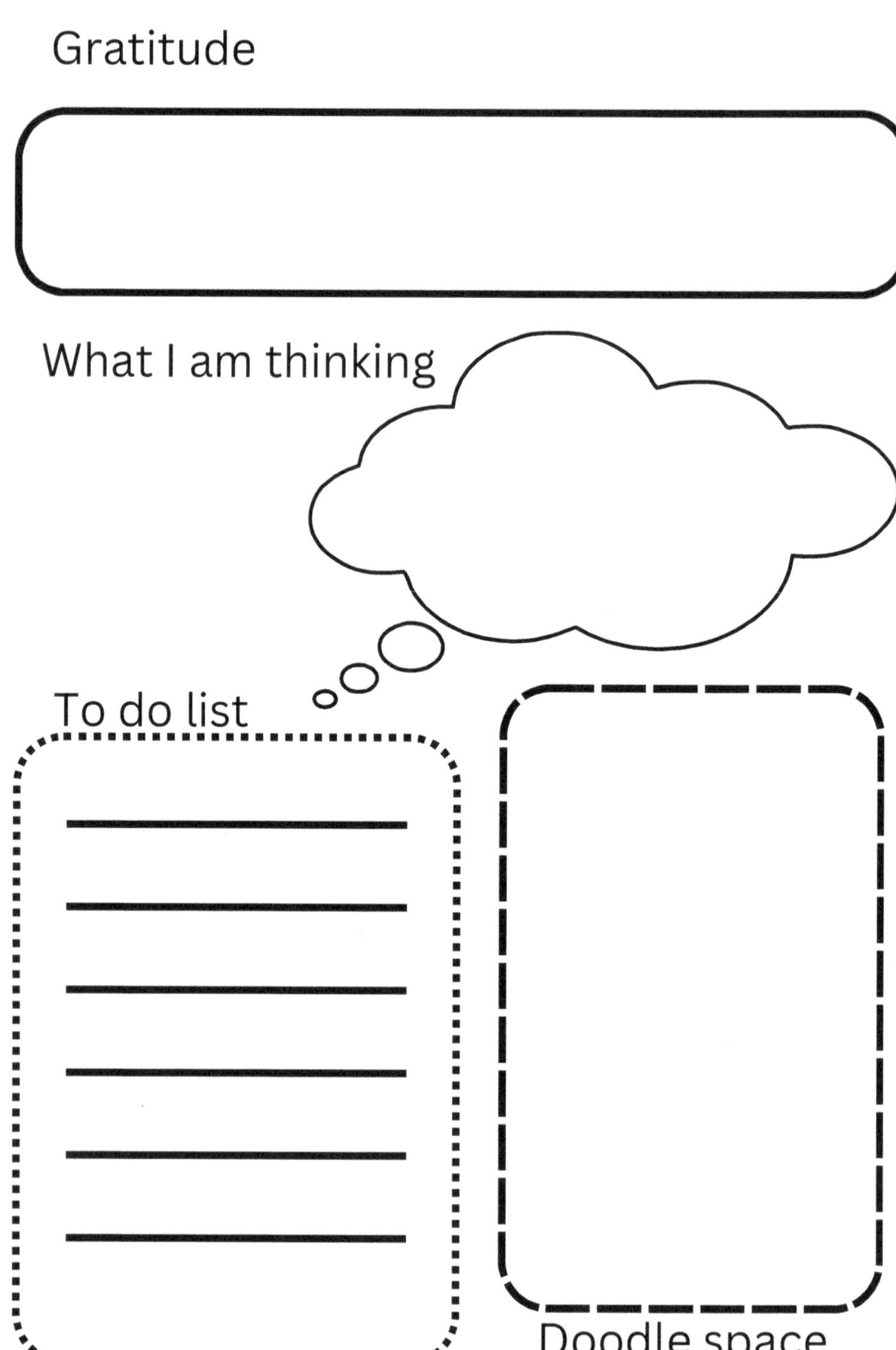

Date:..............

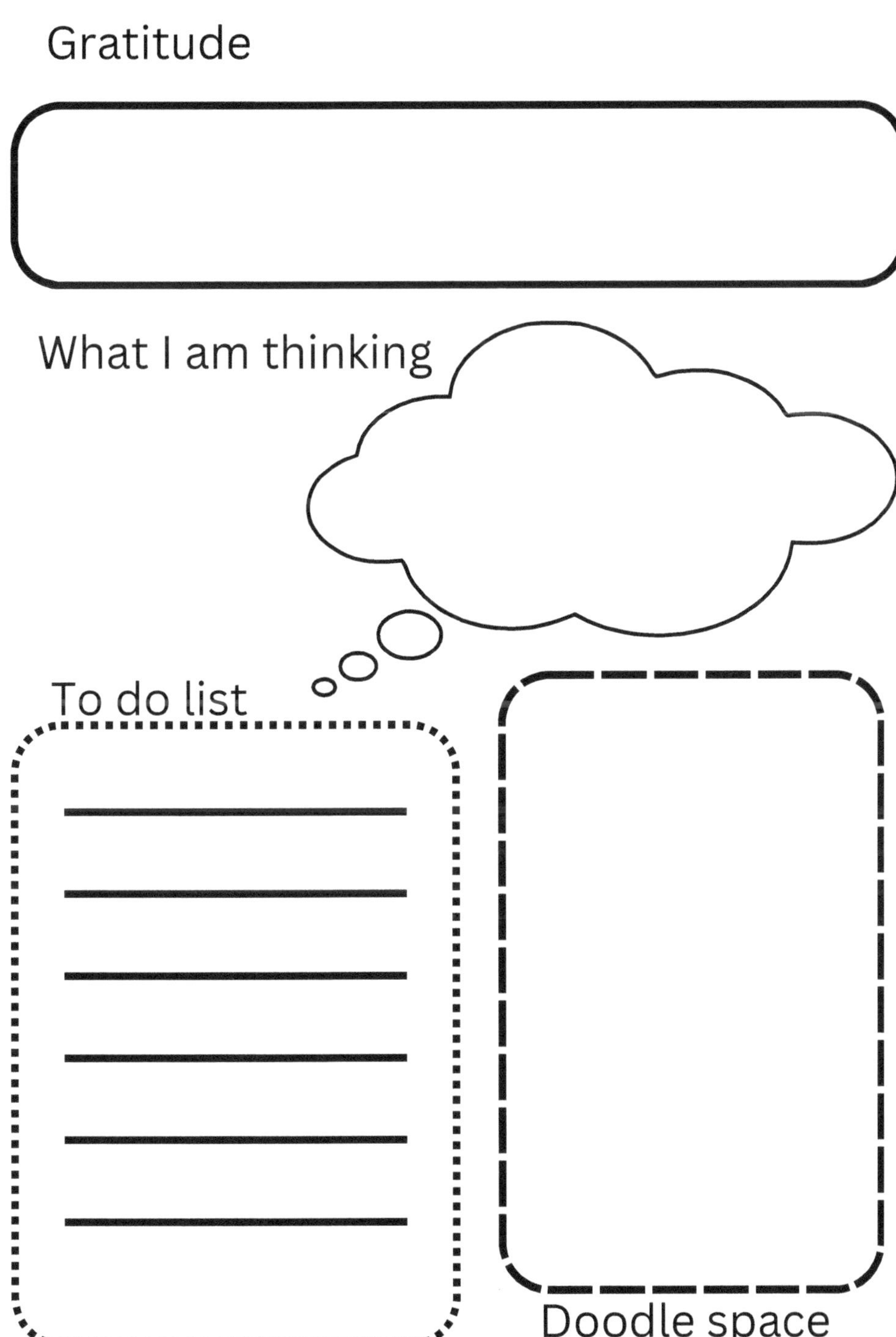

Date:..............

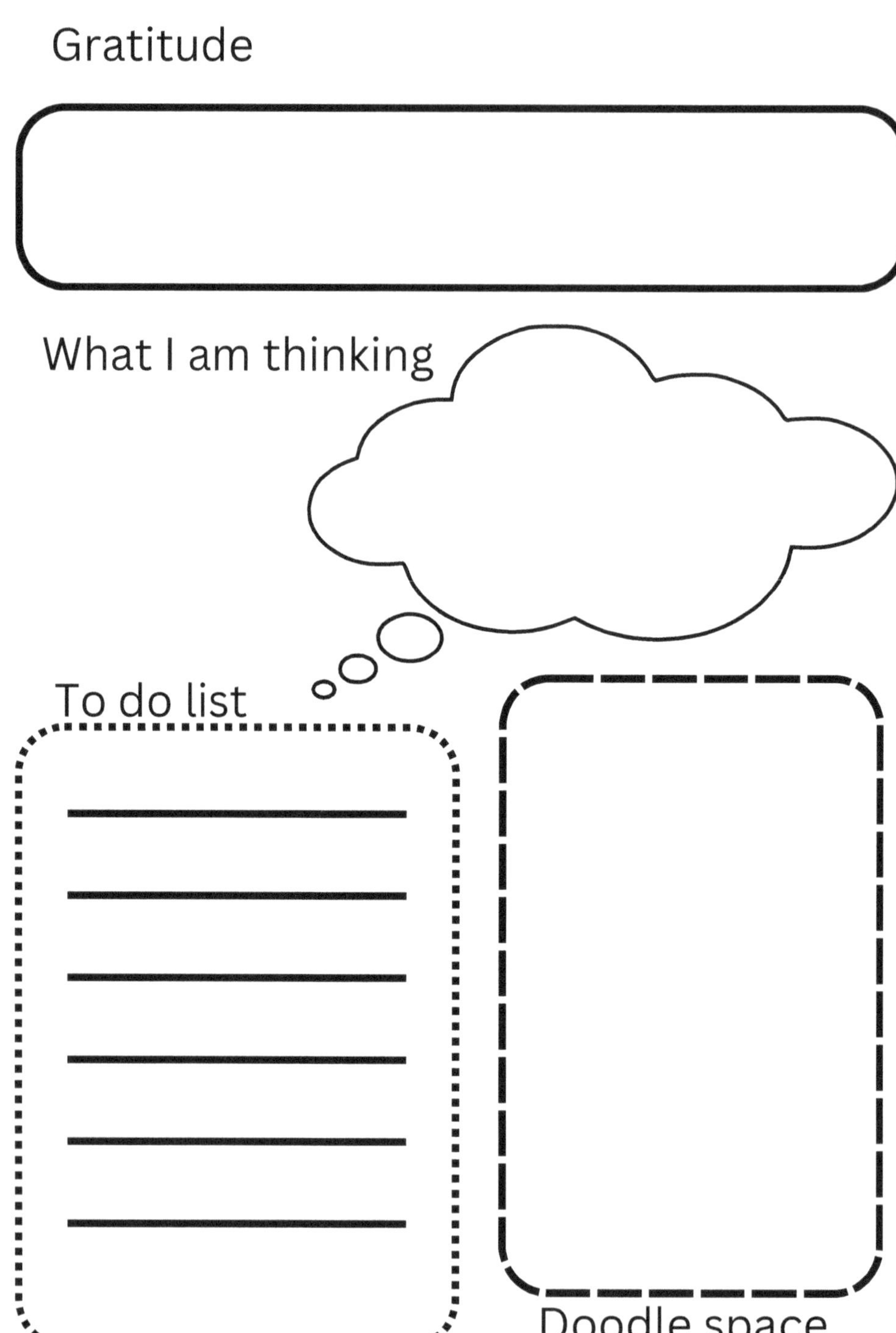

Date:..............

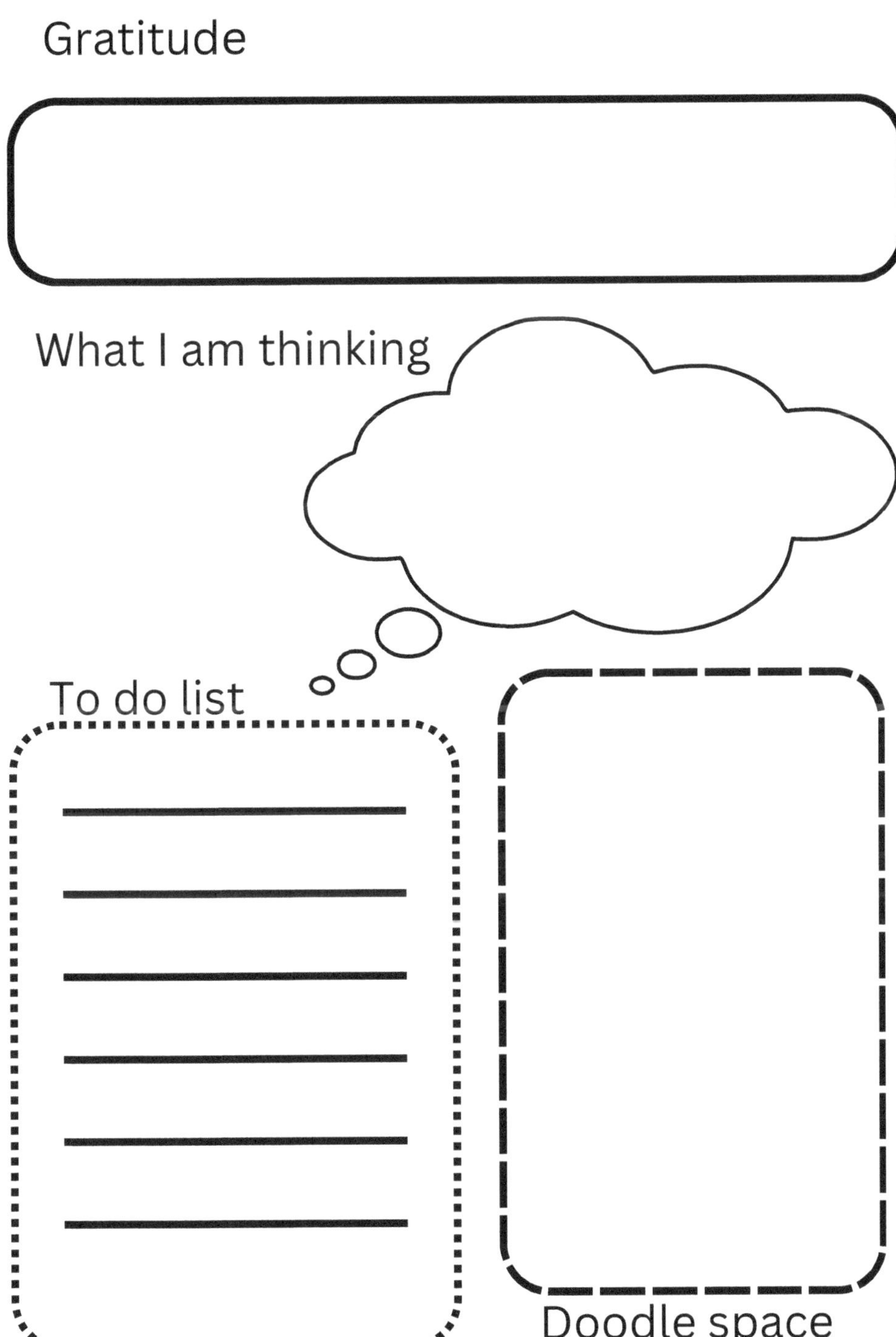

Date:..............

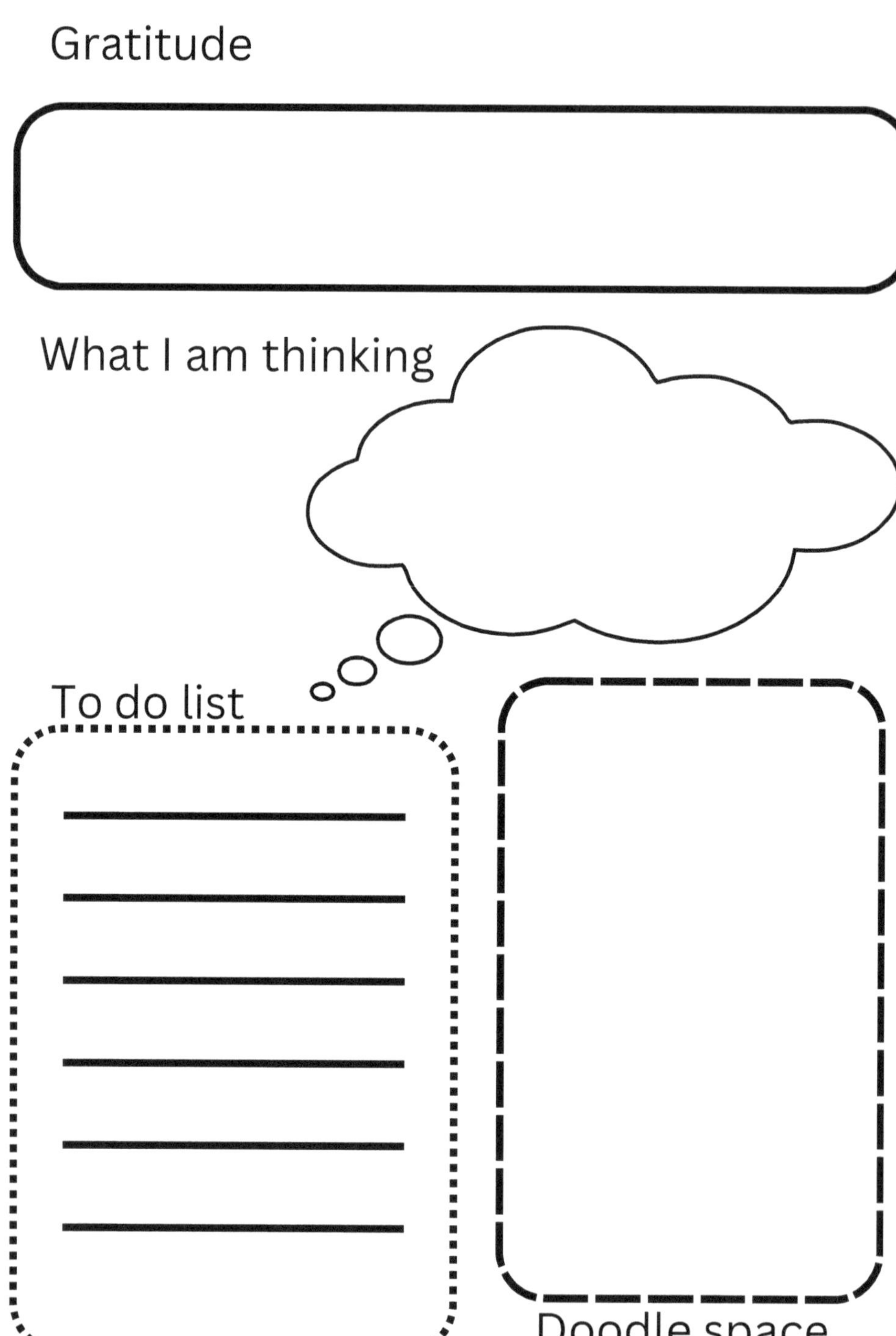

Date:..............

Weekly planner

Date:..../.../.....to..../.../....

MON

TUE

WED

THU

FRI

SAT

SUN

Date:..............

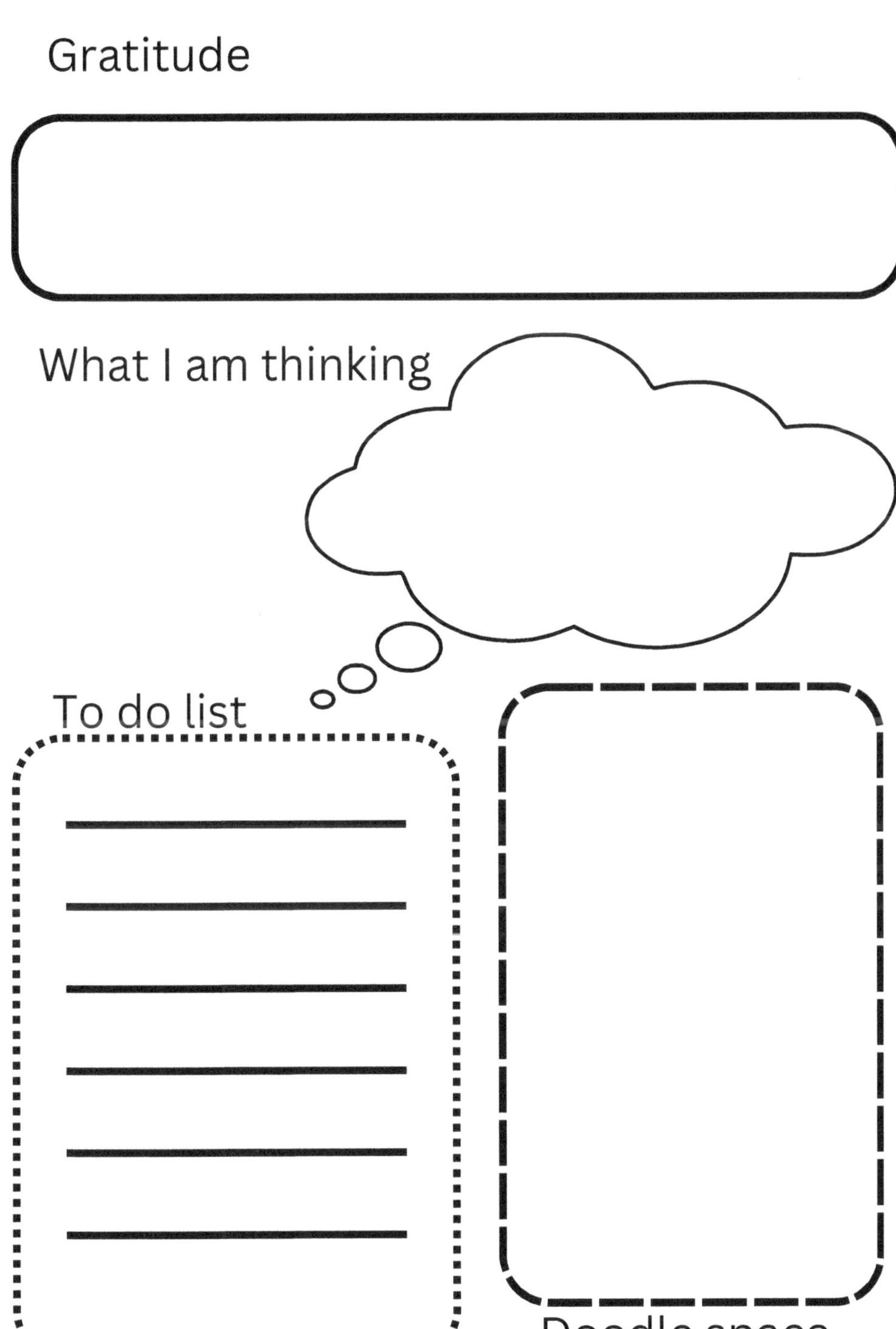

Date:..............

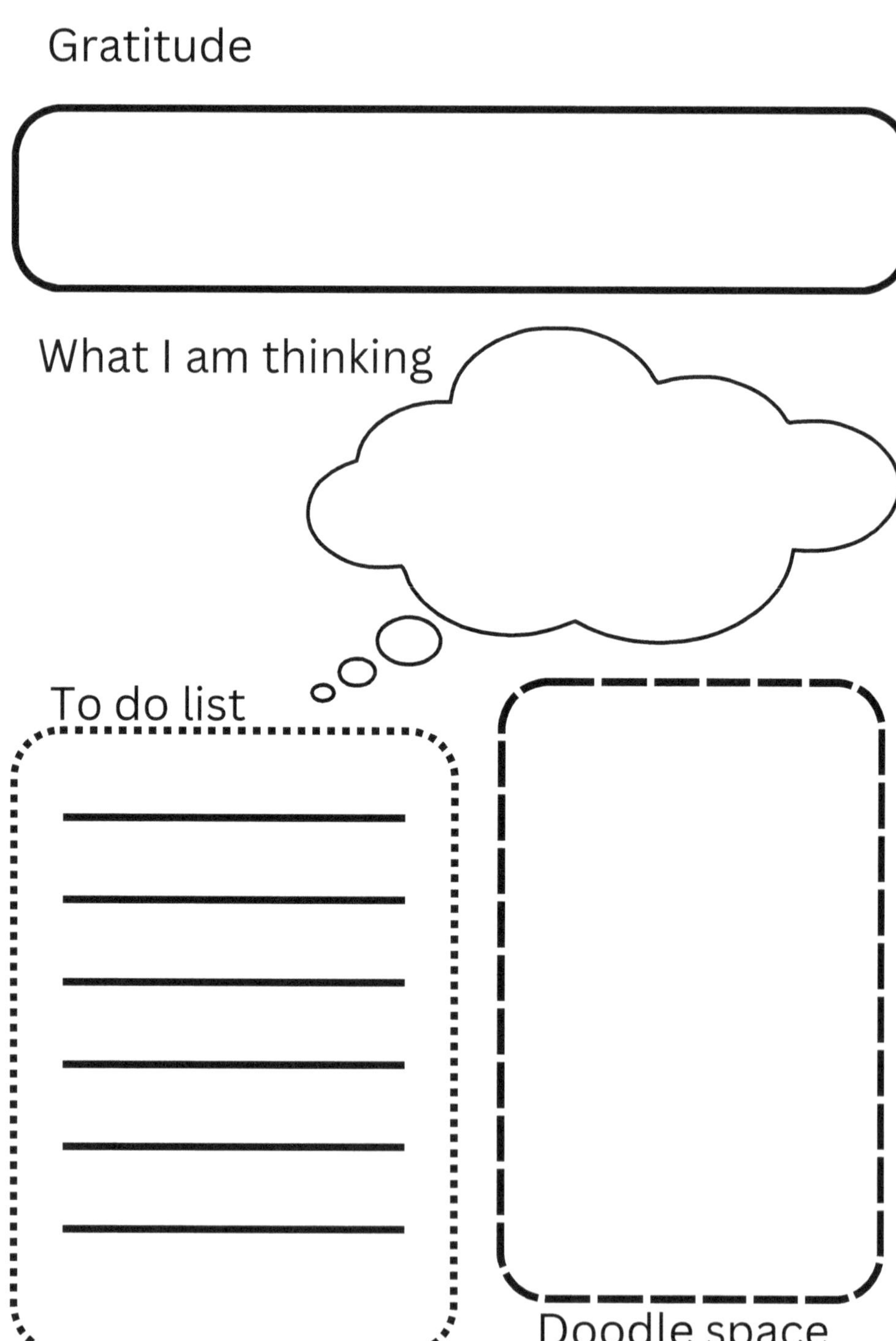

Date:..............

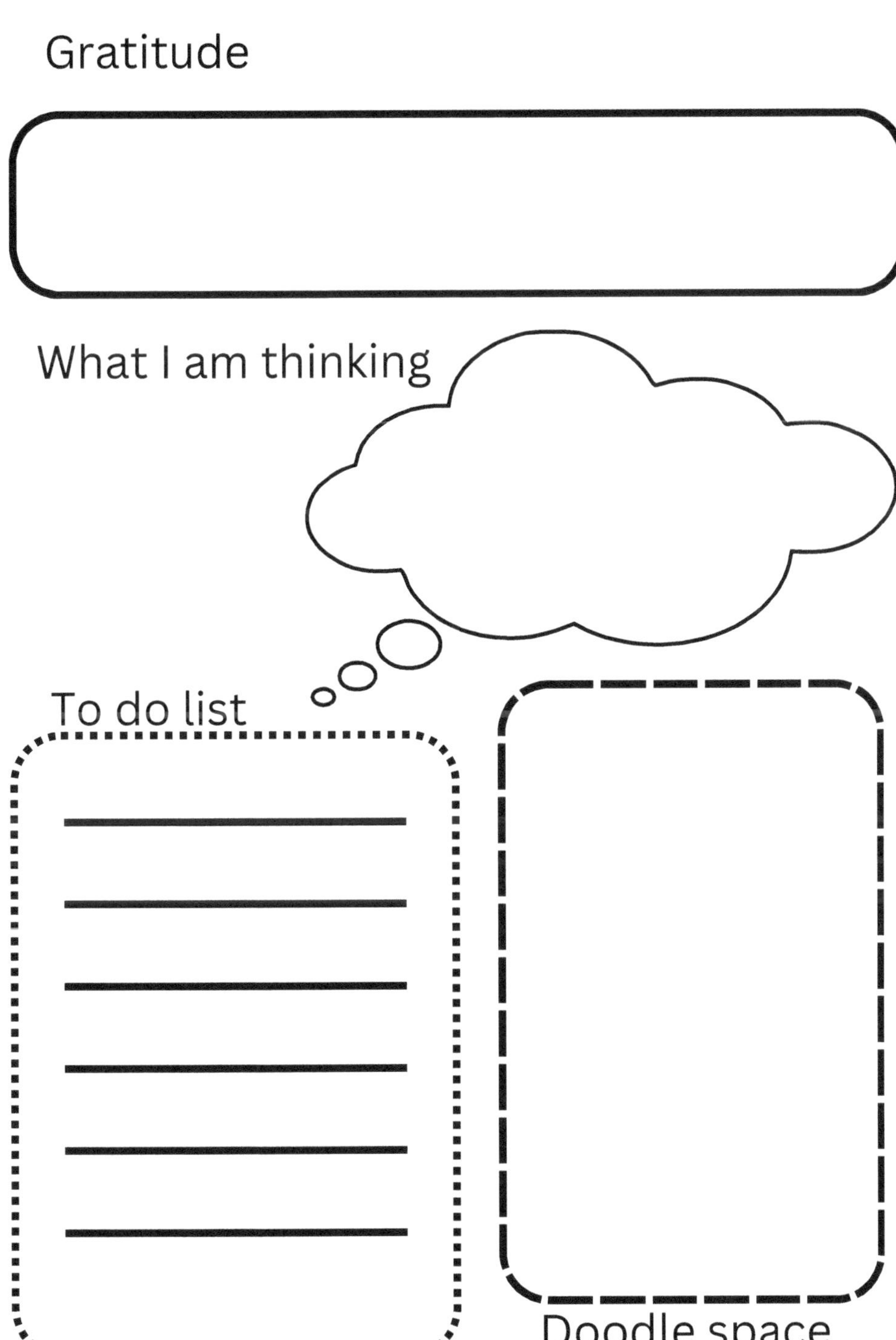

Date:..............
Gratitude
What I am thinking
To do list
Doodle space

Date:..............

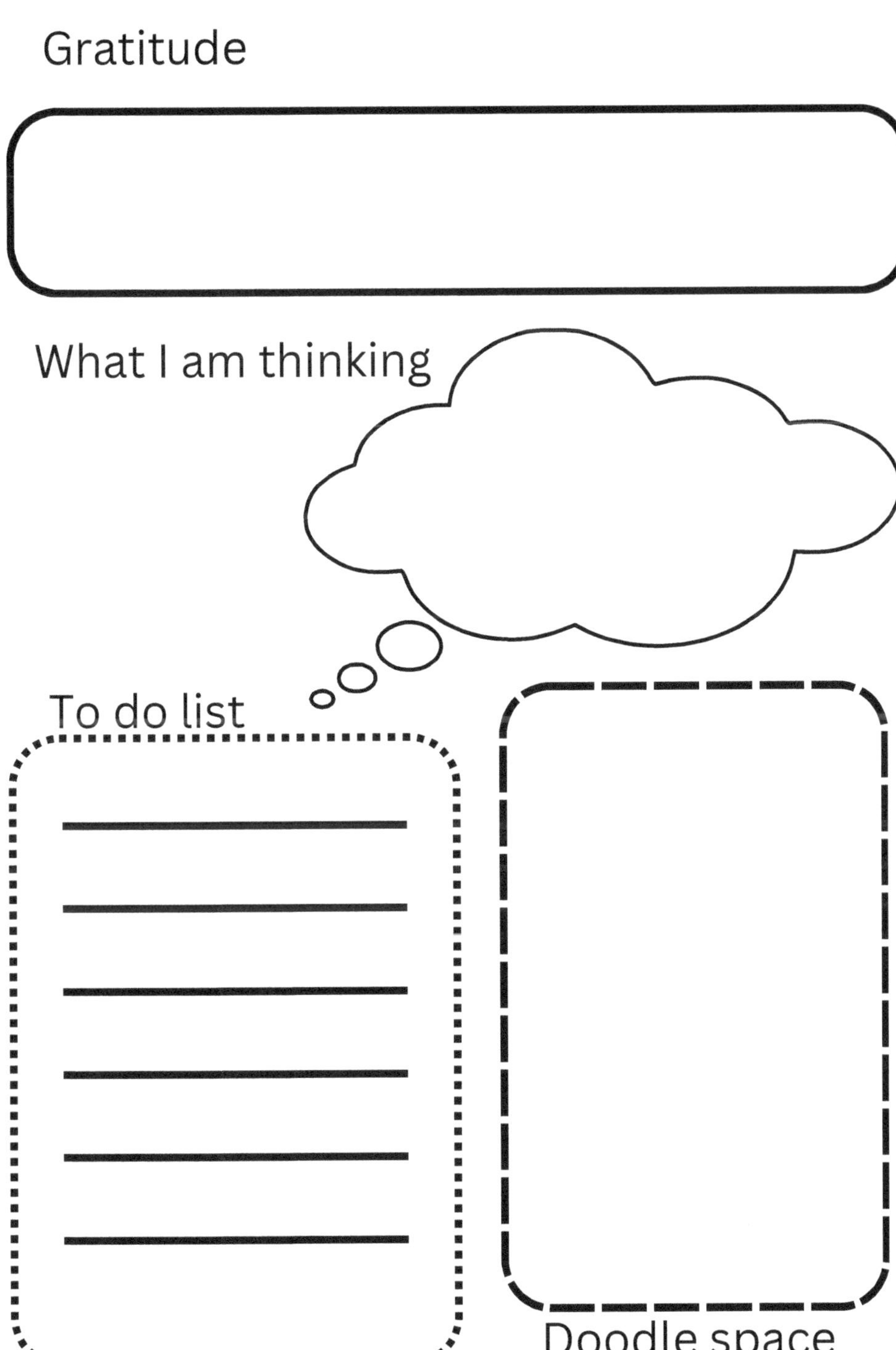

Date:...............

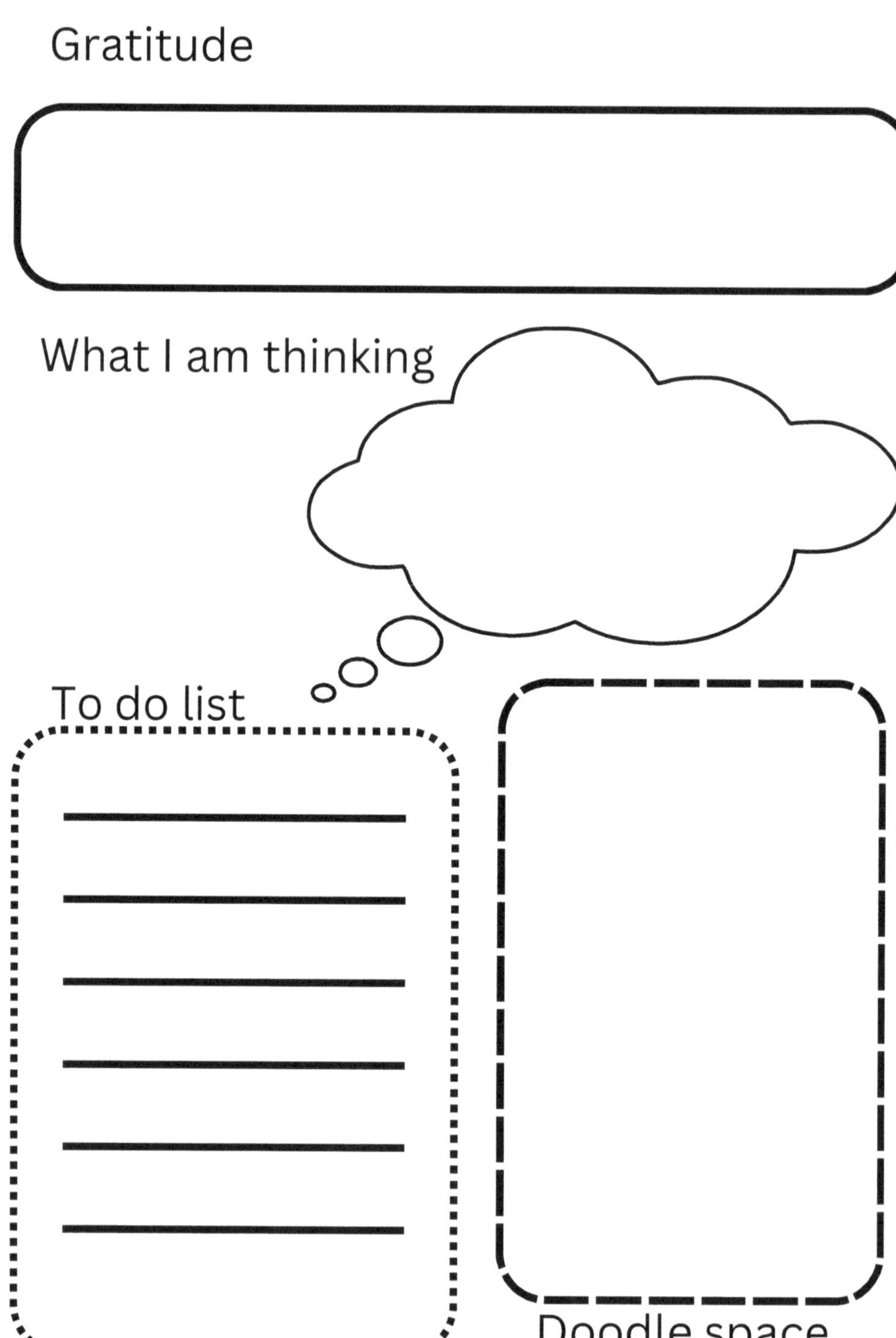

Date:..............

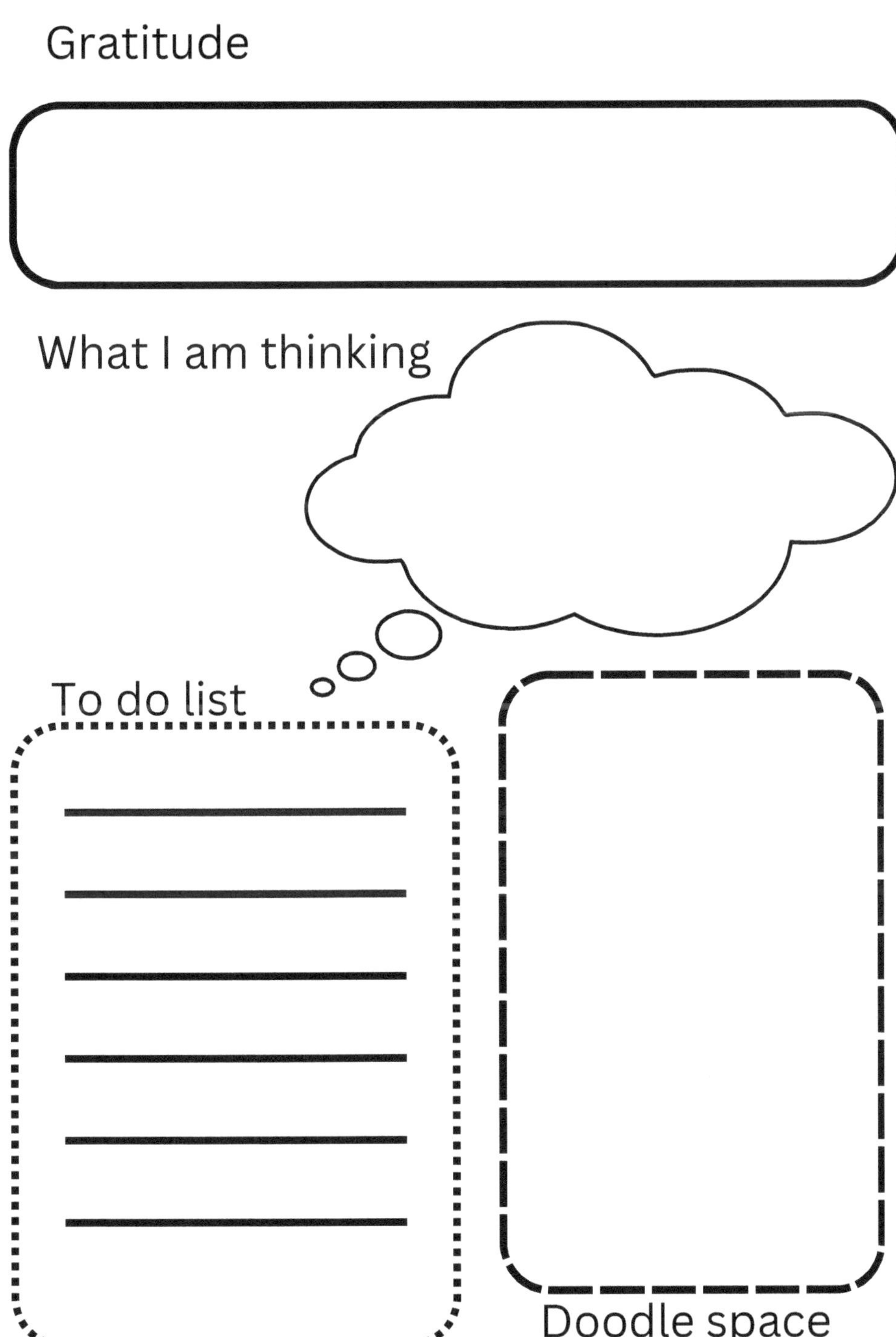

Weekly planner

Date:..../.../.....to..../.../....

MON

TUE

WED

THU

FRI

SAT

SUN

Date:...............

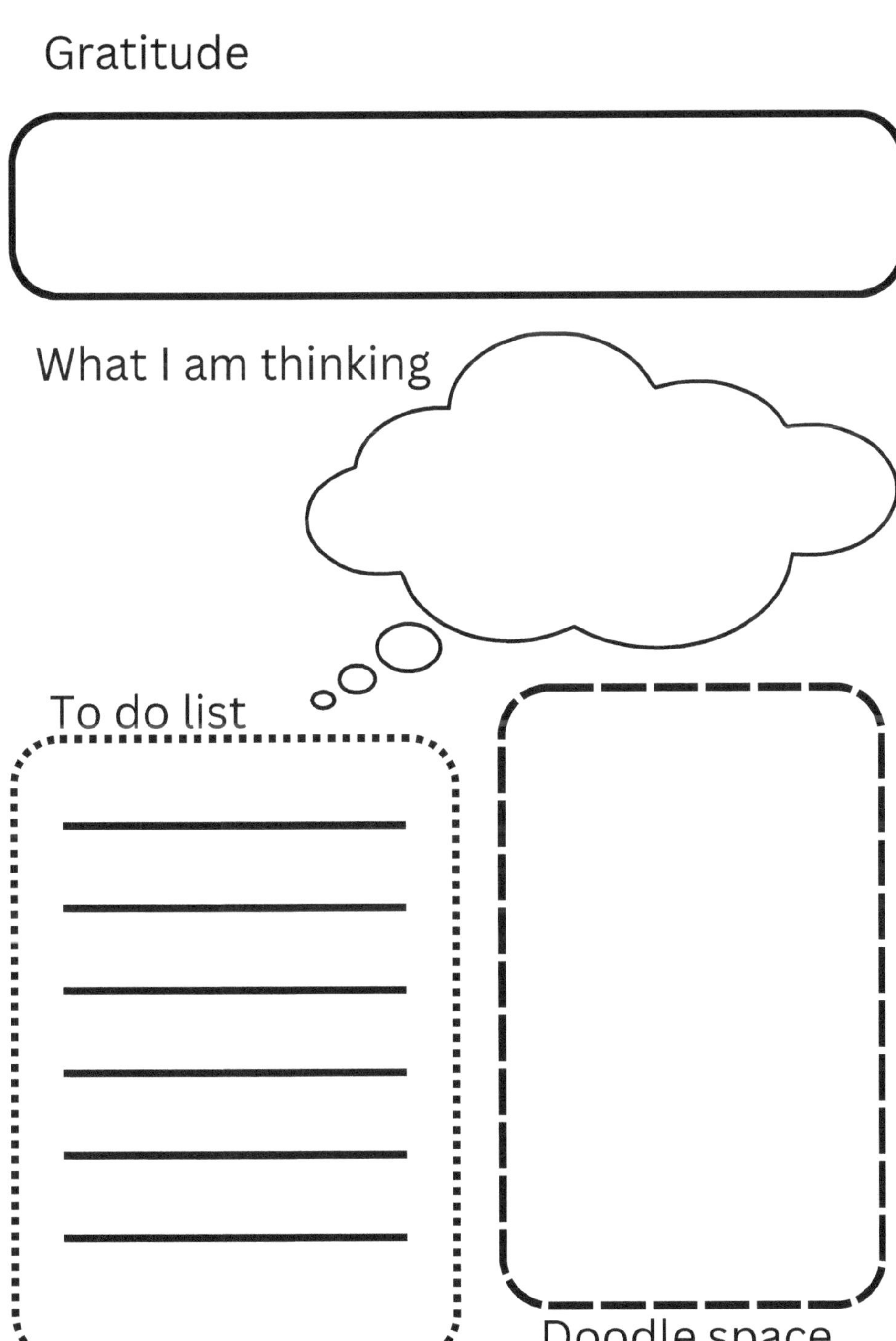

Date:..............

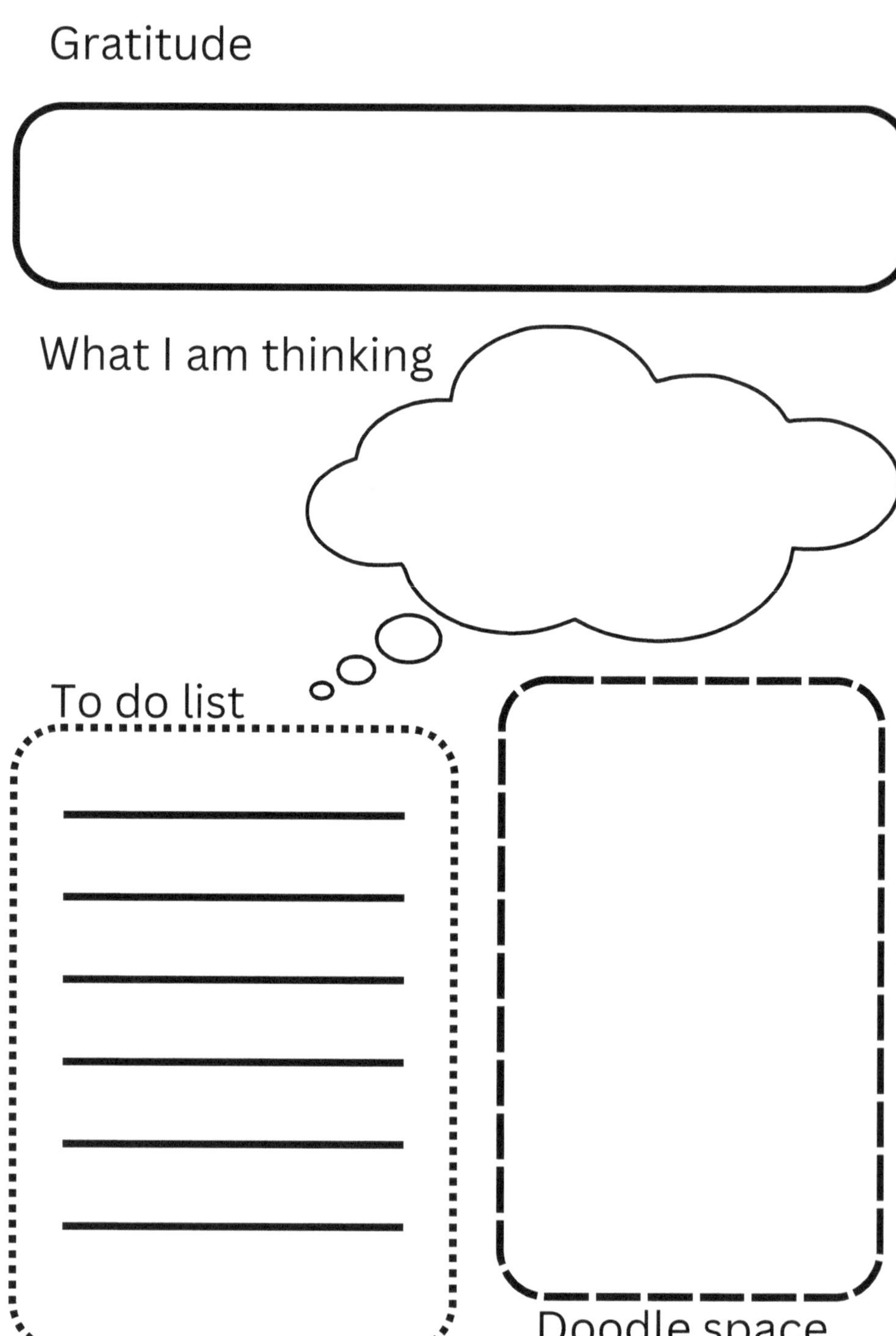

Date:.............

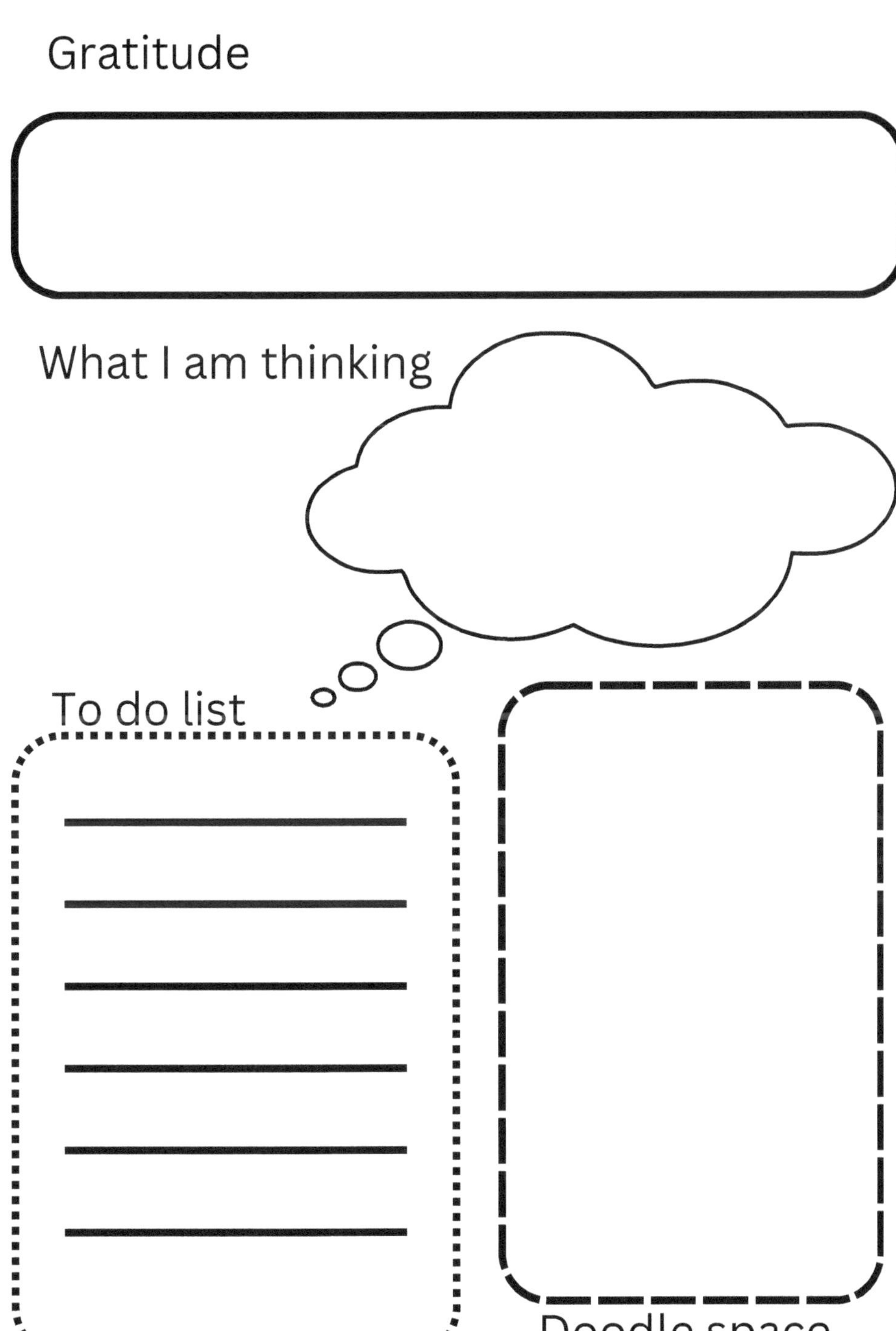

Date:..............

Date:..............

Date:..............

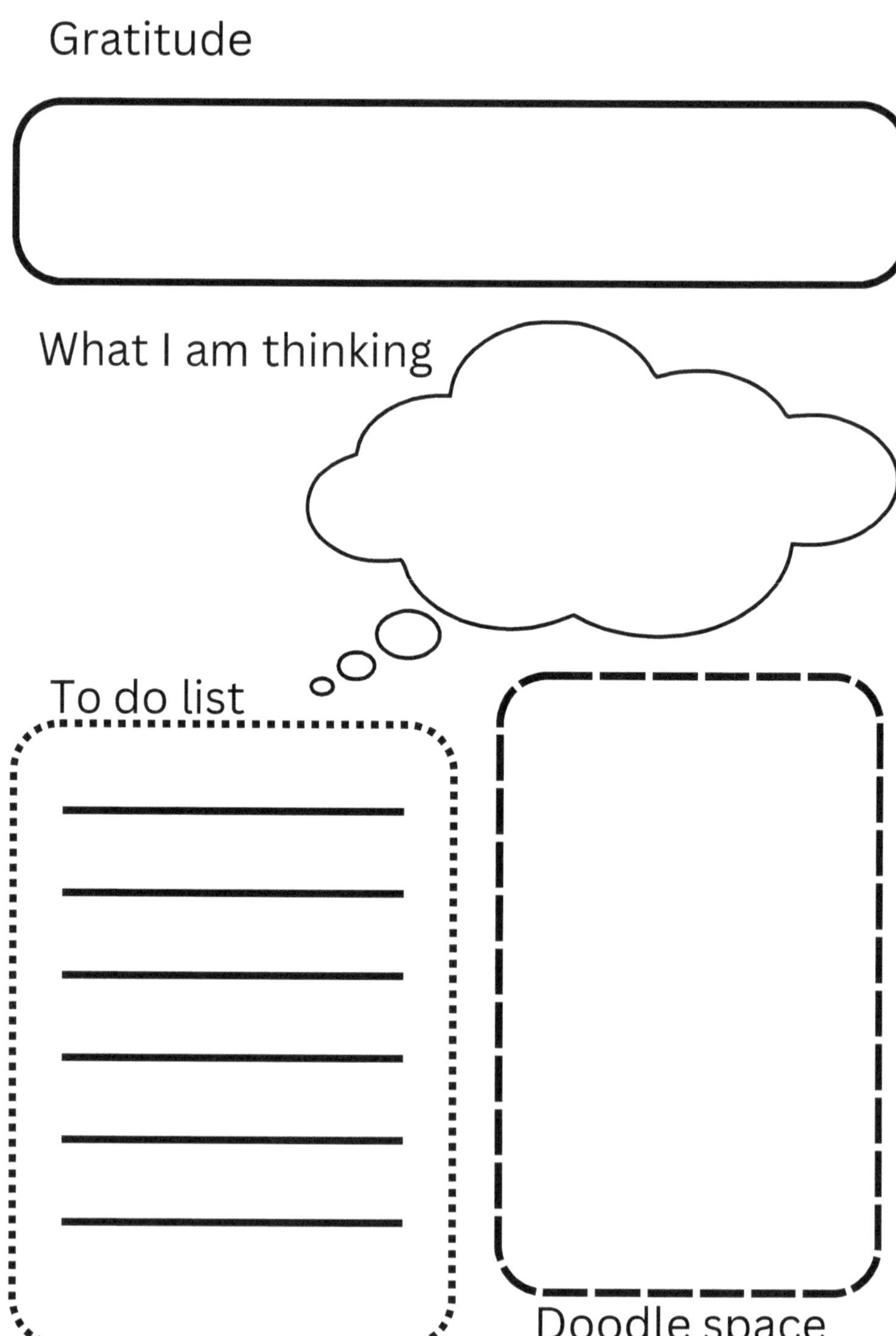

Date:..............

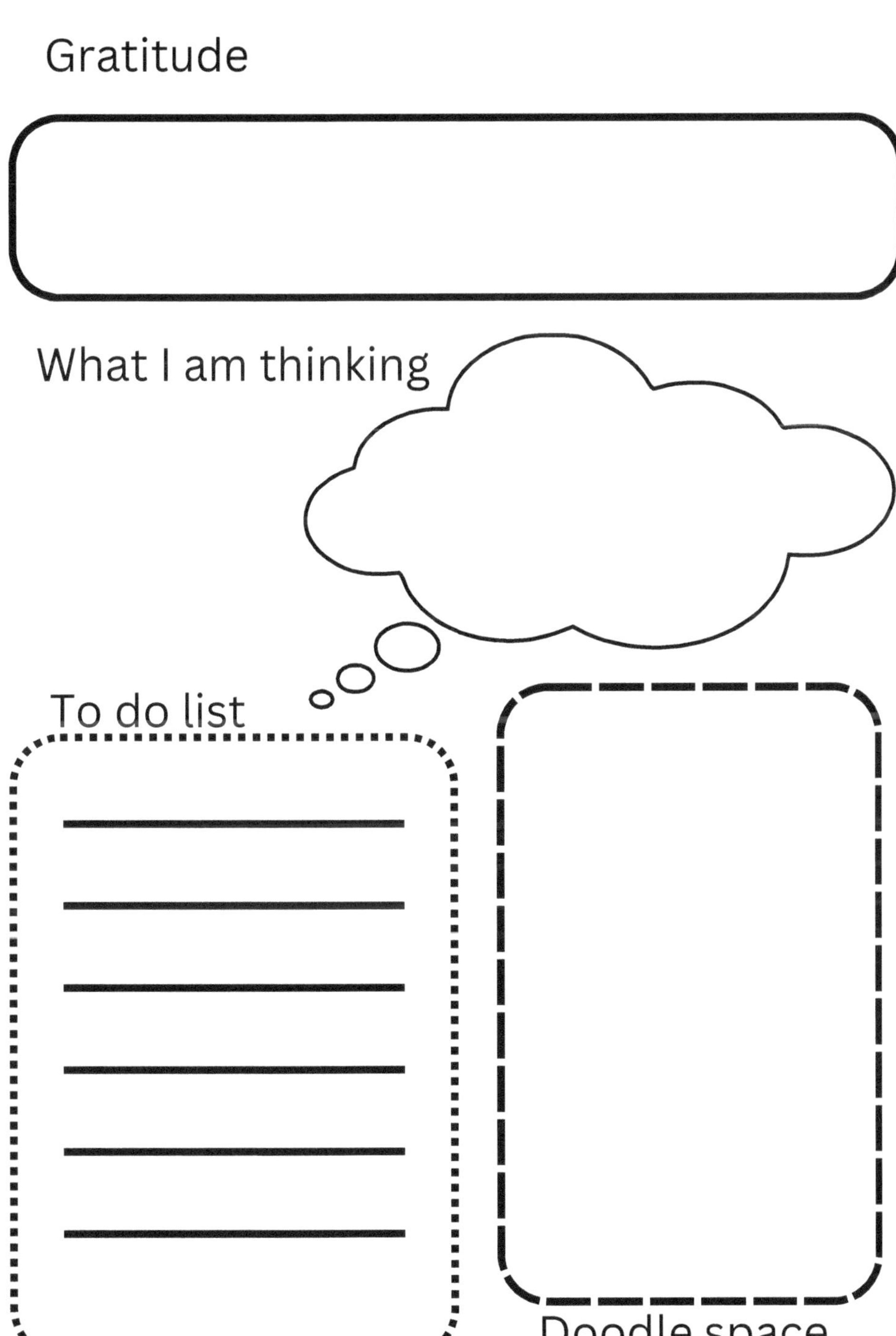

Weekly planner

Date:..../.../.....to..../.../....

MON

TUE

WED

THU

FRI

SAT

SUN

Date:..............

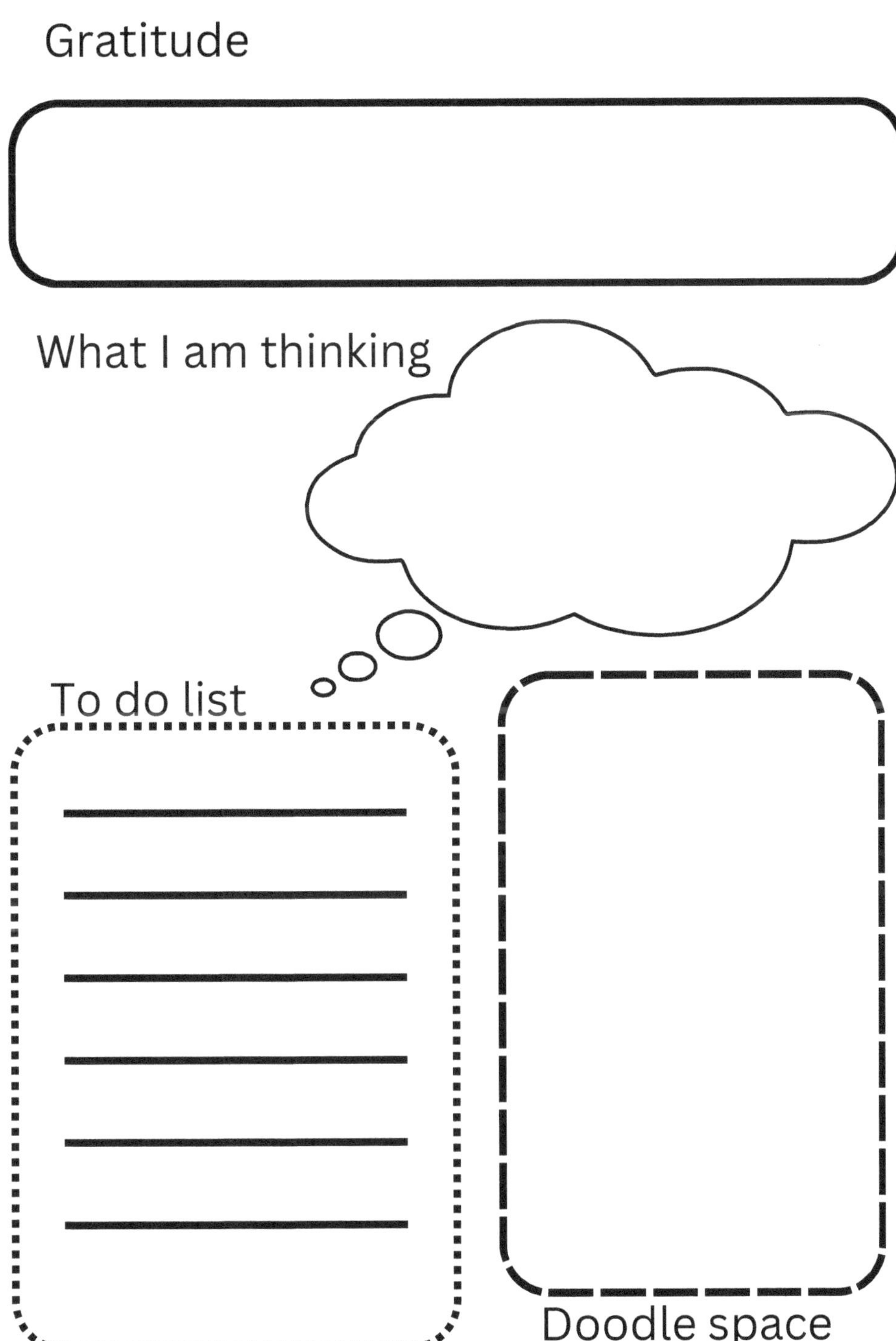

Date:..............

Date:..............

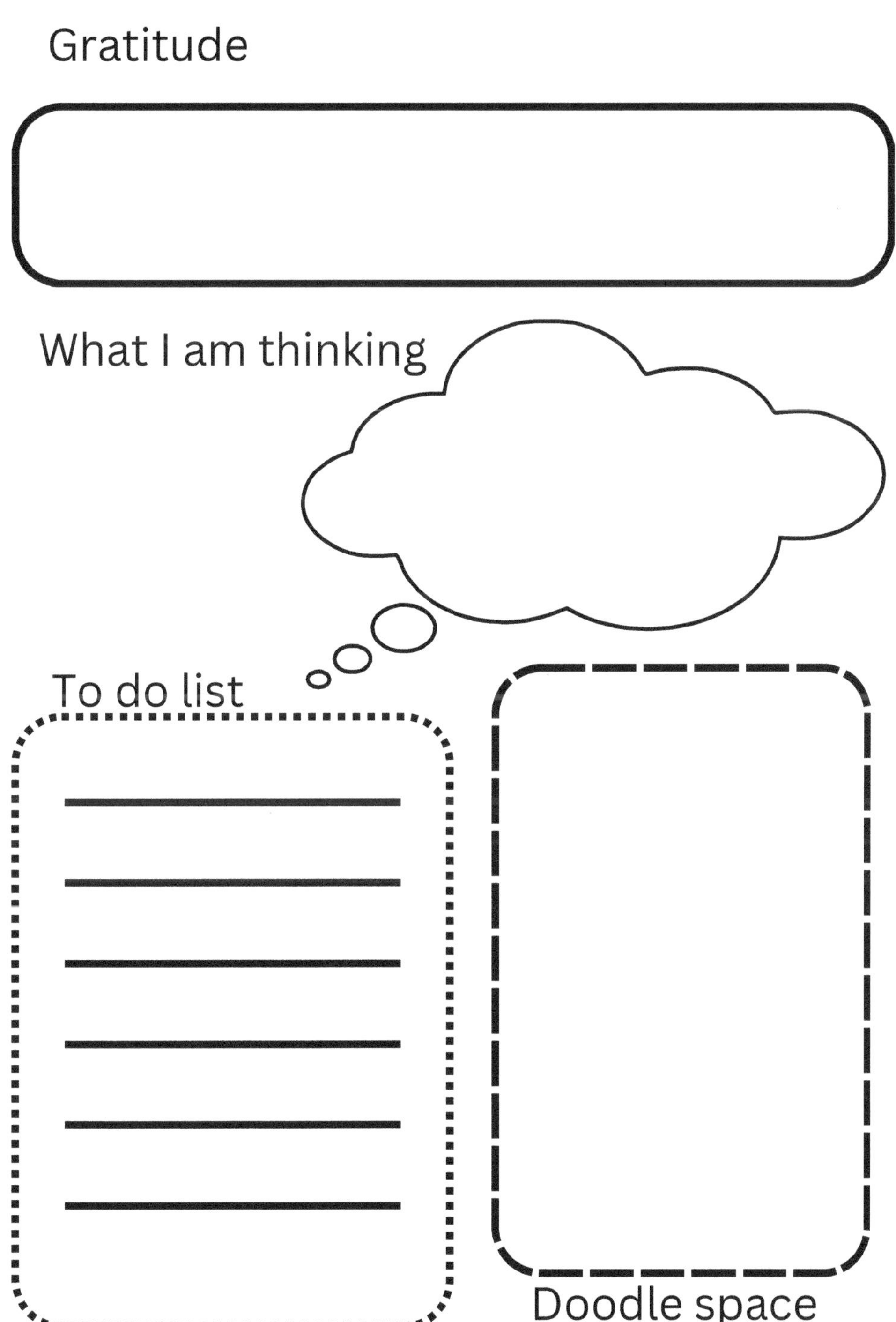

Date:..............
Gratitude
What I am thinking
To do list
Doodle space

Date:..............

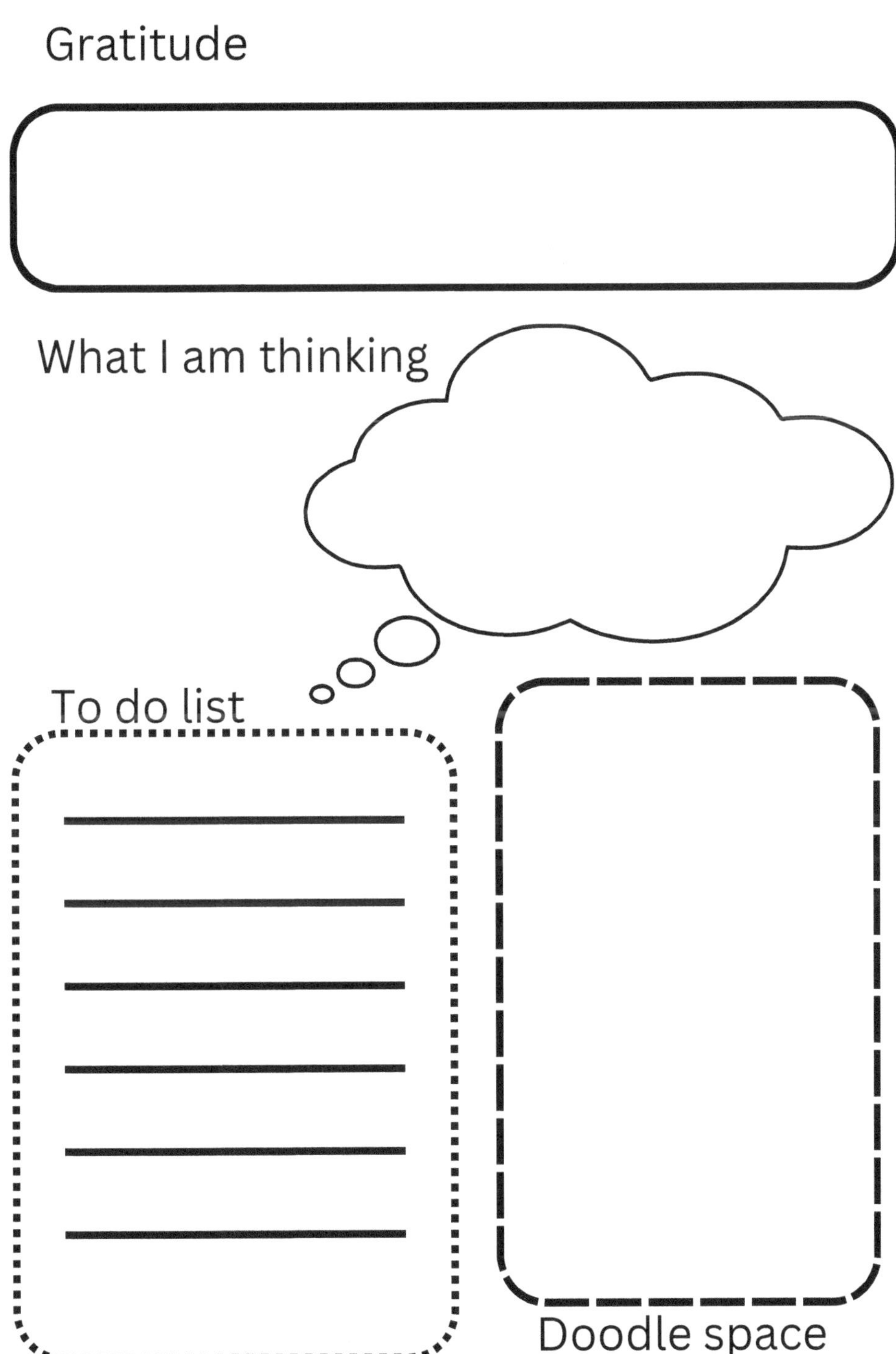

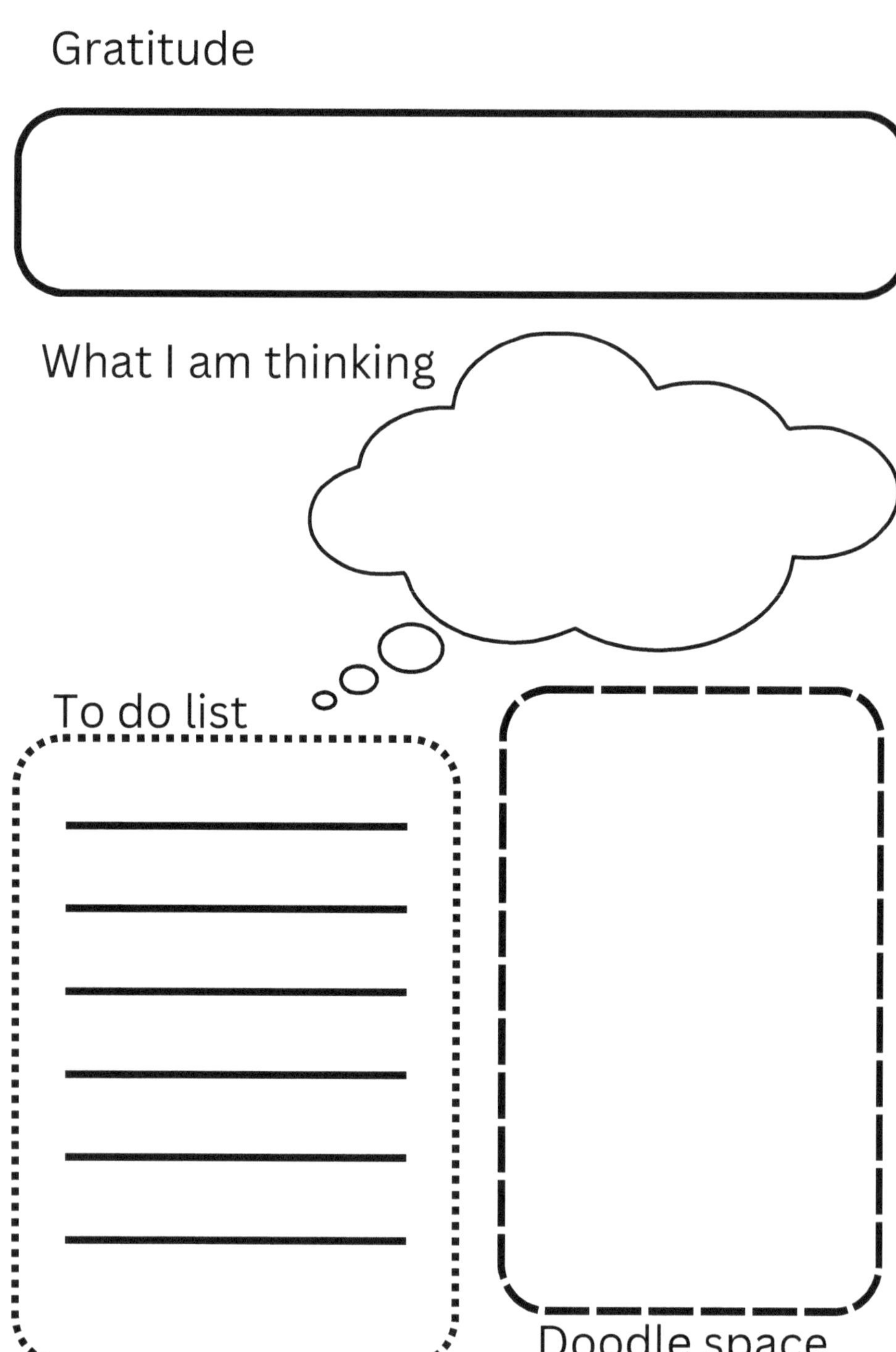
Date:..............
Gratitude
What I am thinking
To do list
Doodle space

Date:..............

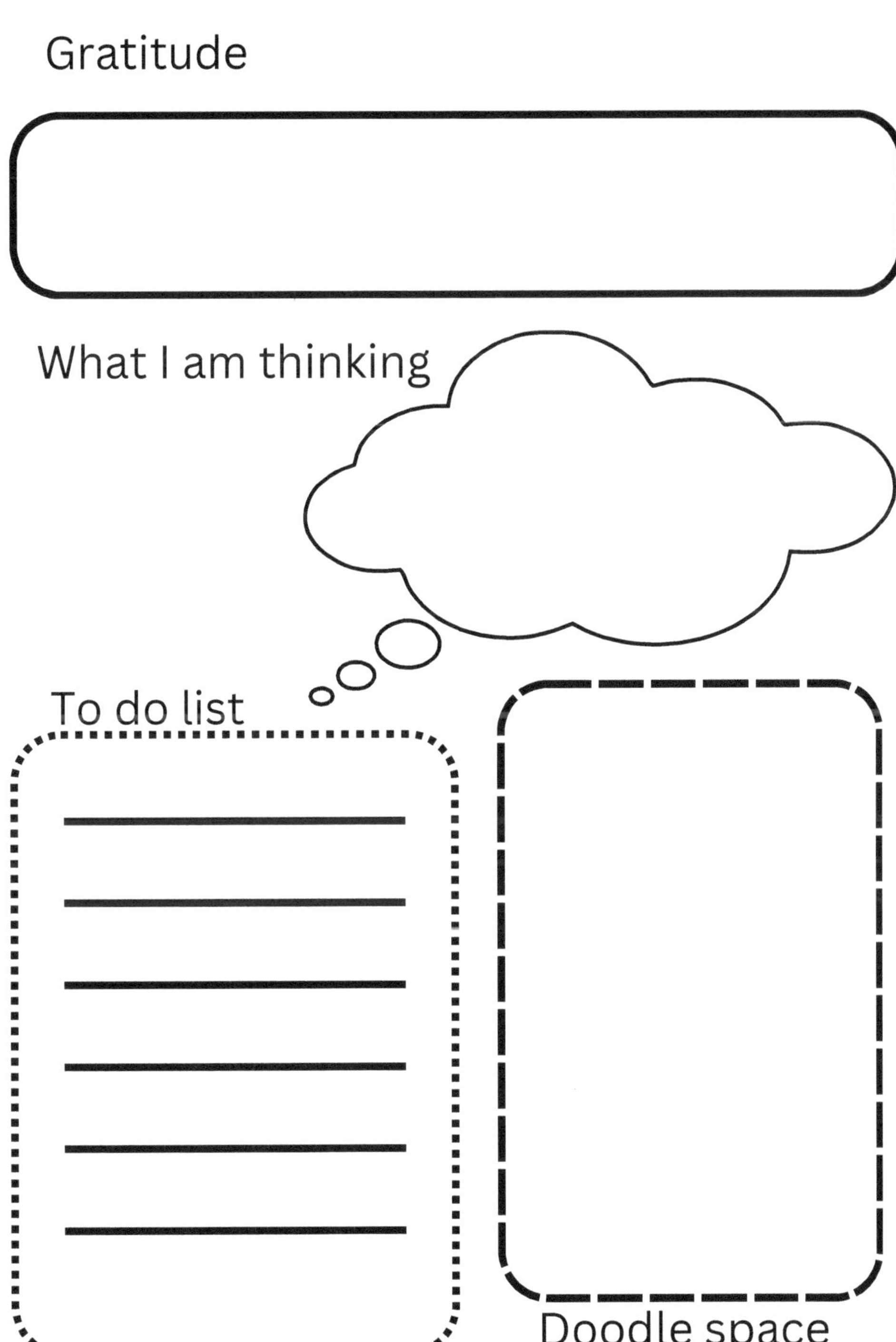

Weekly planner

Date:..../.../.....to..../.../....

MON

TUE

WED

THU

FRI

SAT

SUN

Date:..............

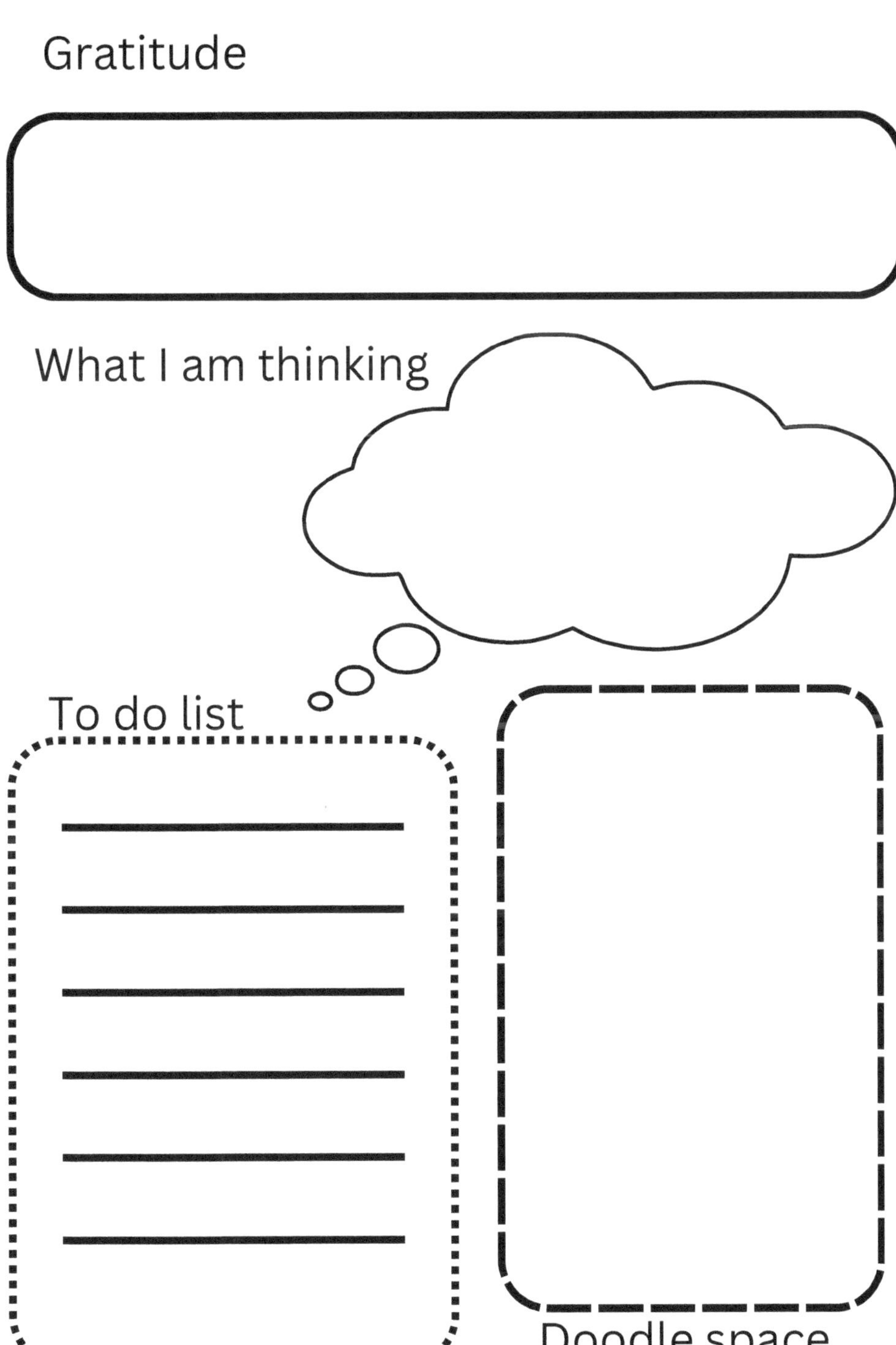

Date:..............

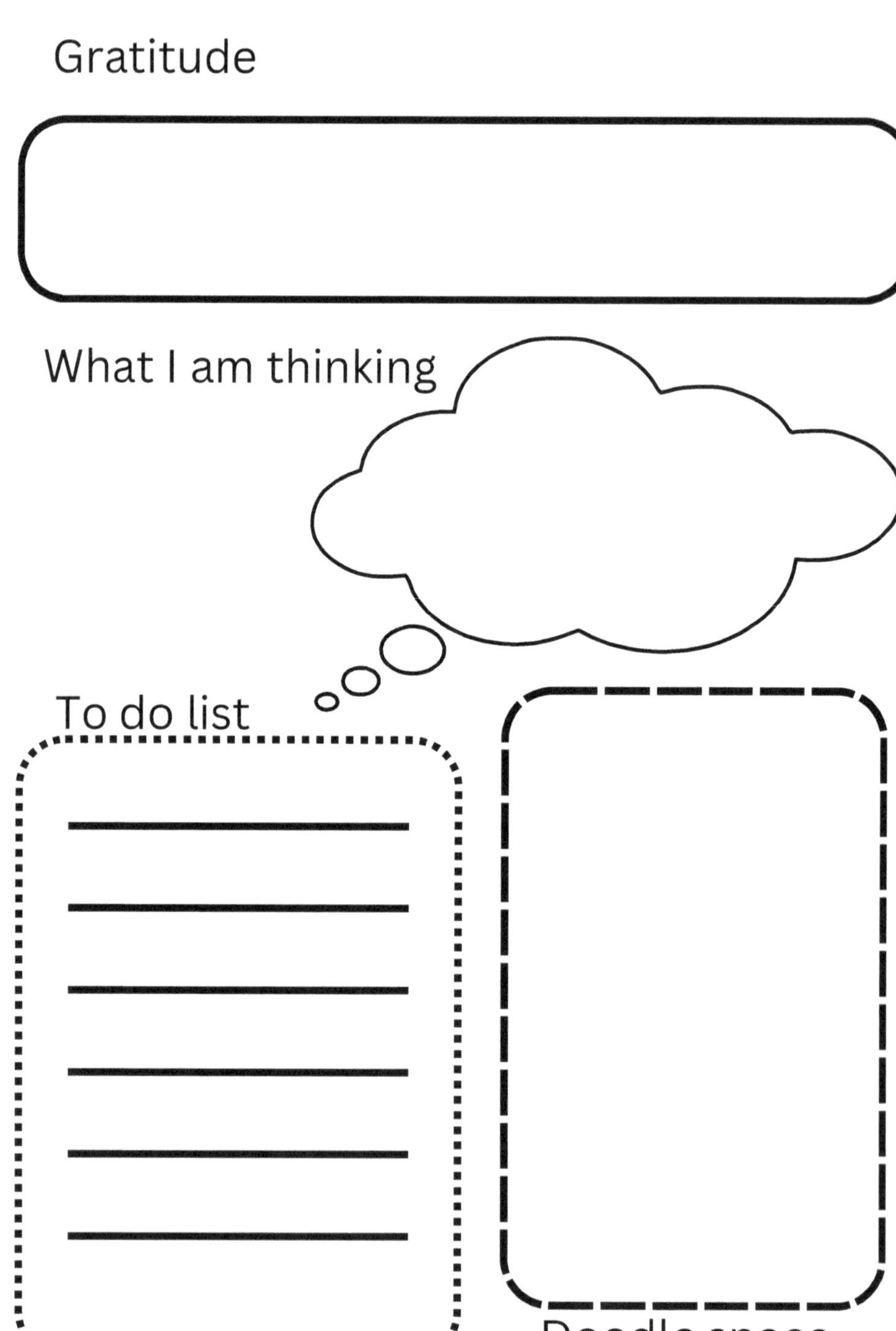

Date:..............

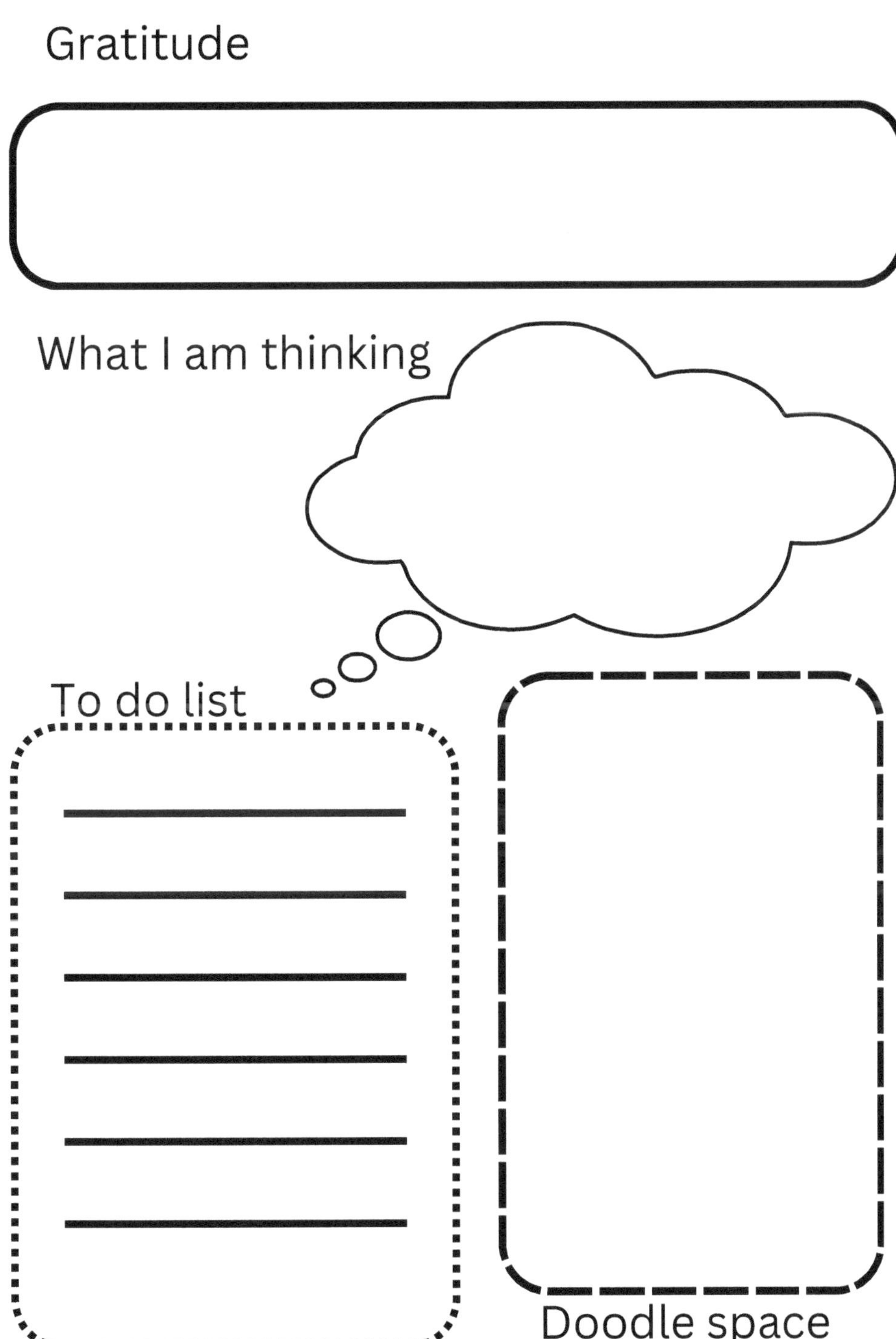

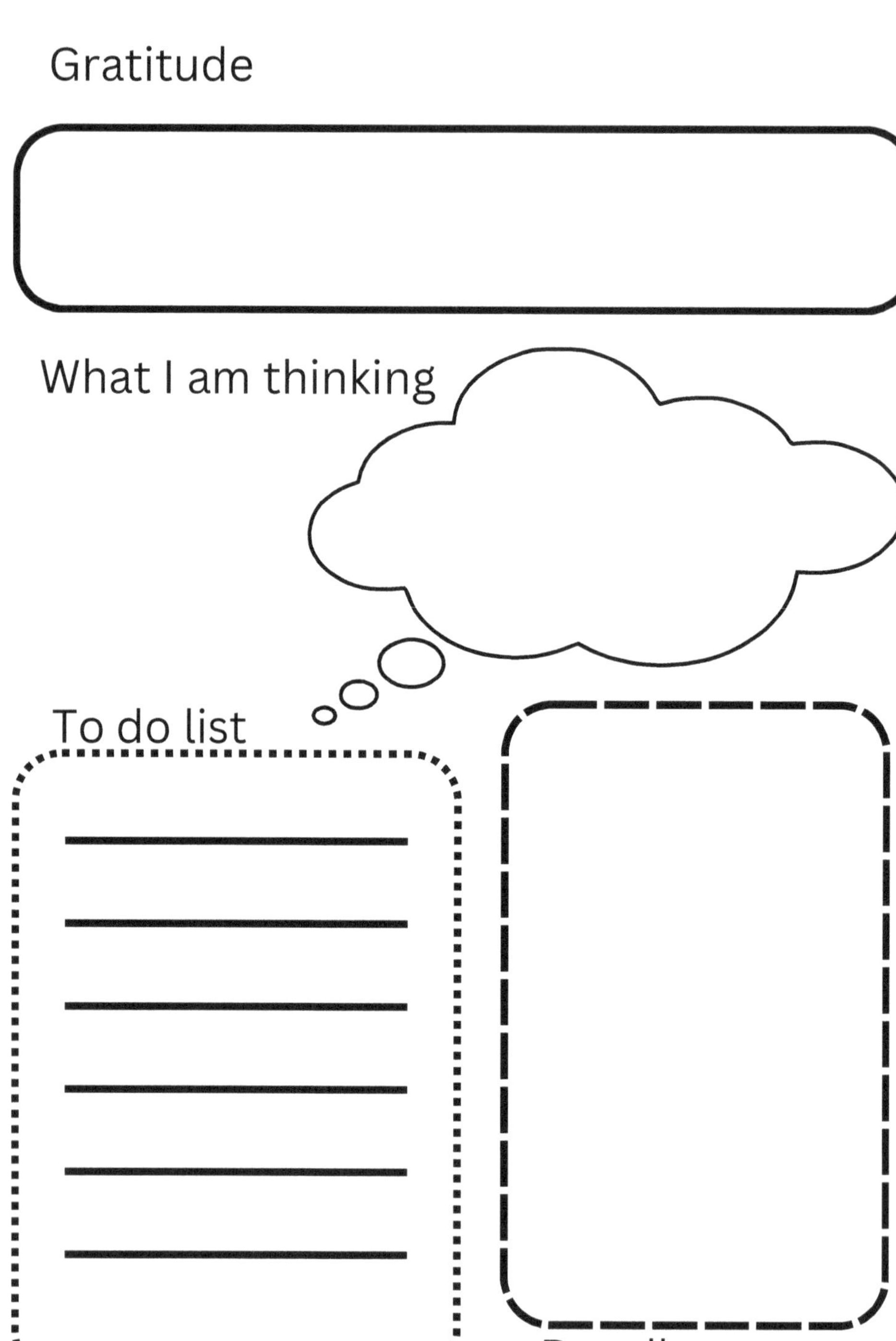
Date:..............
Gratitude
What I am thinking
To do list
Doodle space

Date:...............

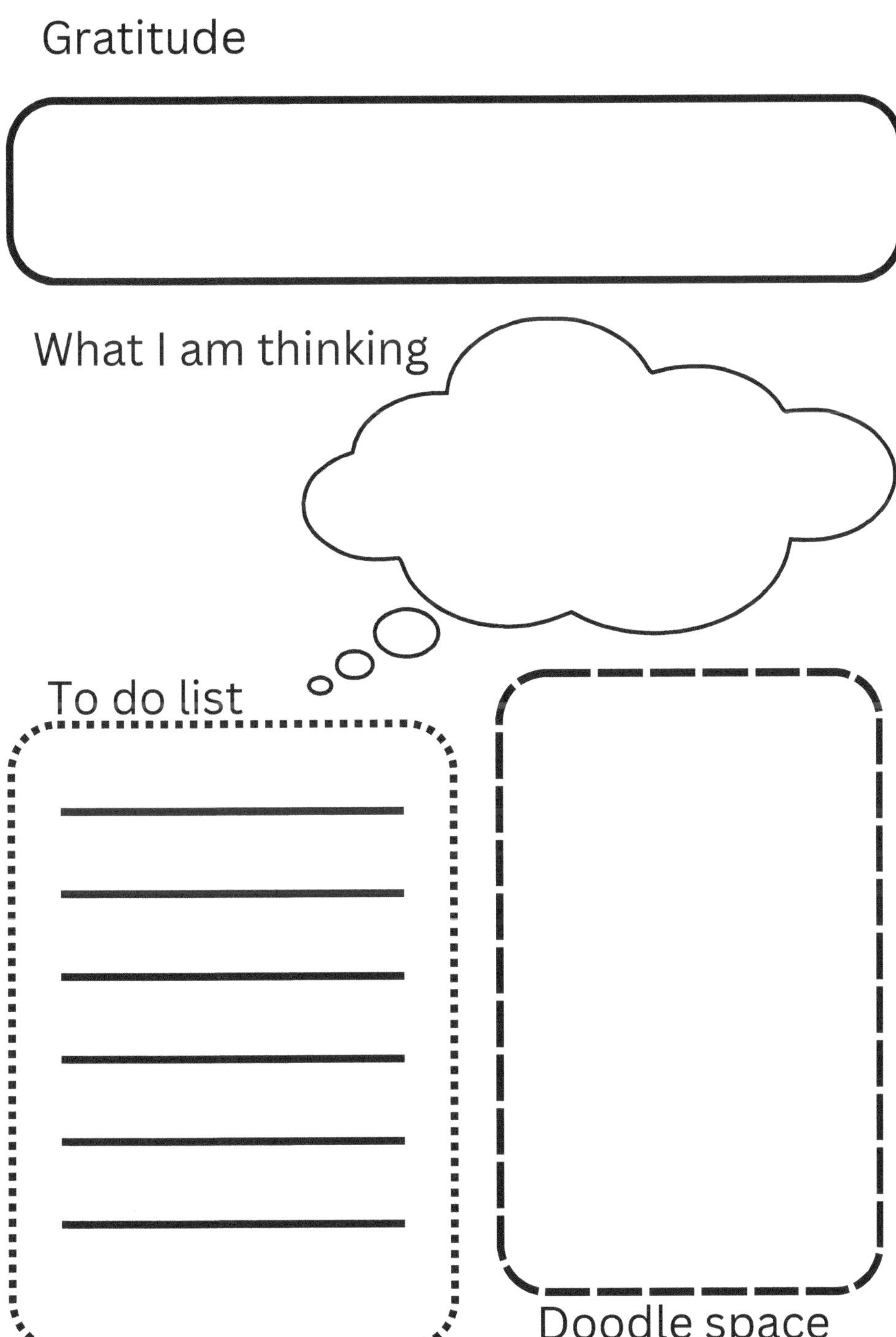

Date:..............

Date:..............

Weekly planner

Date:..../.../.....to..../.../....

MON

TUE

WED

THU

FRI

SAT

SUN

Date:...............

Date:..............

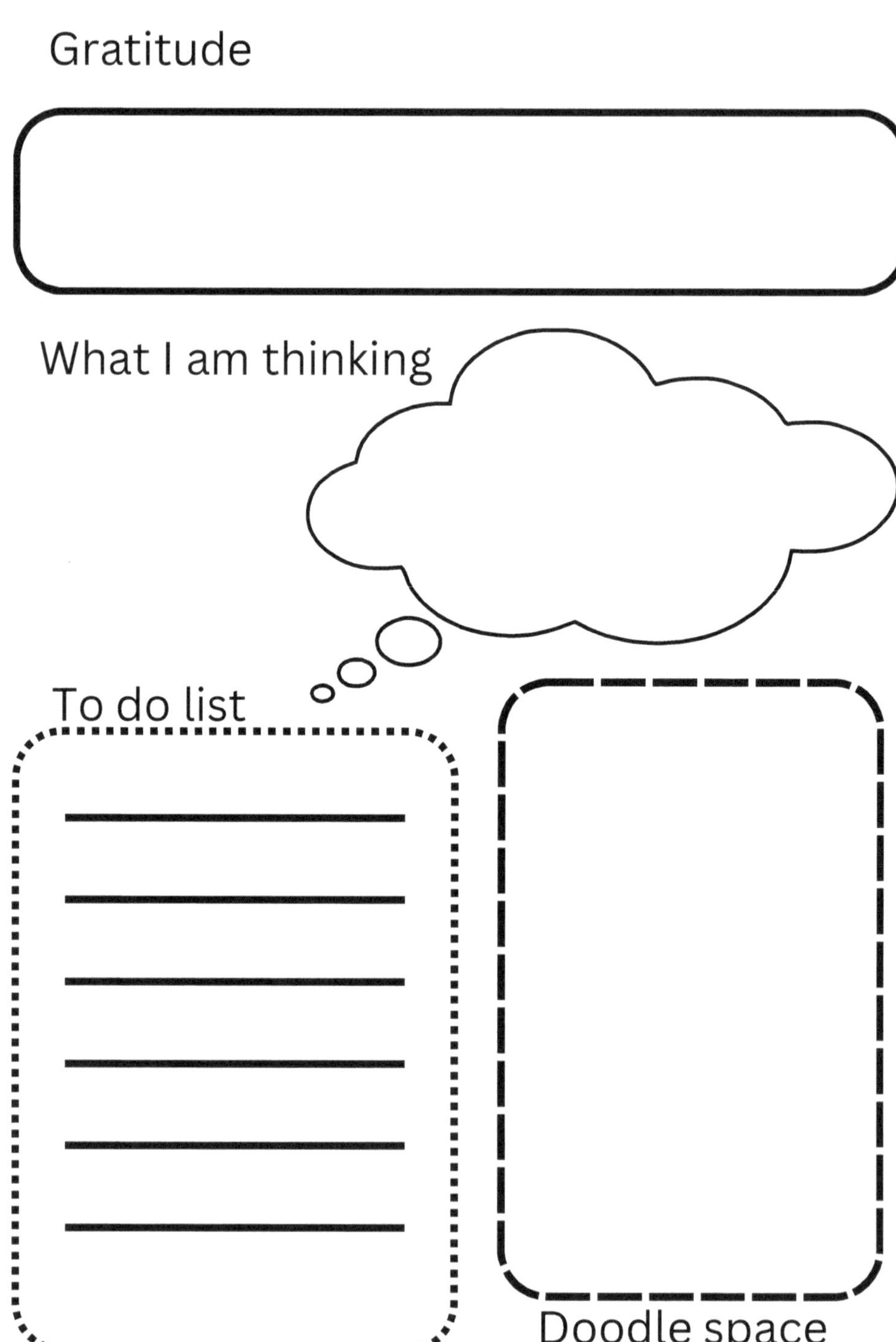

Date:..............

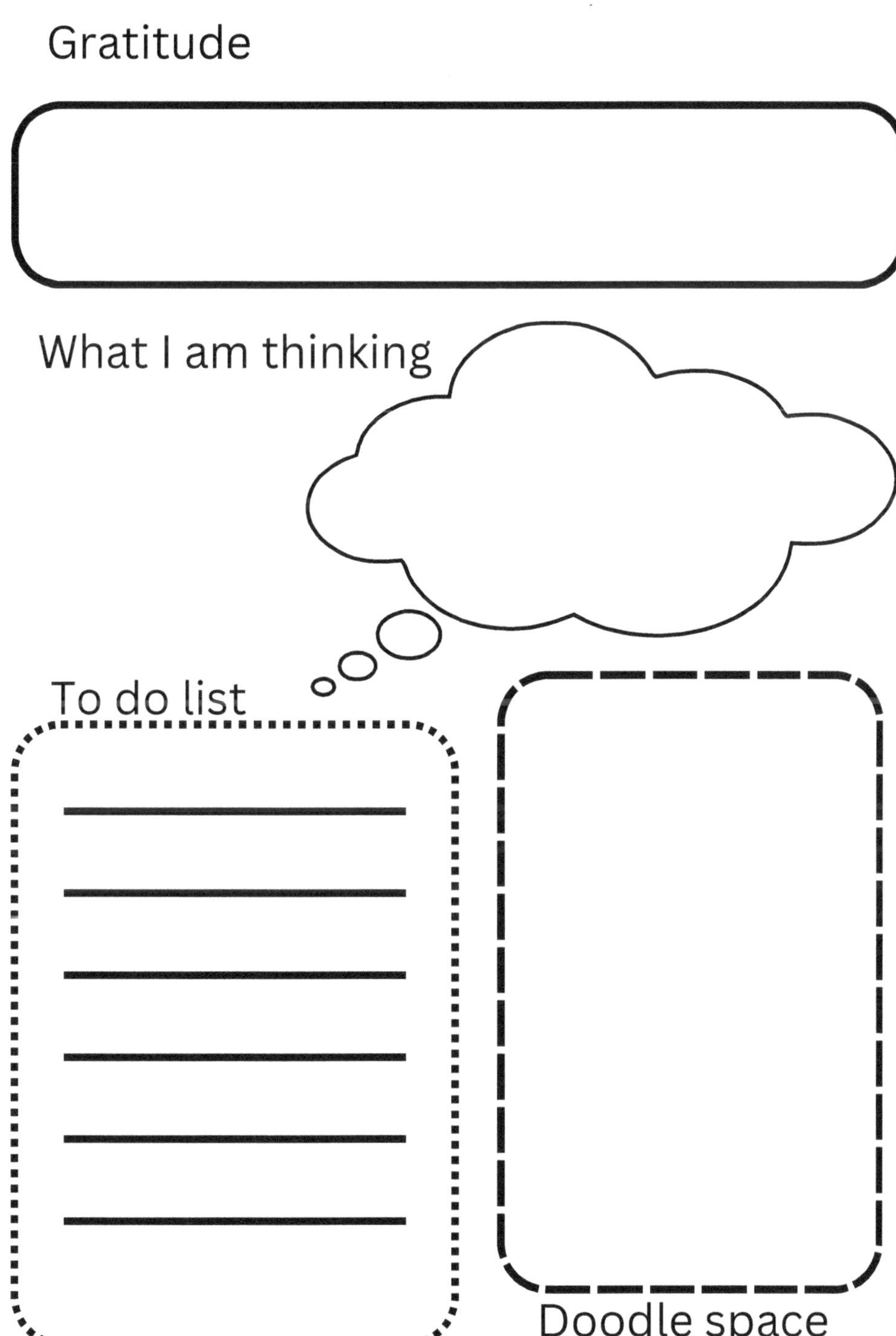

Date:..............
Gratitude
What I am thinking
To do list
Doodle space

Date:..............

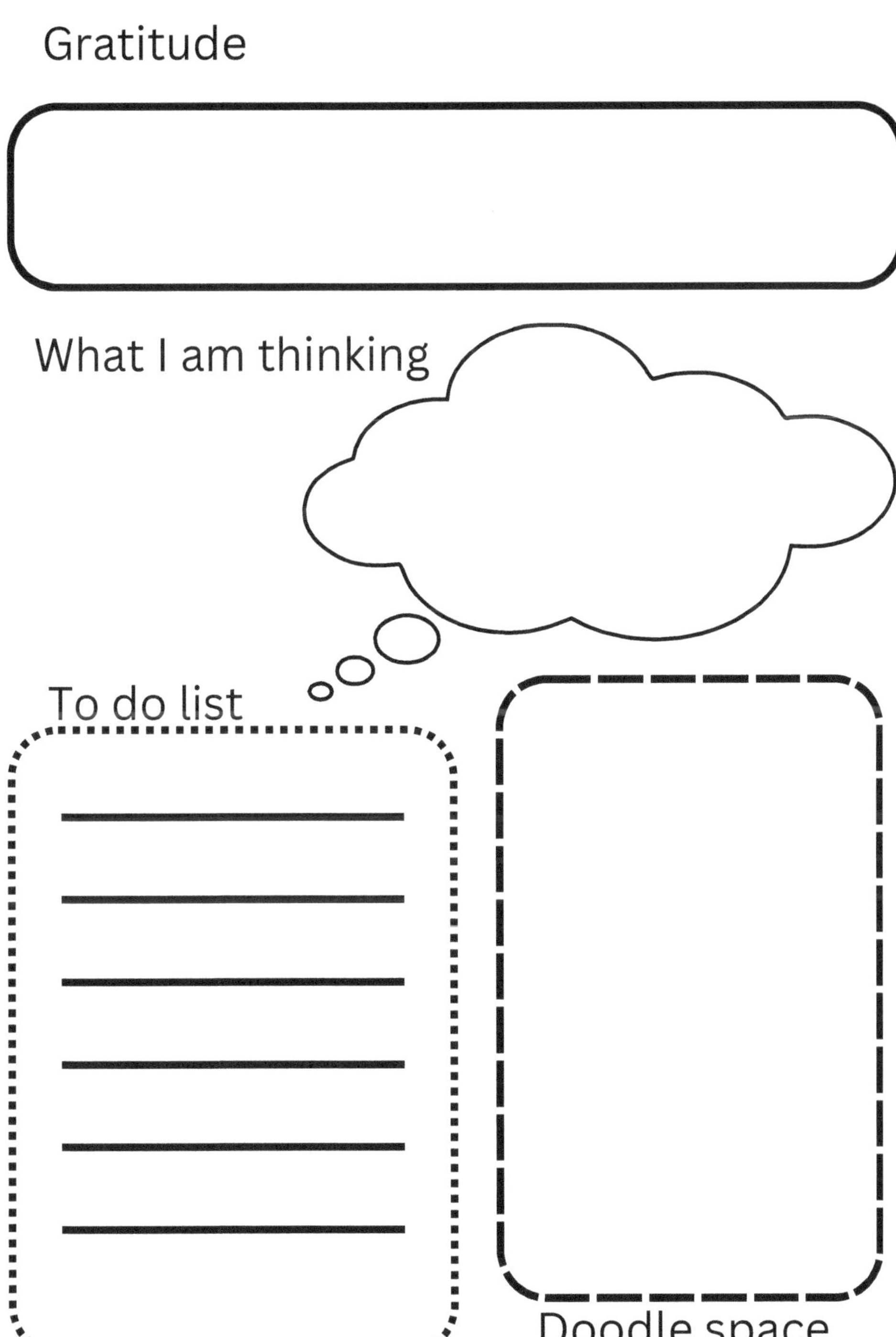

Date:..............

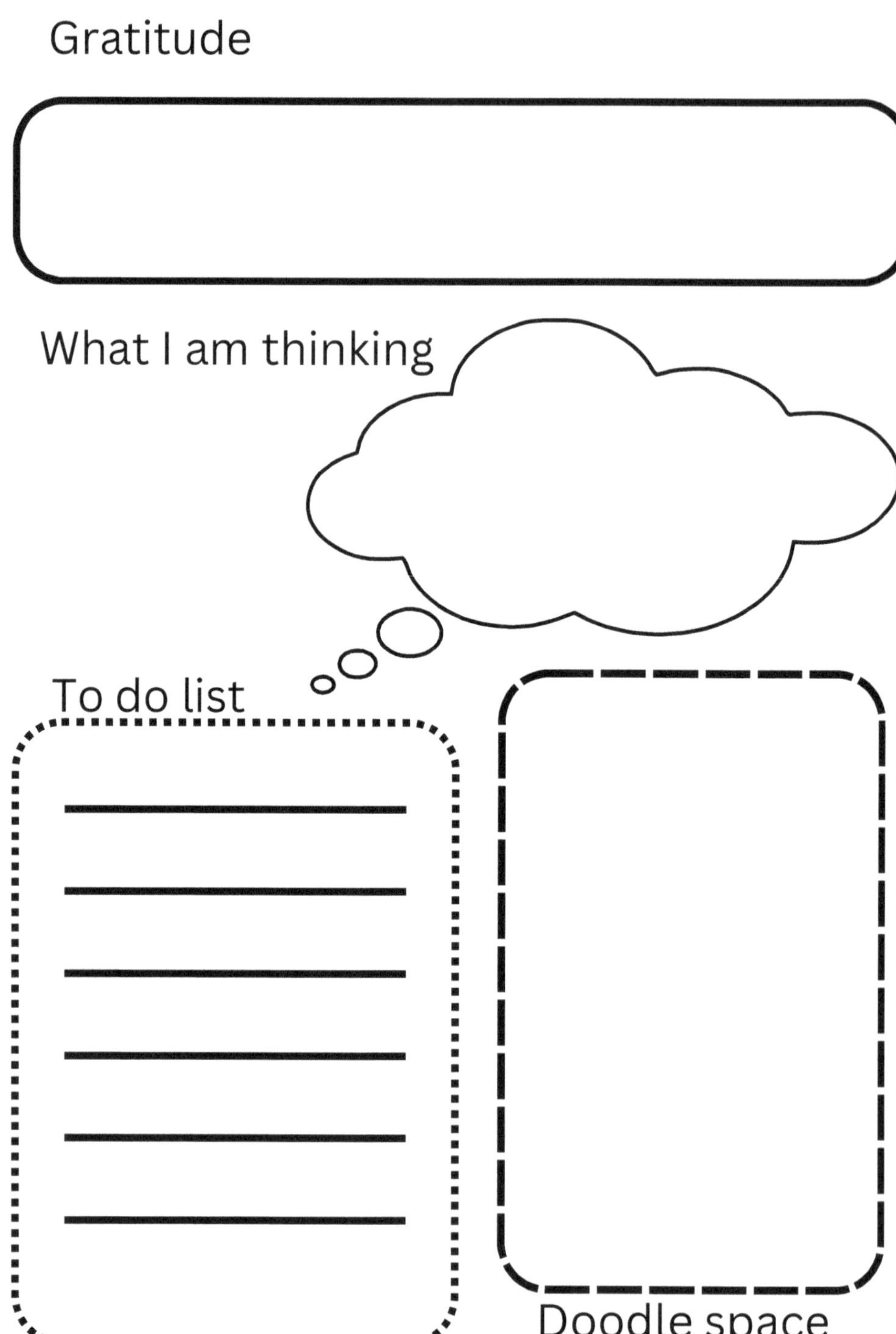

Date:..............

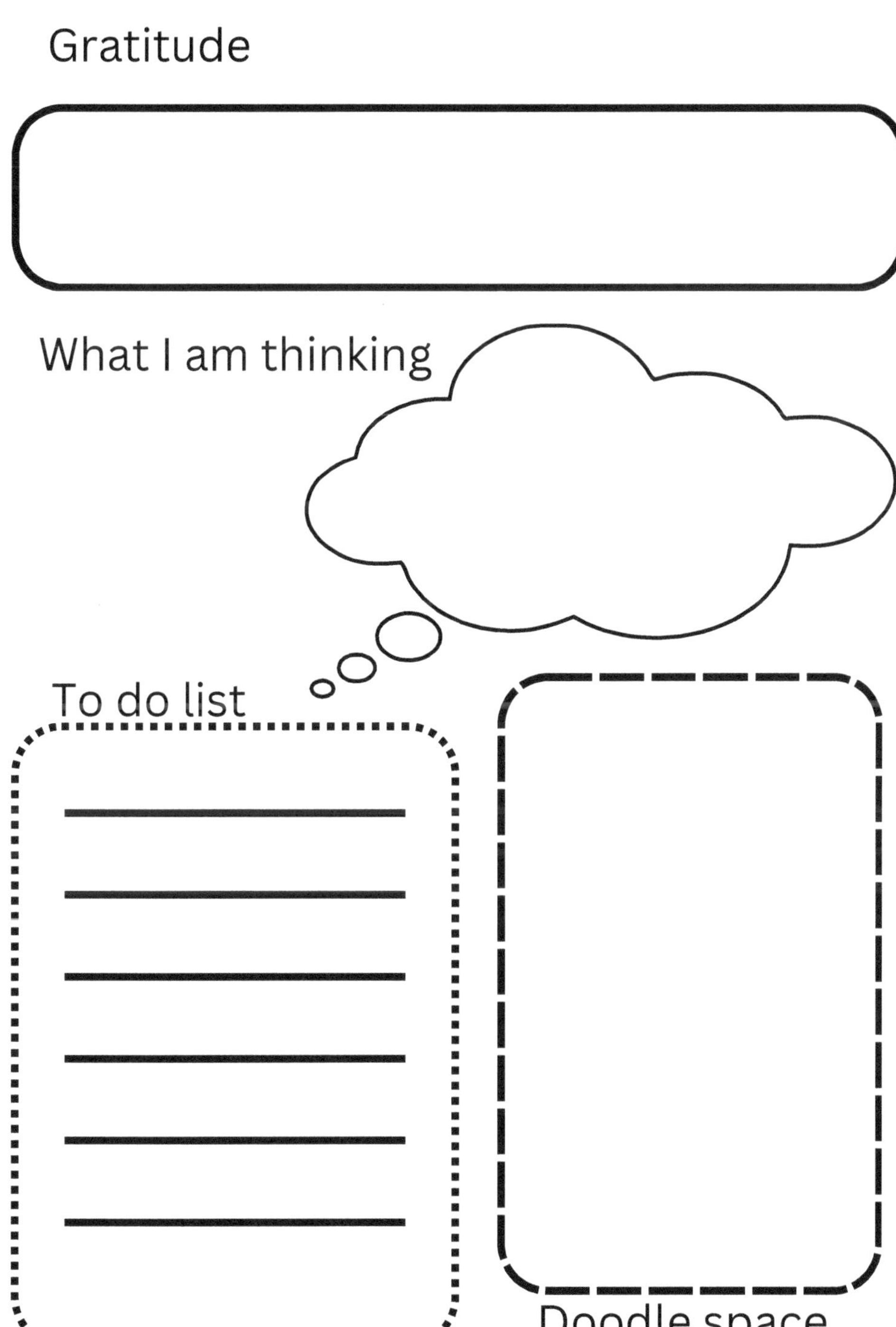

Weekly planner

Date:..../.../...../to..../.../....

MON

TUE

WED

THU

FRI

SAT

SUN

Date:..............

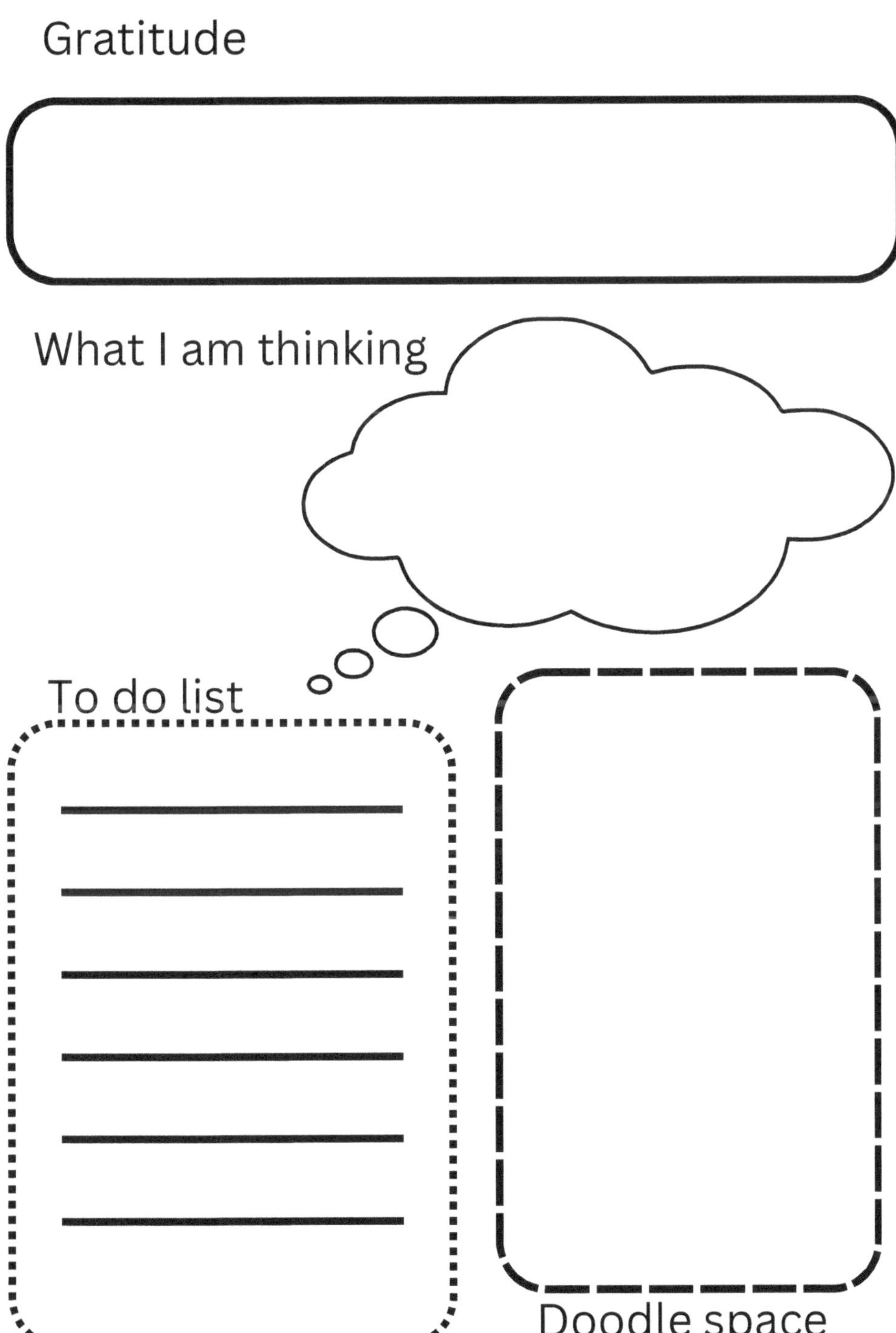

Date:..............

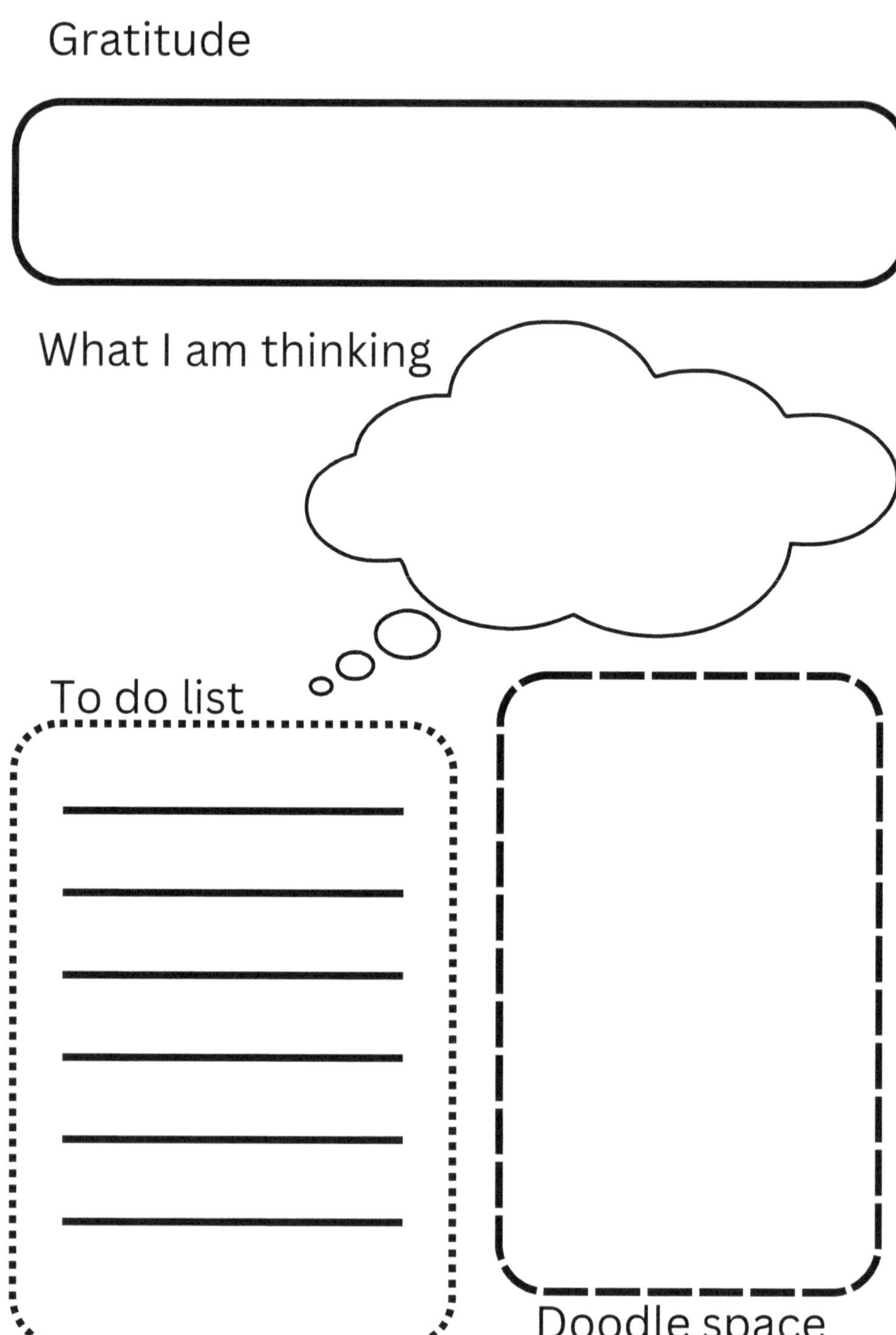

Date:.............

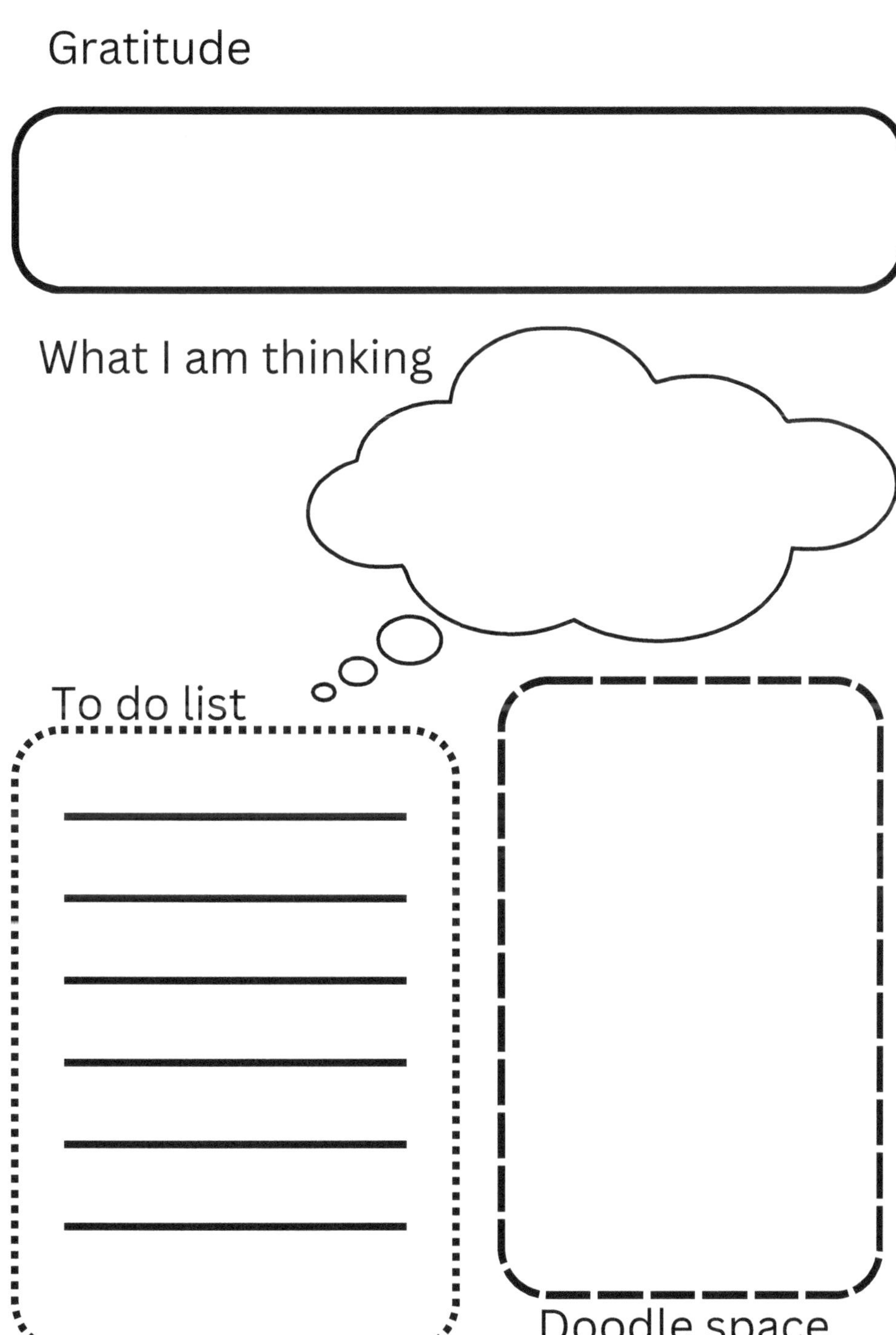

Date:..............

Date:..............

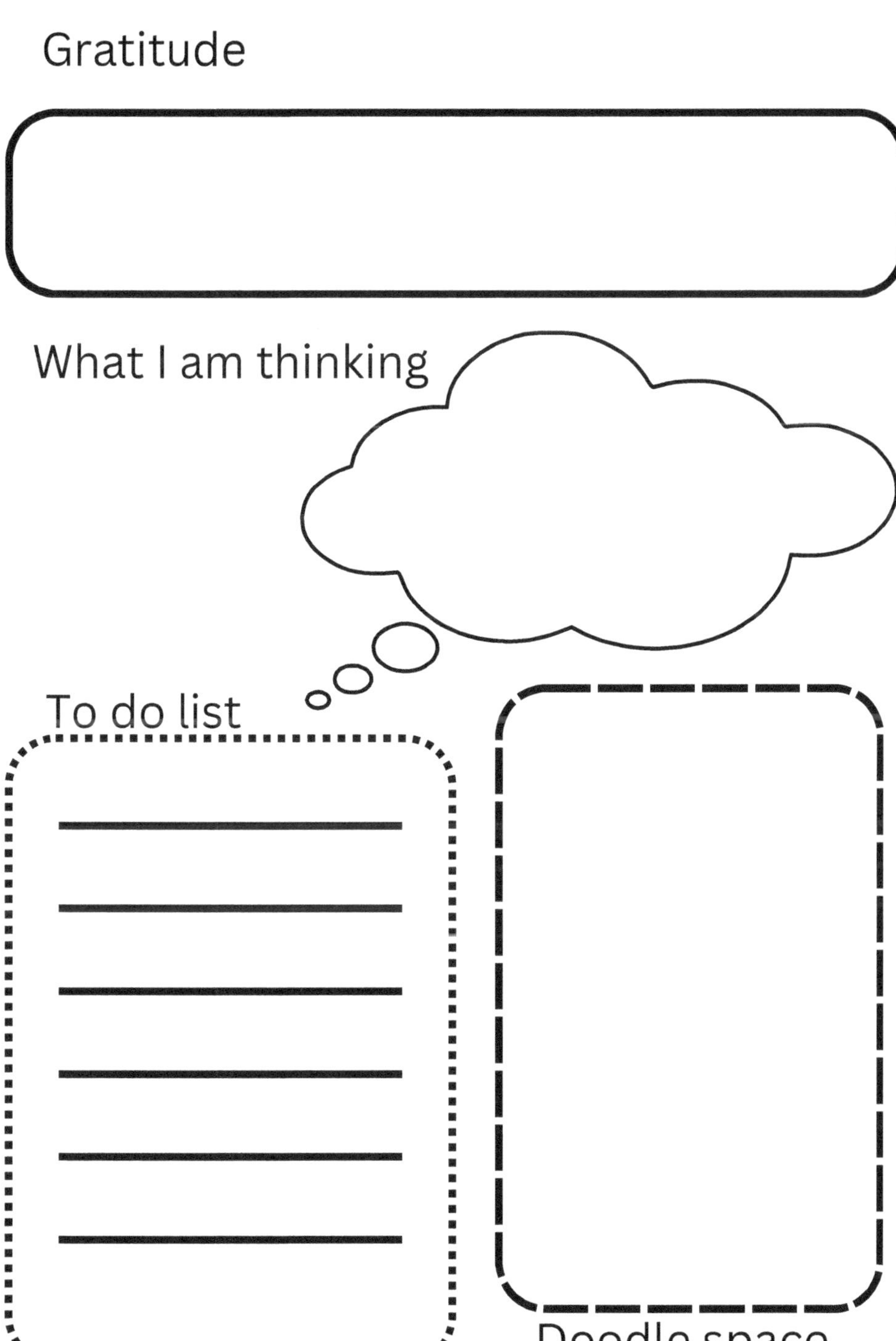

Date:..............

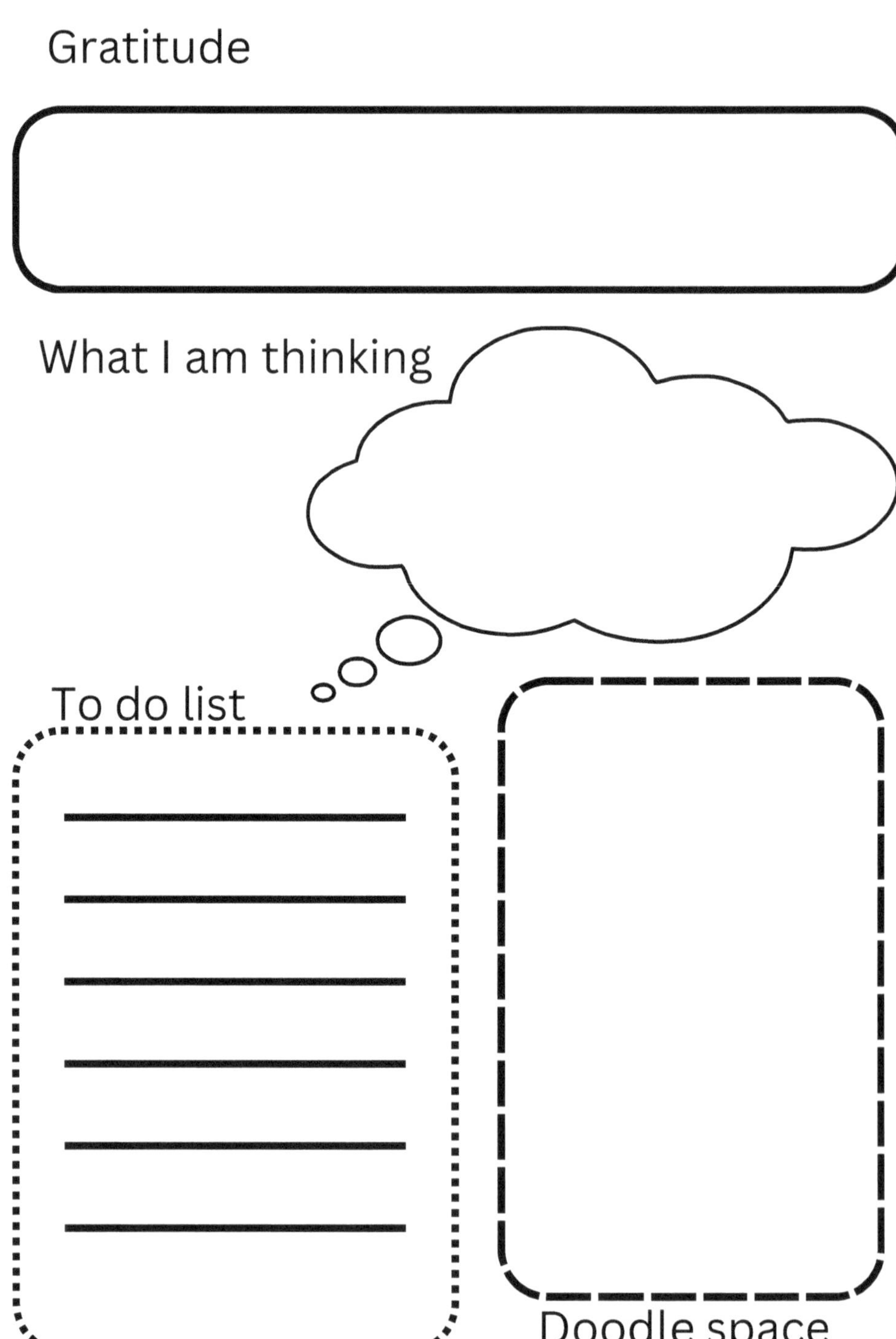

Date:..............

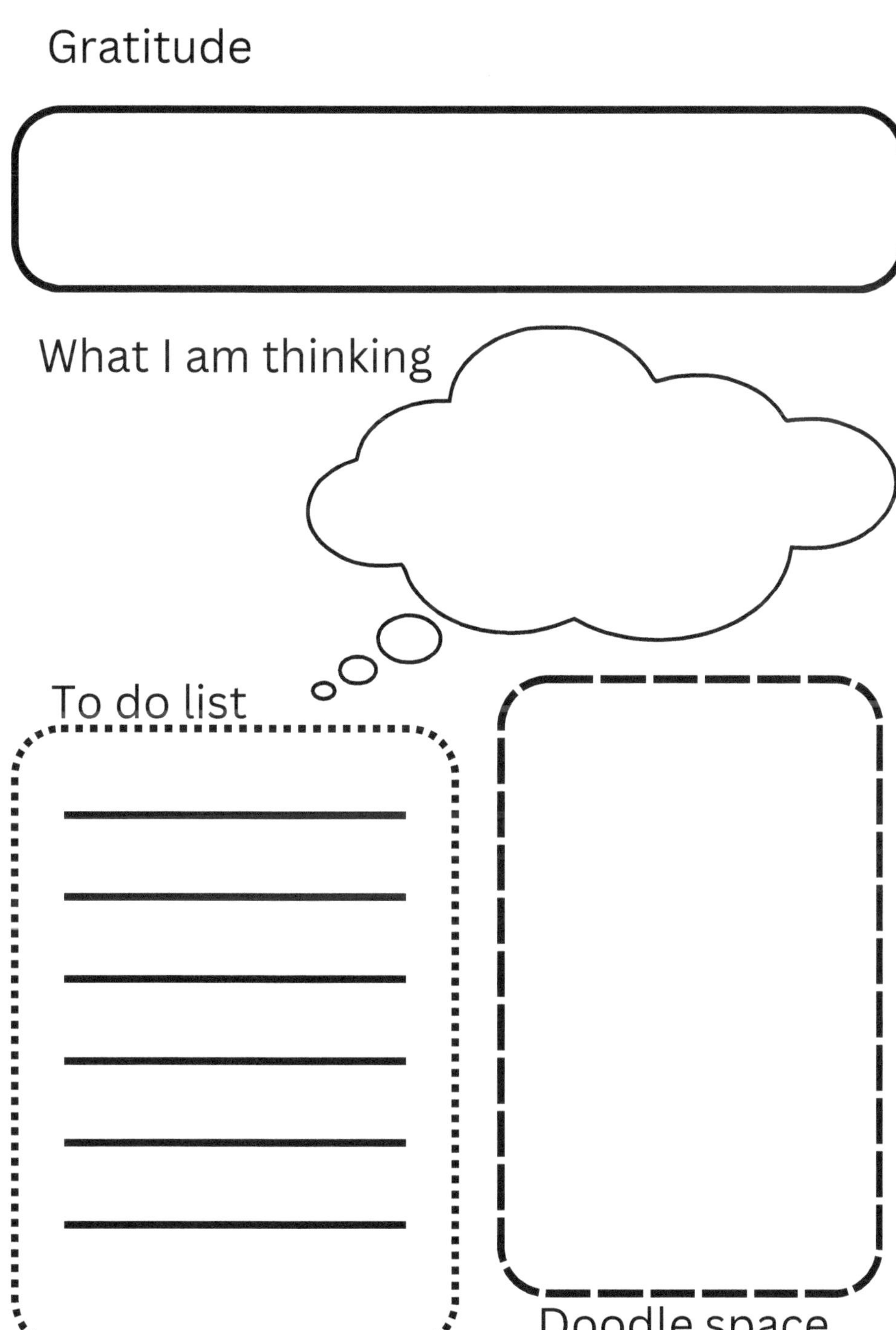

Weekly planner

Date:..../.../.....to..../.../....

MON

TUE

WED

THU

FRI

SAT

SUN

Date:..............

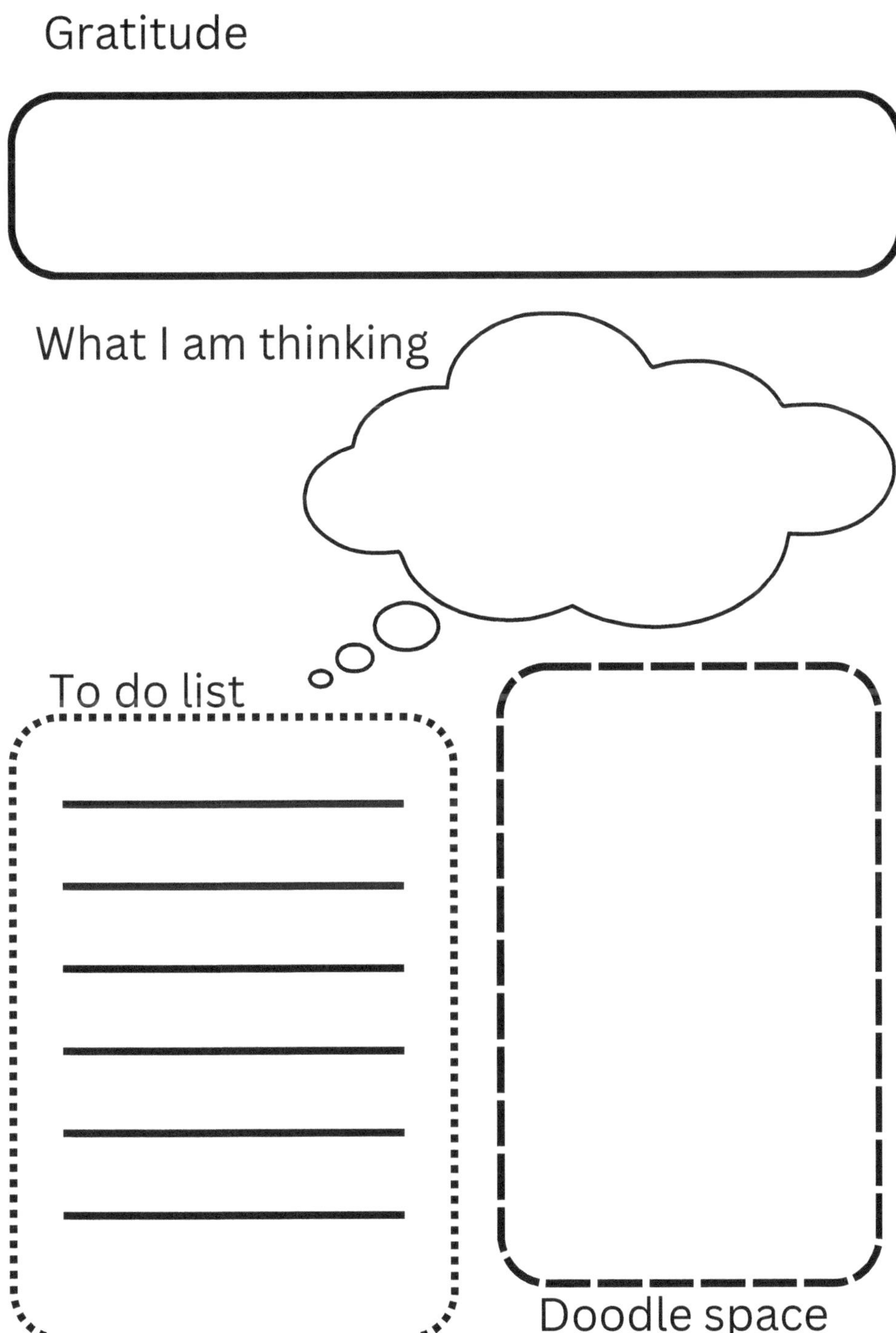

Date:..............

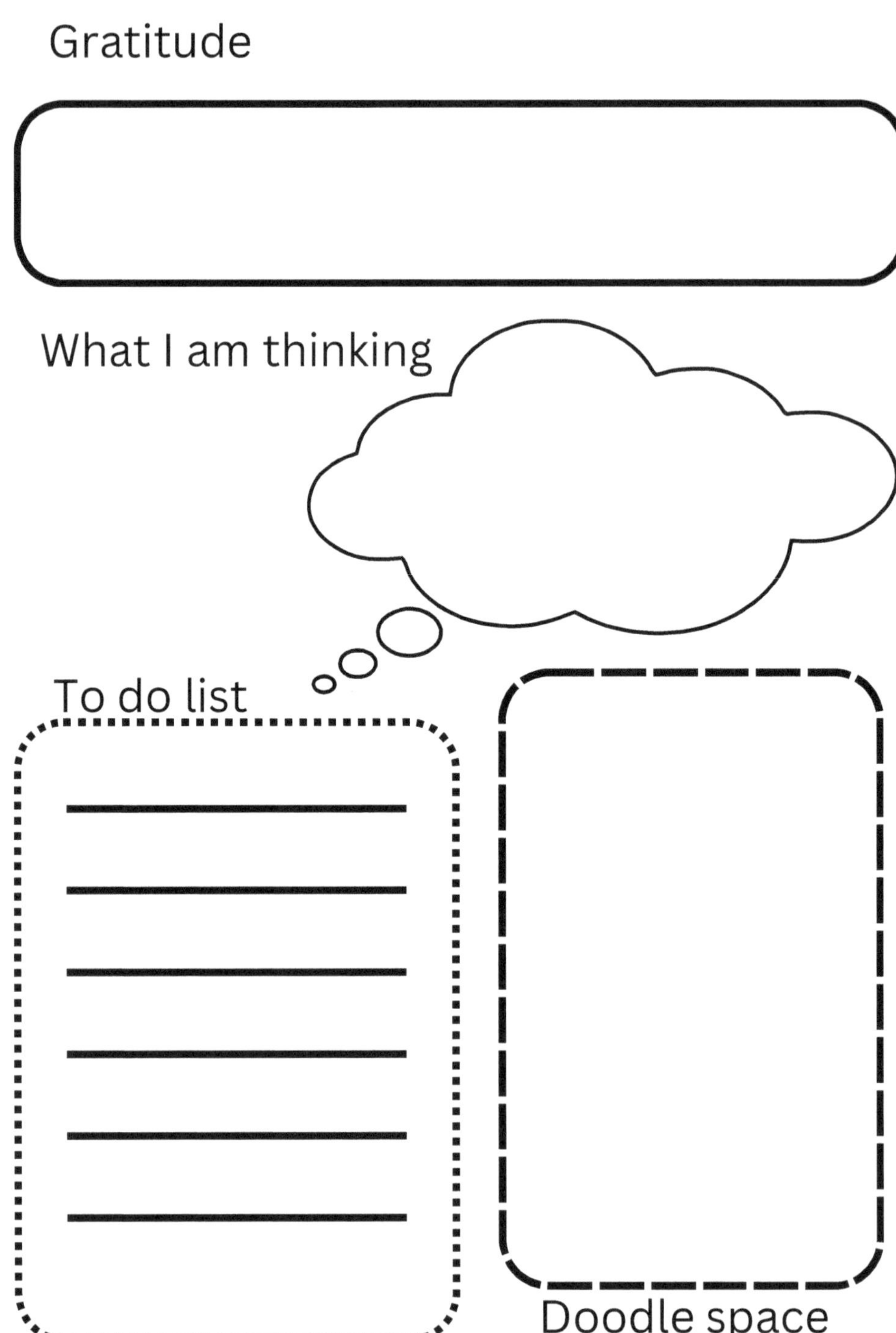

Date:..............

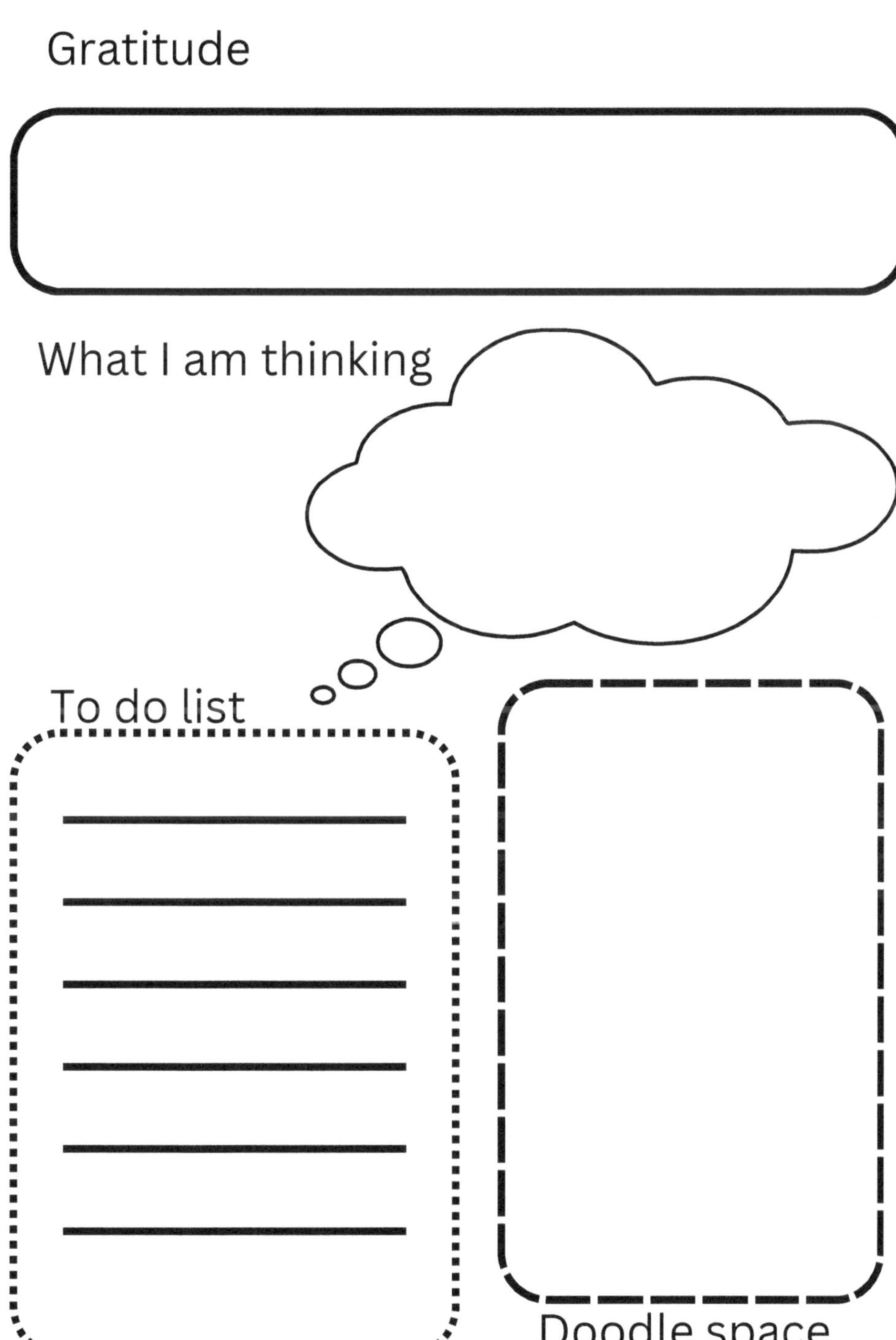

Date:..............

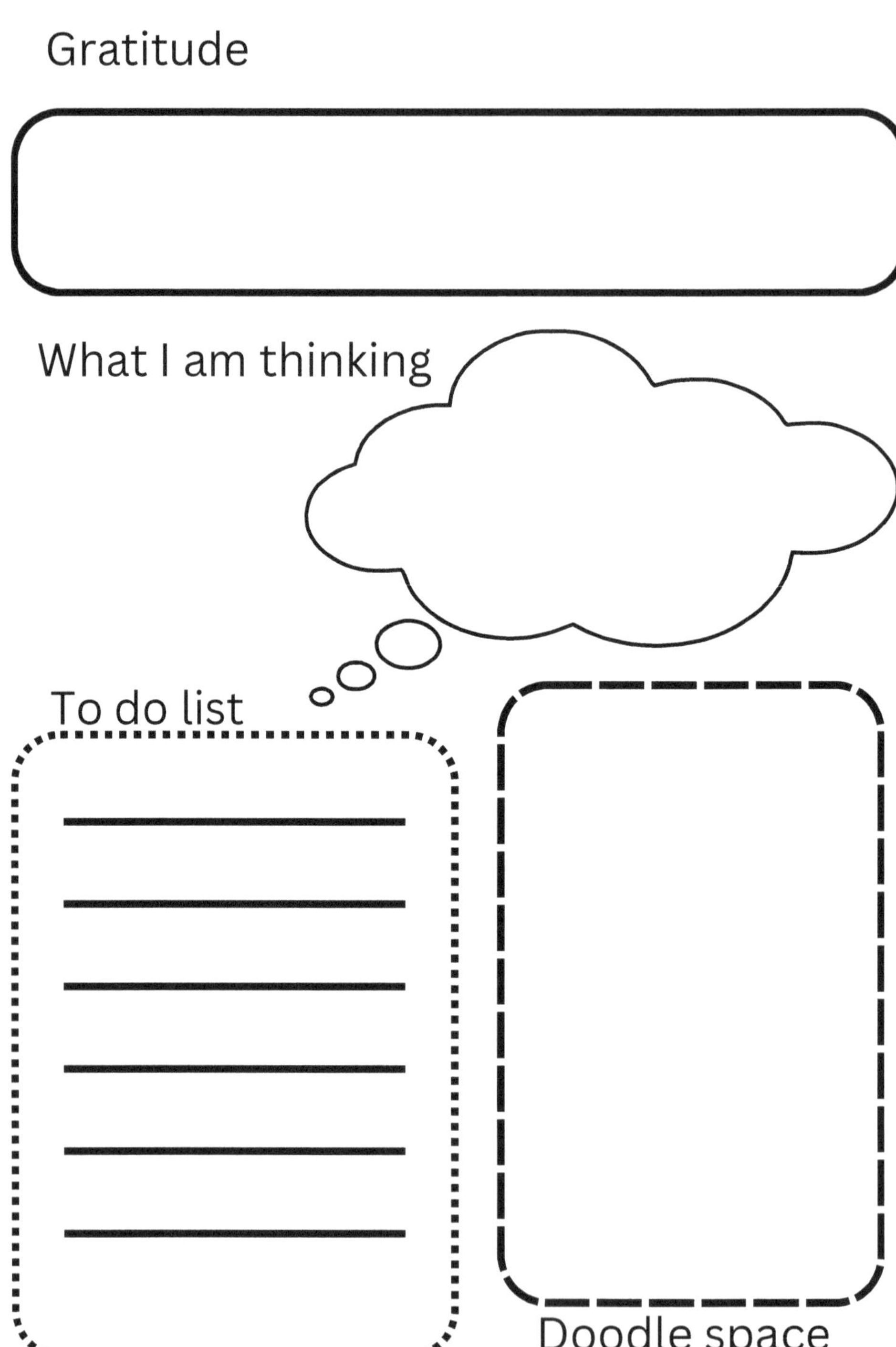

Date:..............

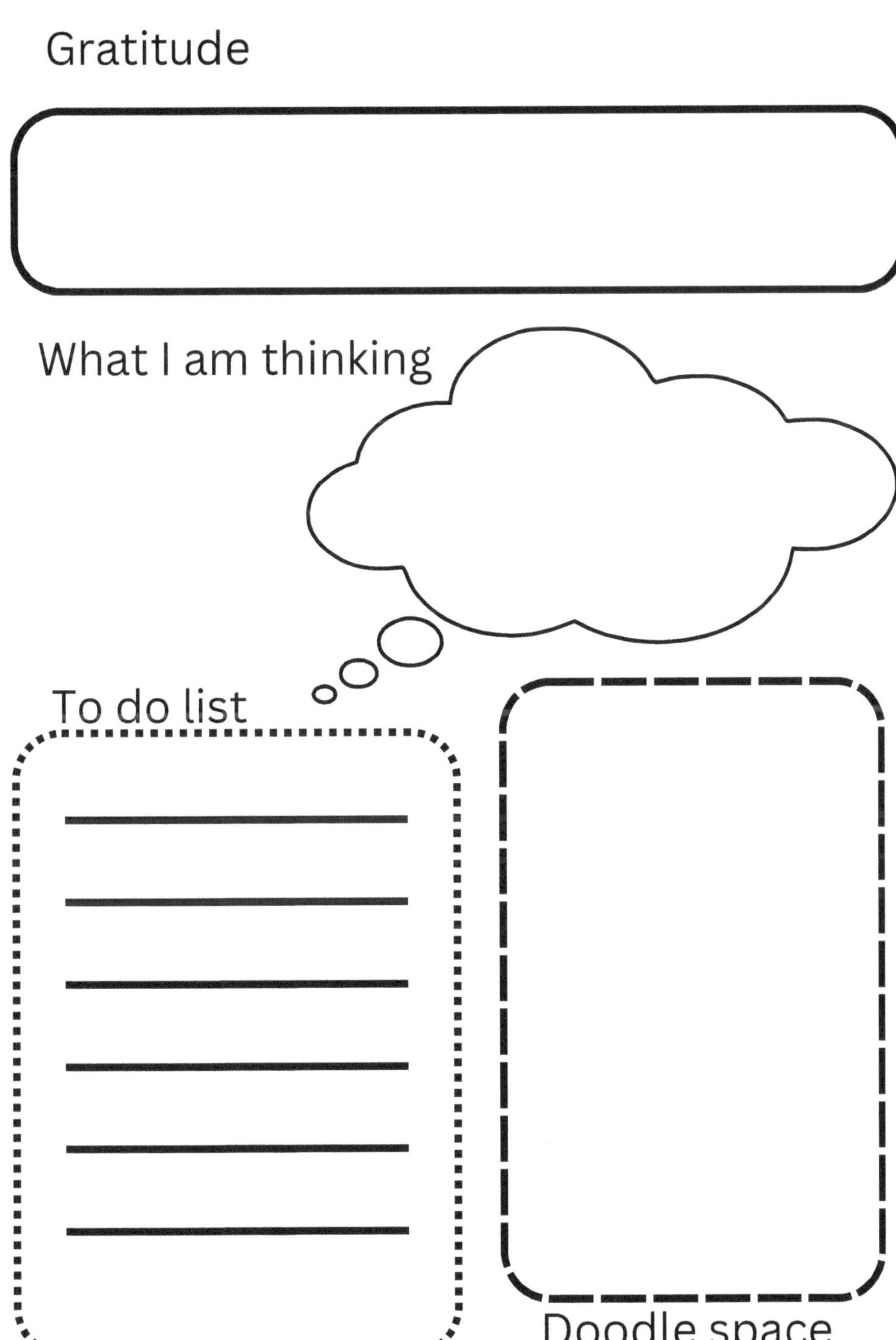

Date:..............

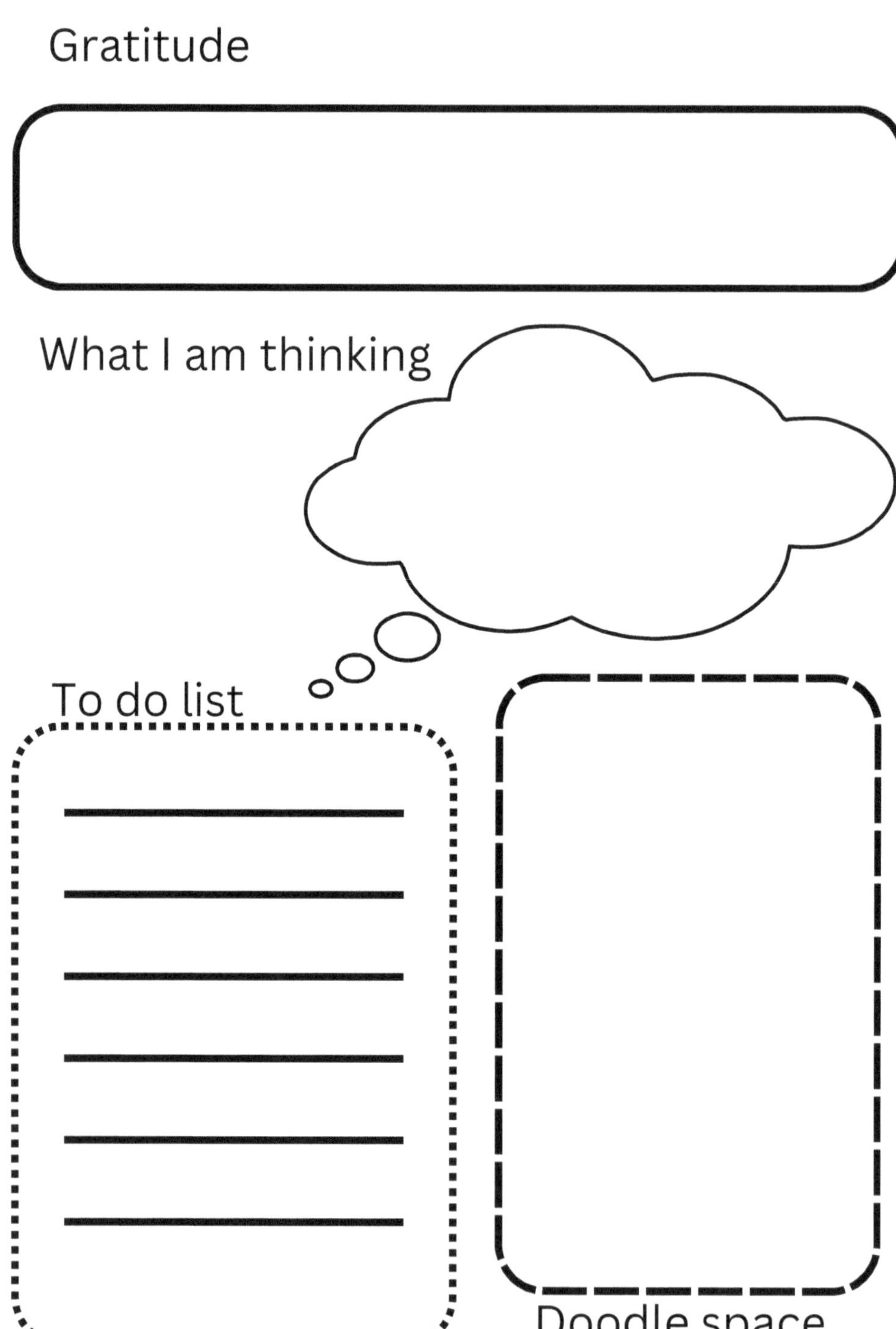

Date:..............

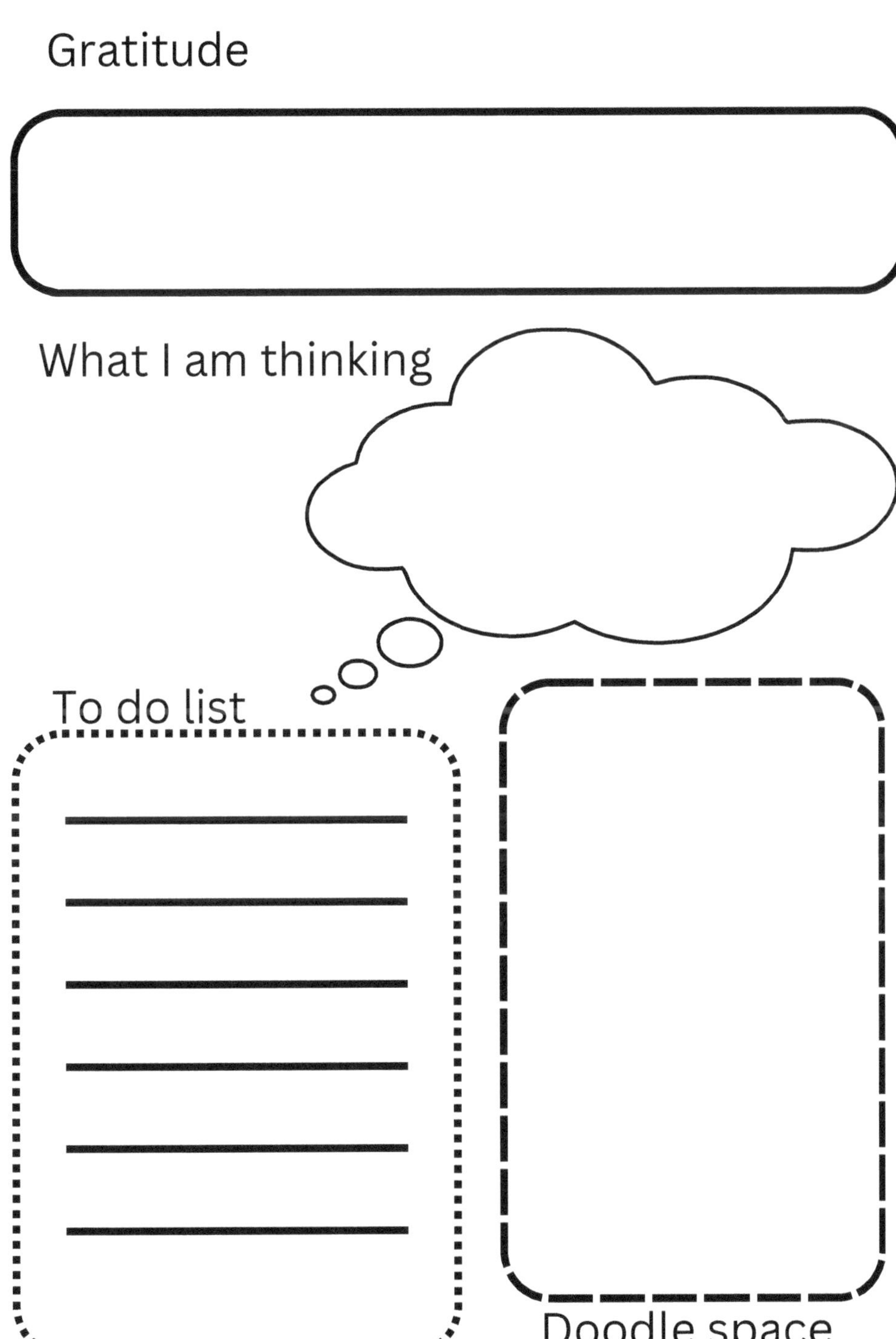

Weekly planner

Date:..../.../...../to..../.../....

MON

TUE

WED

THU

FRI

SAT

SUN

Date:..............

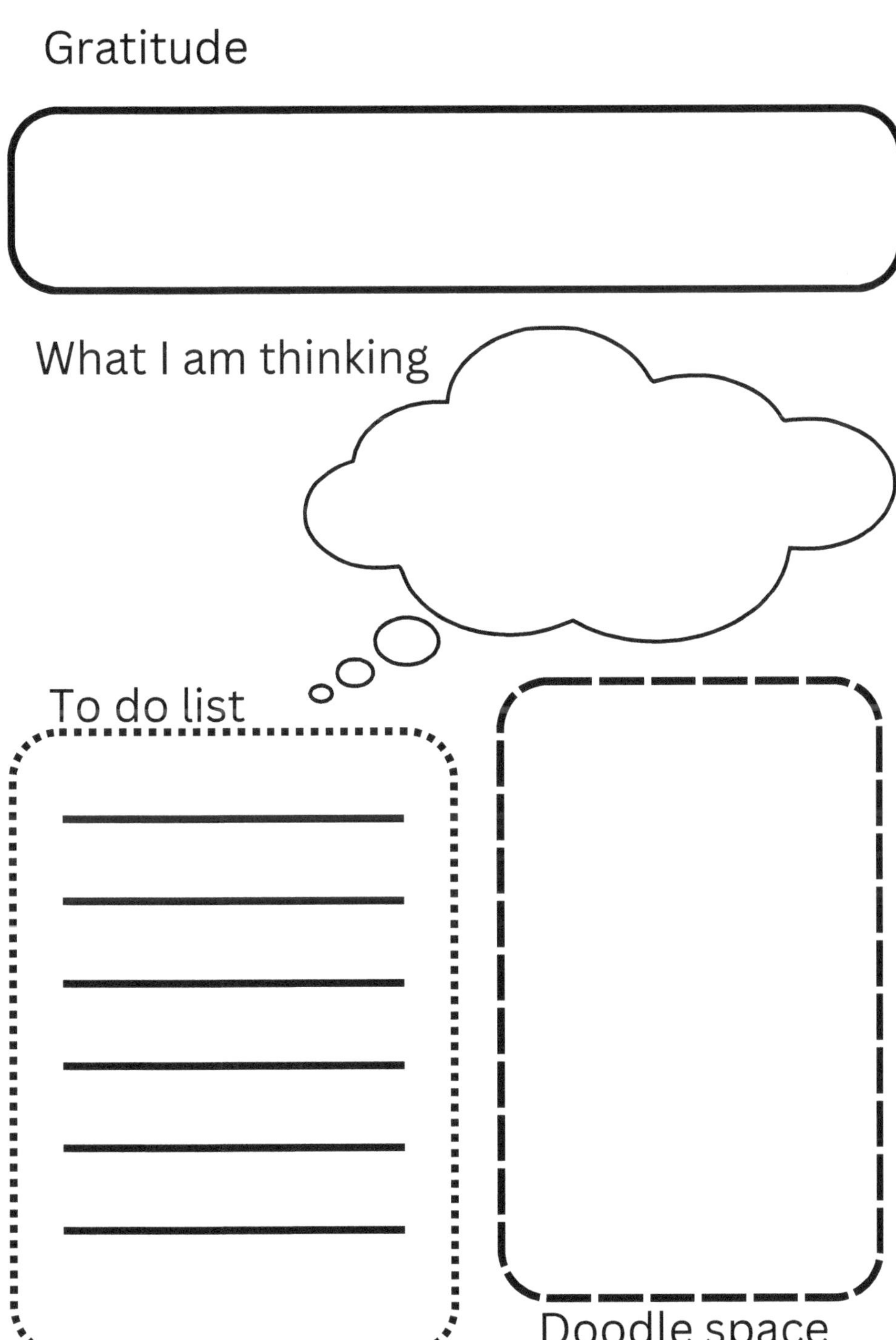

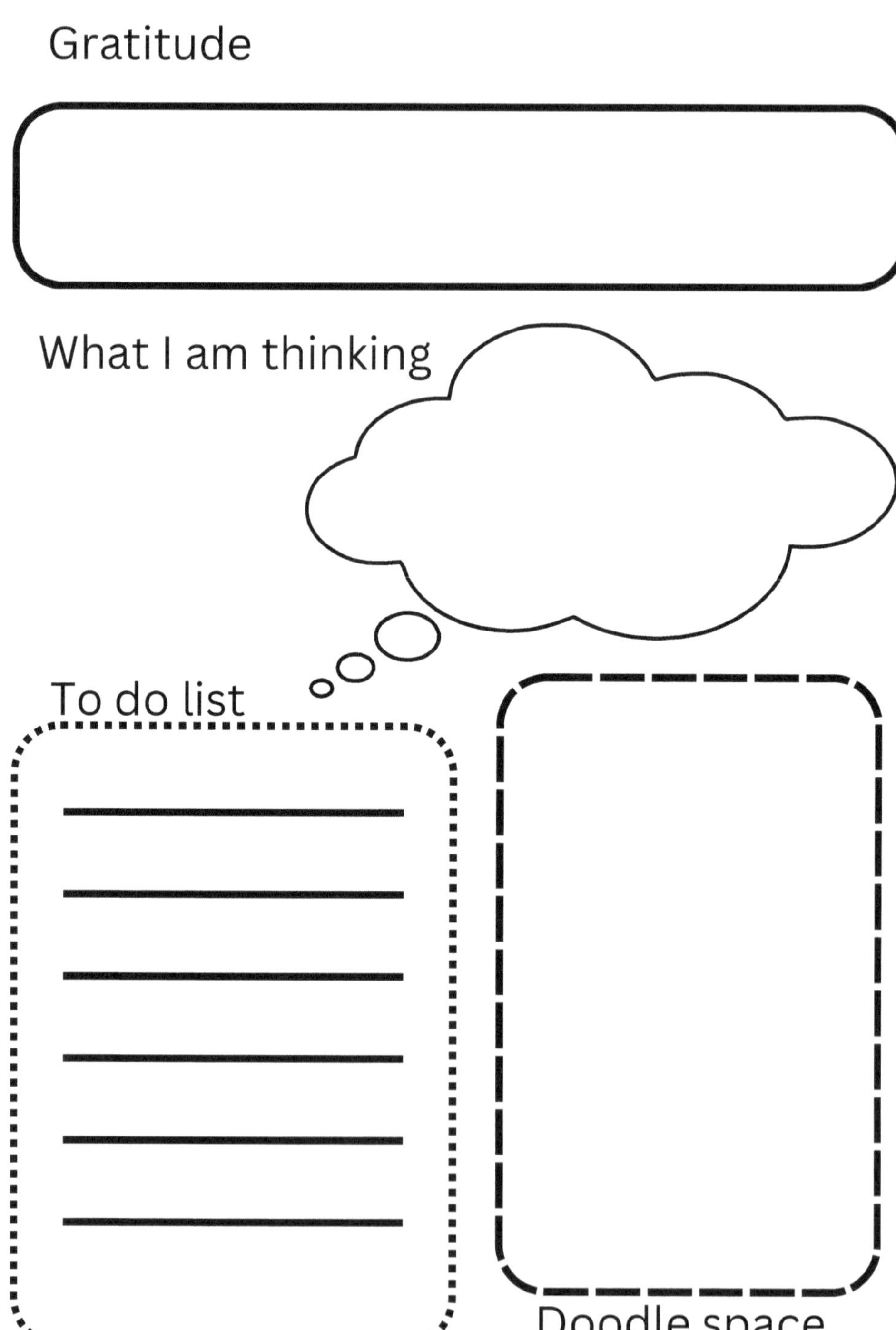
Date:..............
Gratitude
What I am thinking
To do list
Doodle space

Date:..............

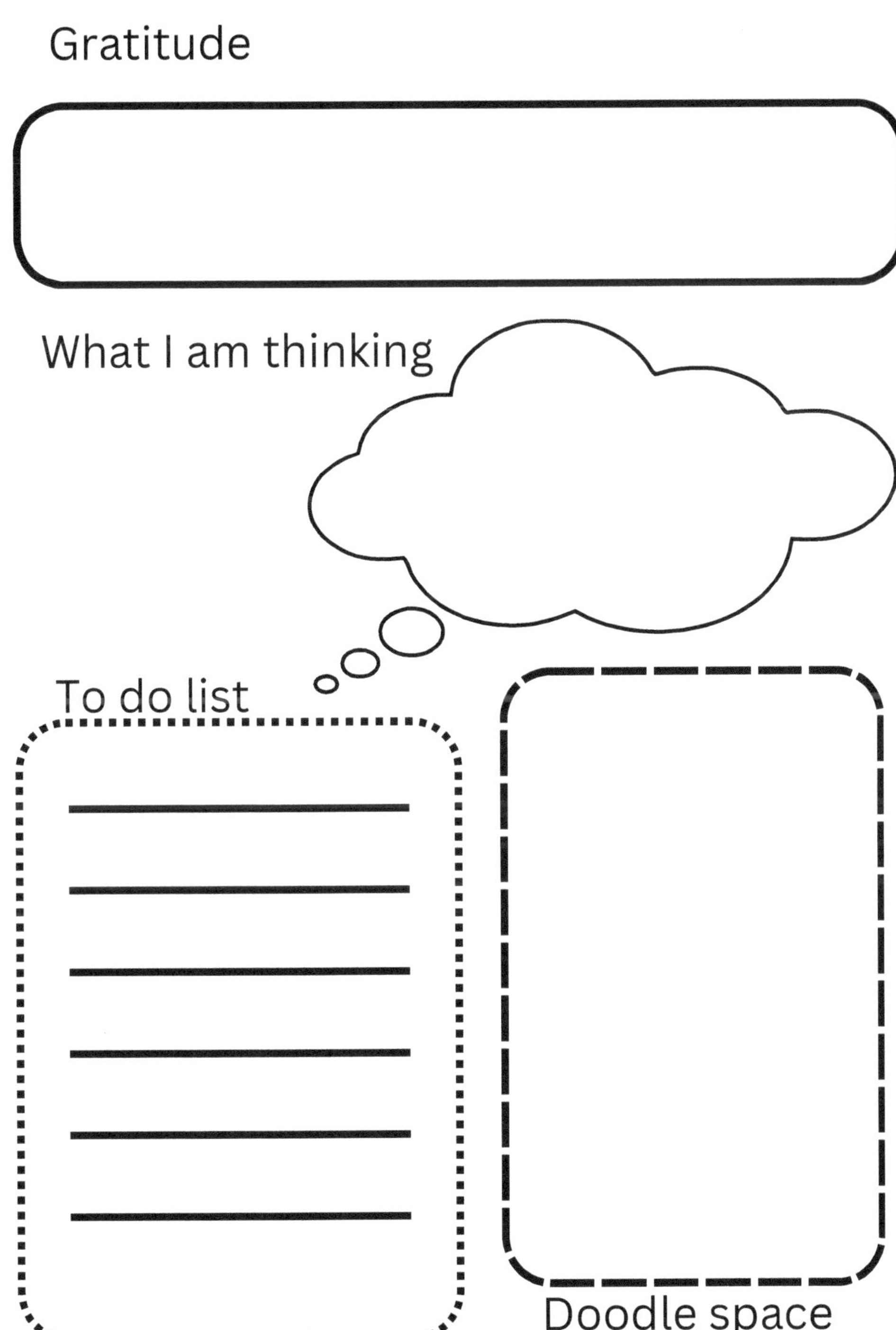

Date:..............

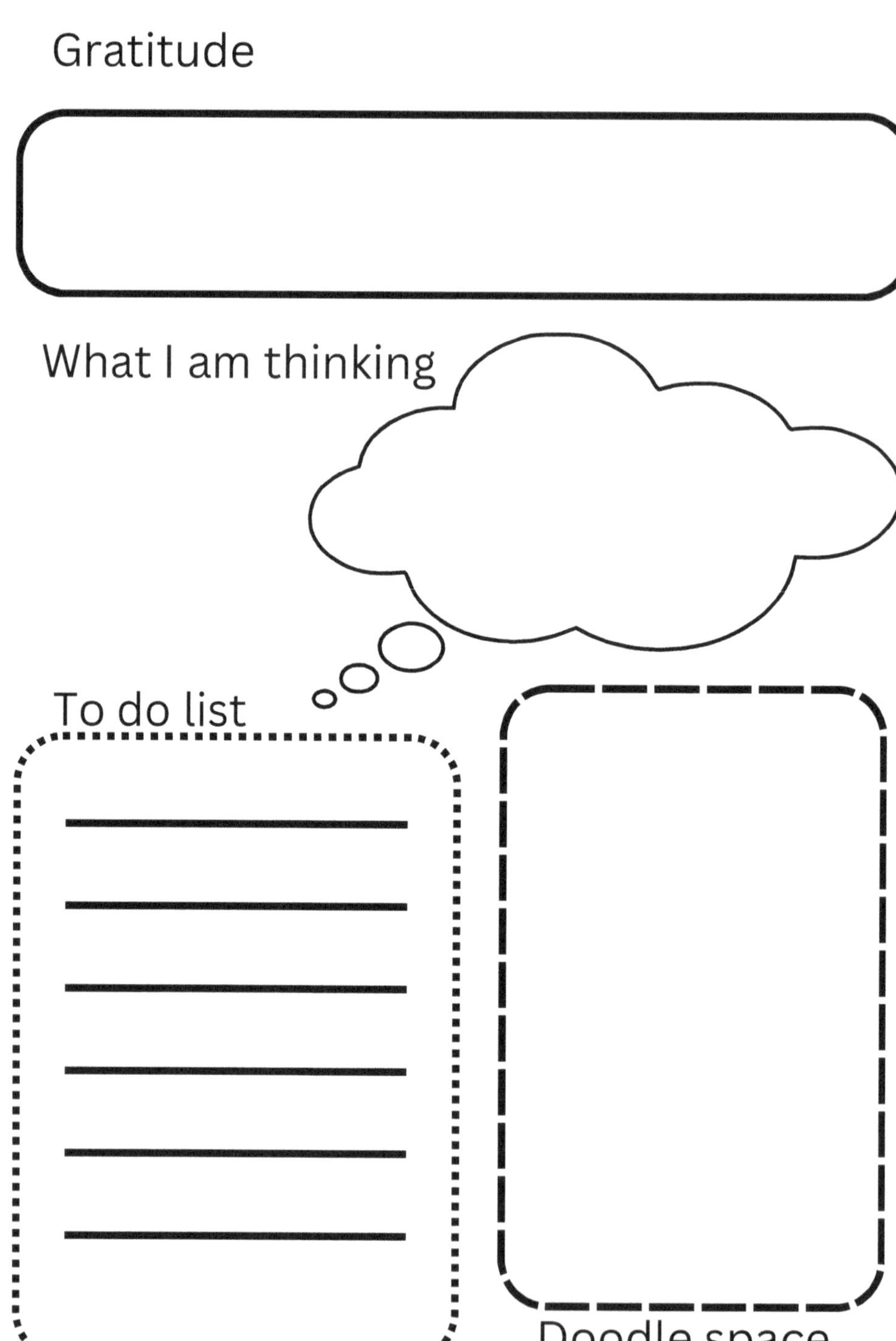

Date:..............

Date:..............

Date:..............

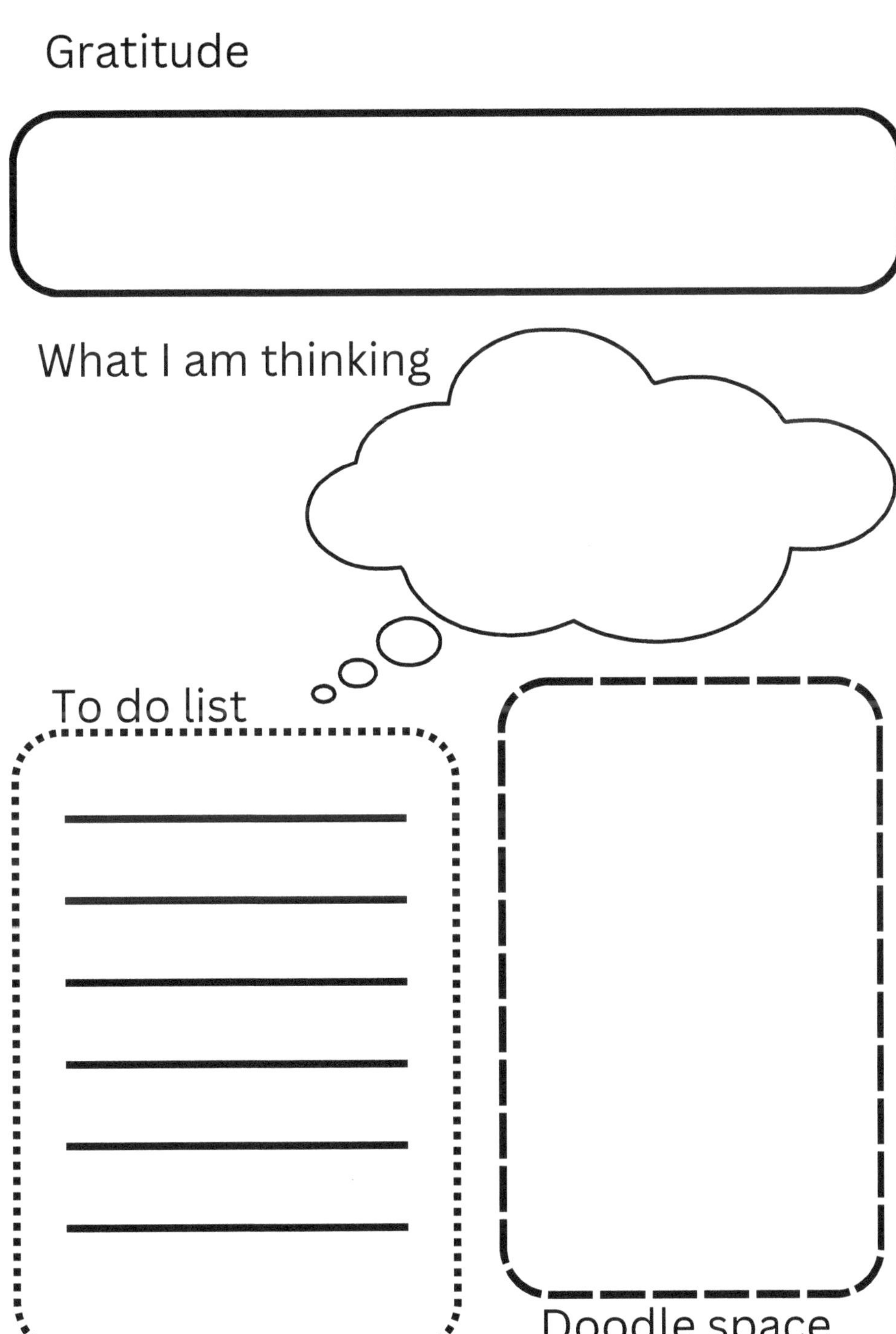

Weekly planner

Date:..../.../.....to..../.../....

MON

TUE

WED

THU

FRI

SAT

SUN

Date:..............

Gratitude

What I am thinking

To do list

Doodle space

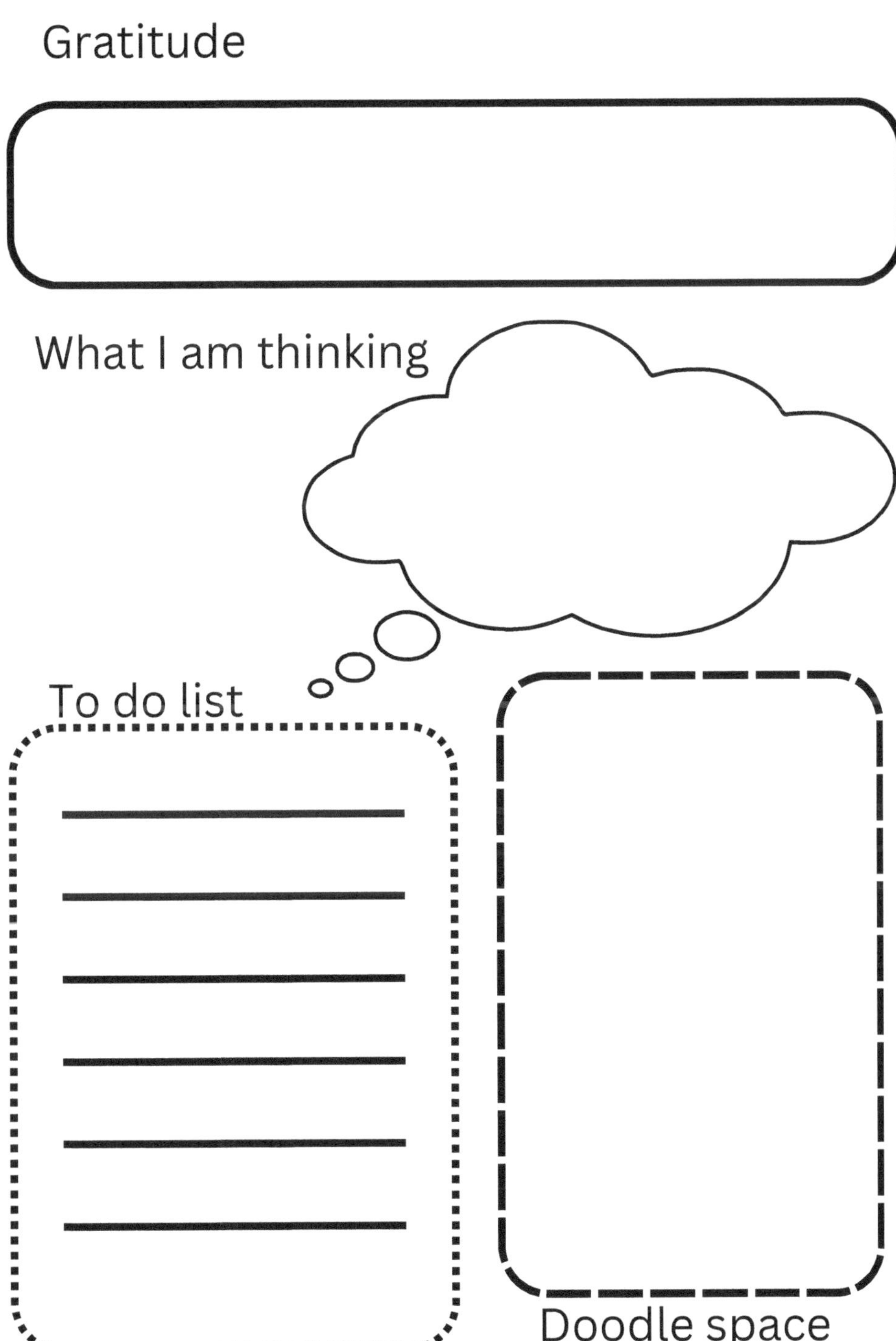

Date:..............

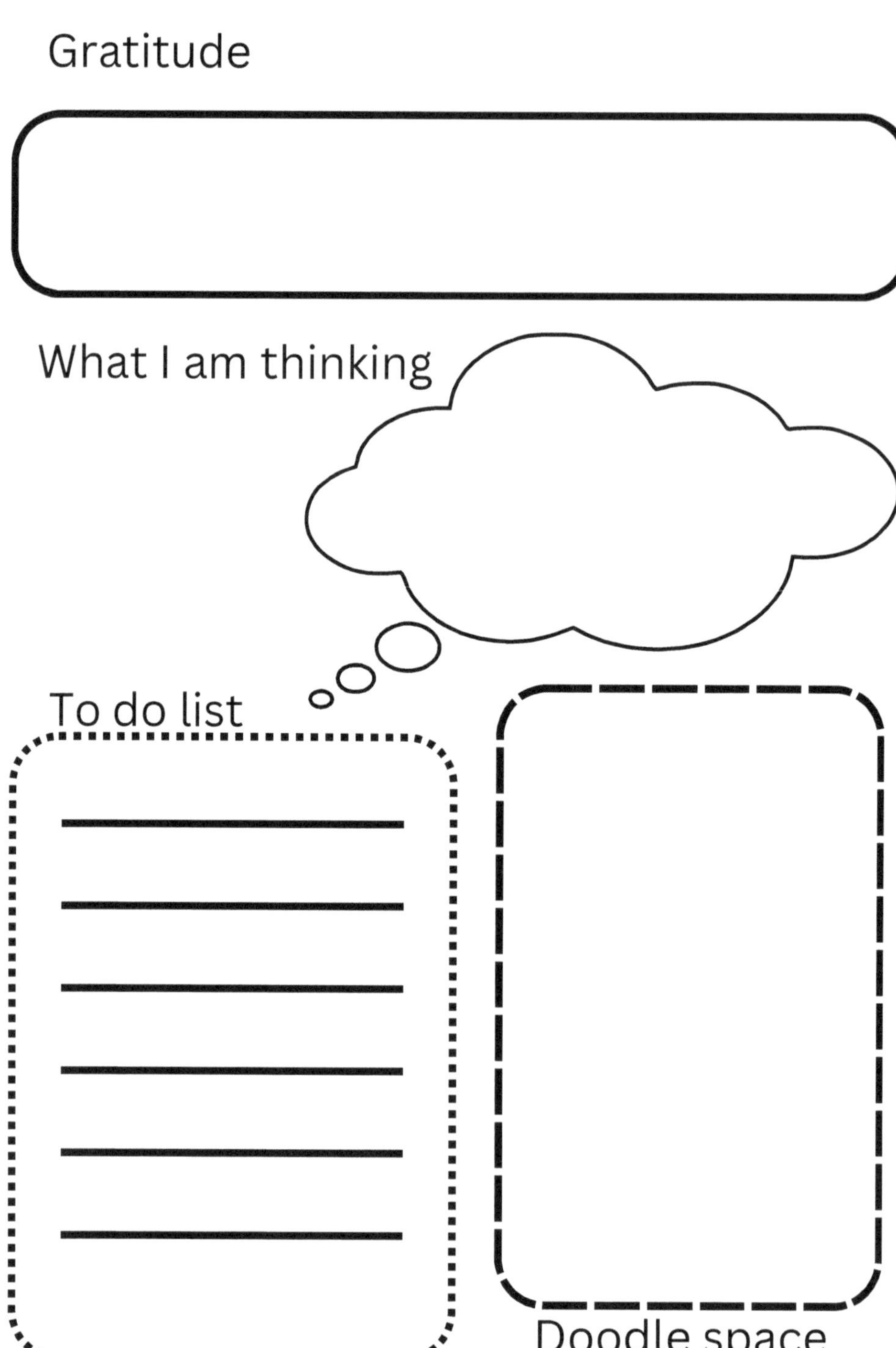

Date:..............

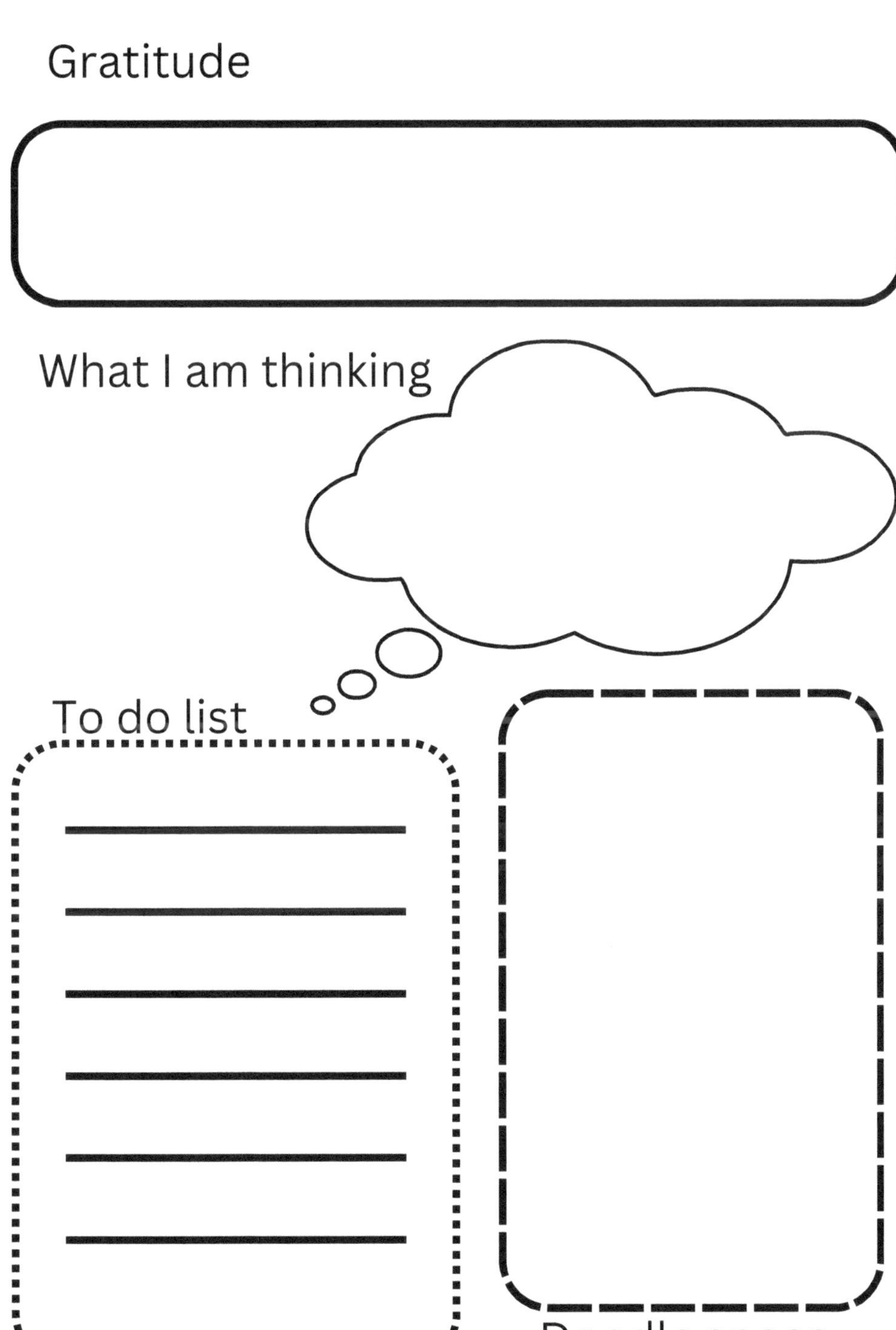

Date:..............

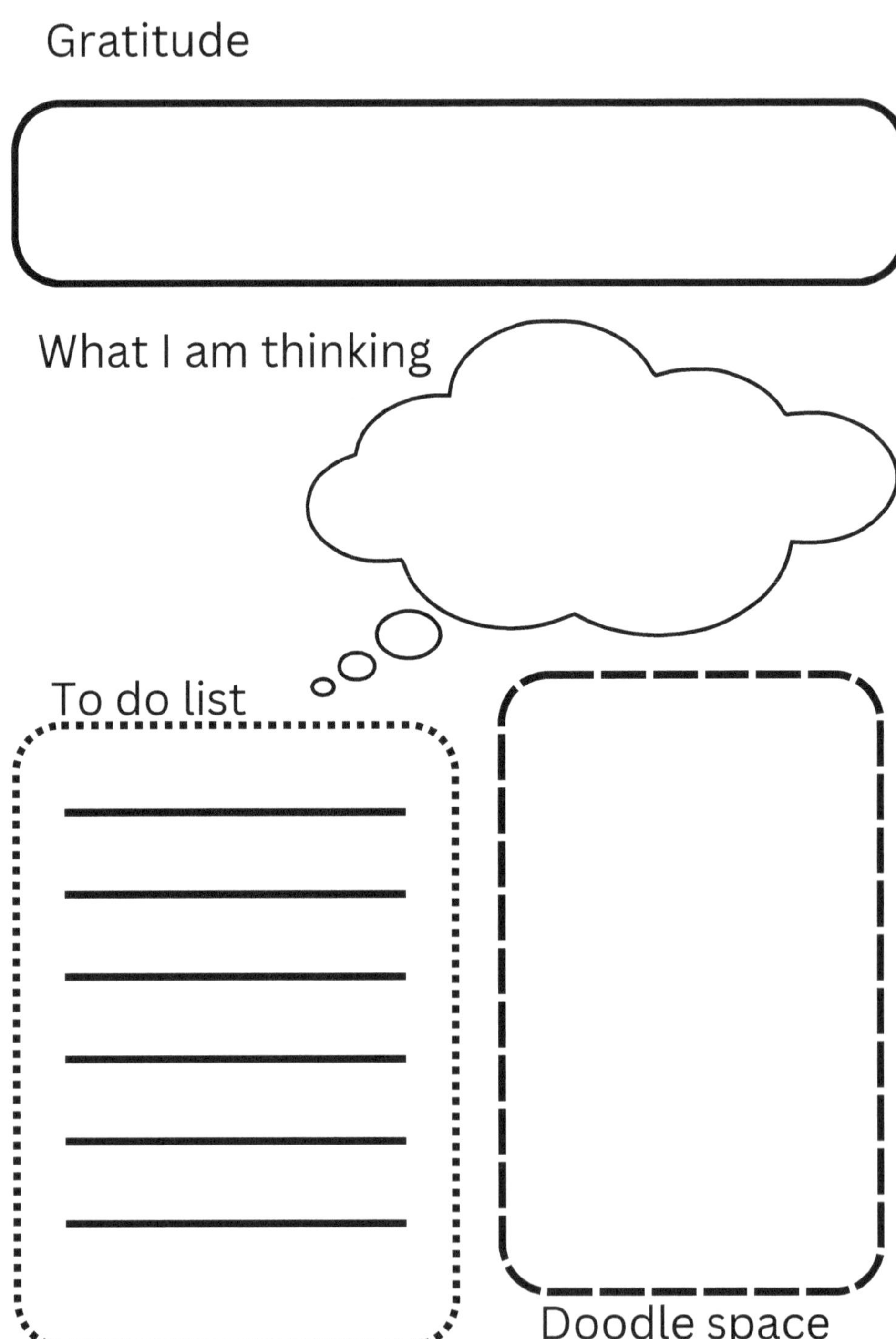

Date:..............

Gratitude

Date:..............

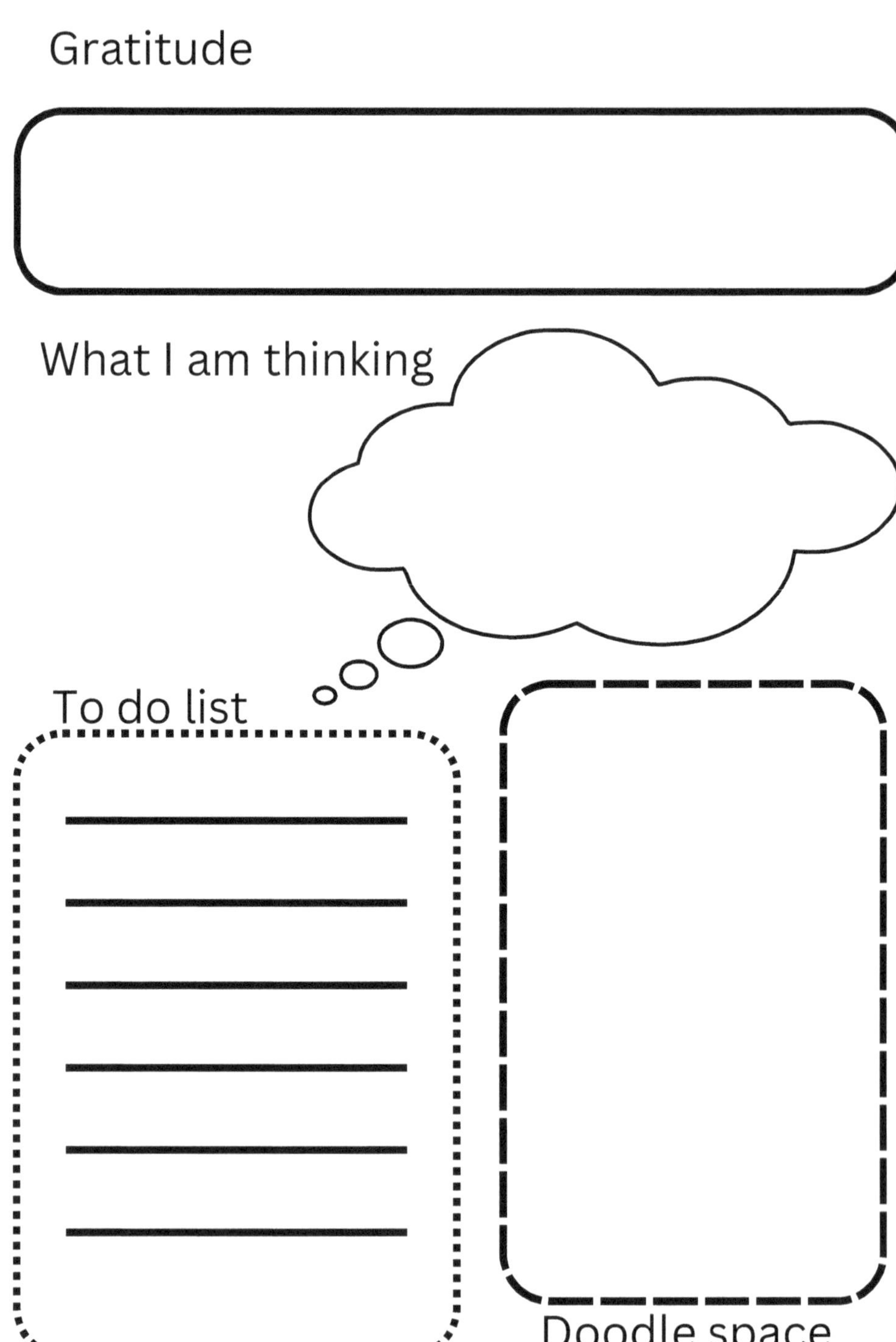

Date:...............

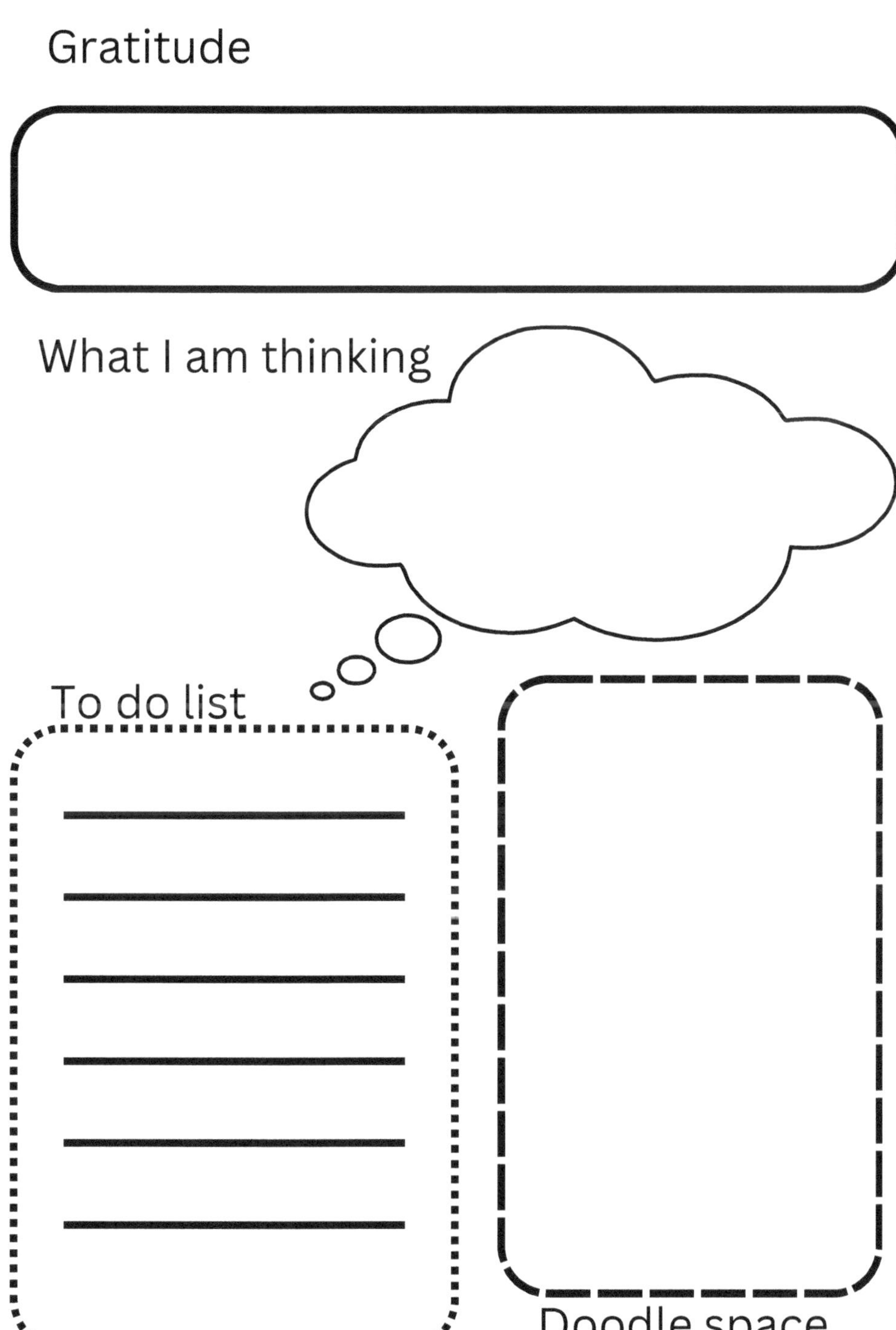

Weekly planner

Date:..../.../.....to..../.../....

MON

TUE

WED

THU

FRI

SAT

SUN

Date:..............

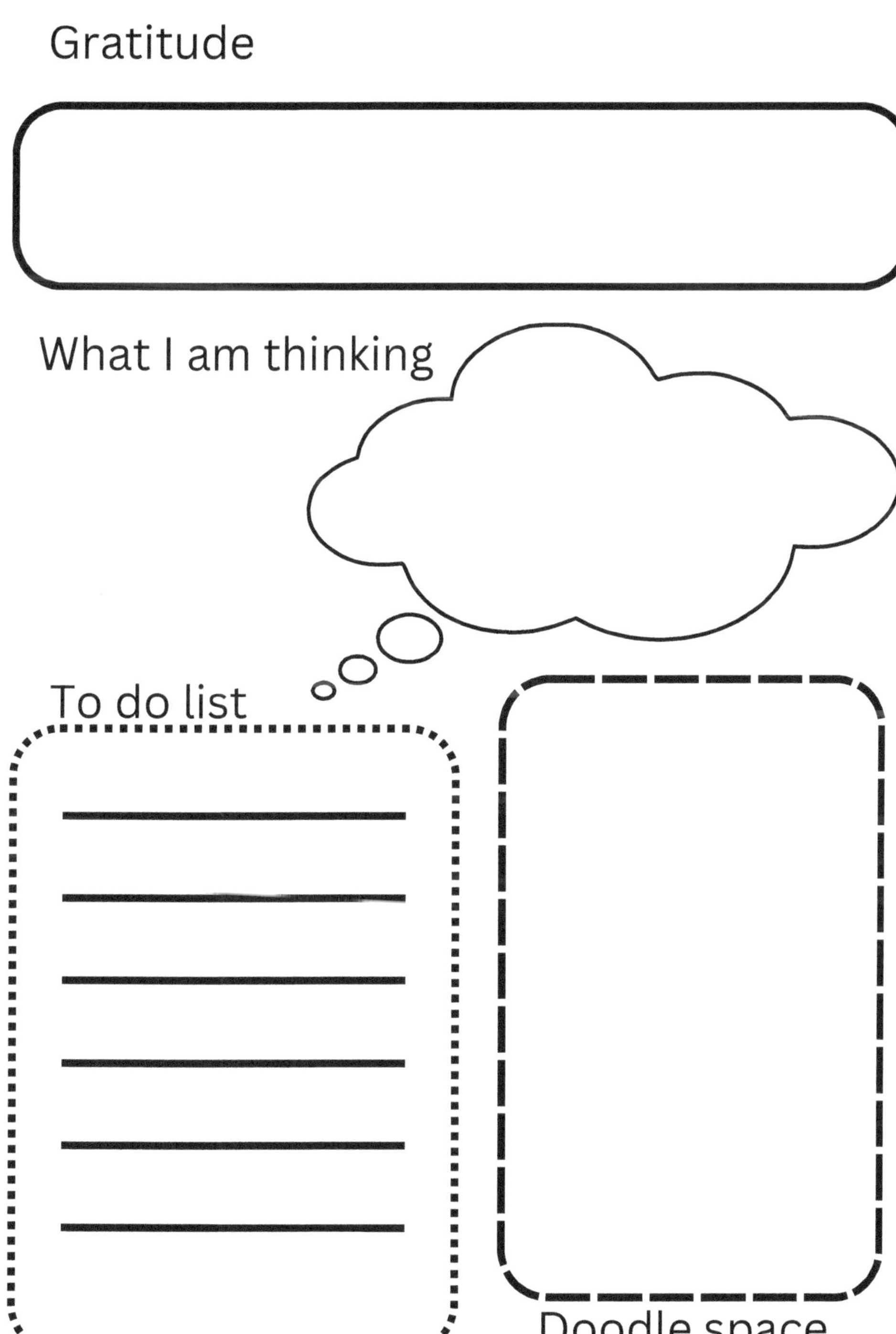

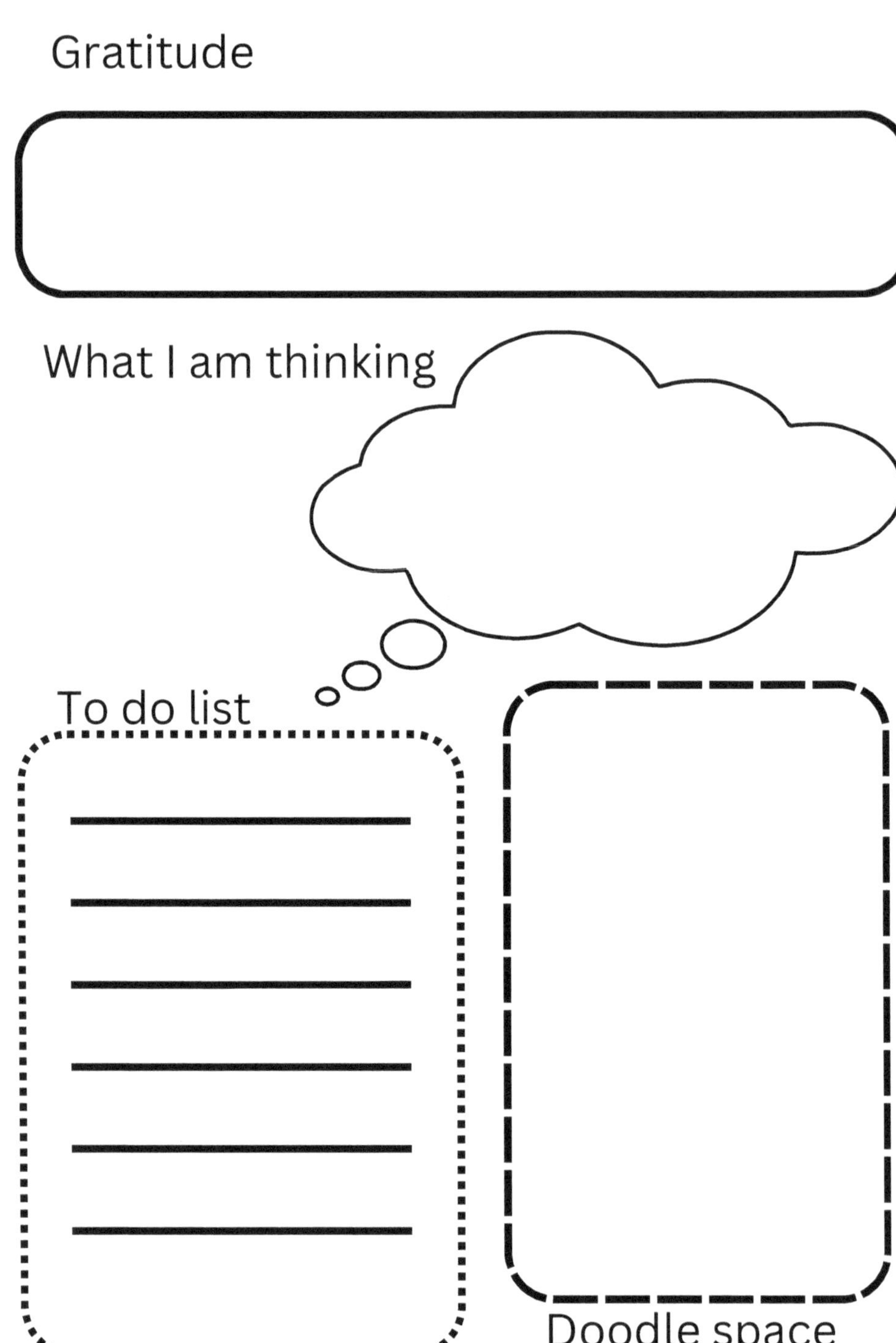
Date:..............
Gratitude
What I am thinking
To do list
Doodle space

Date:...............

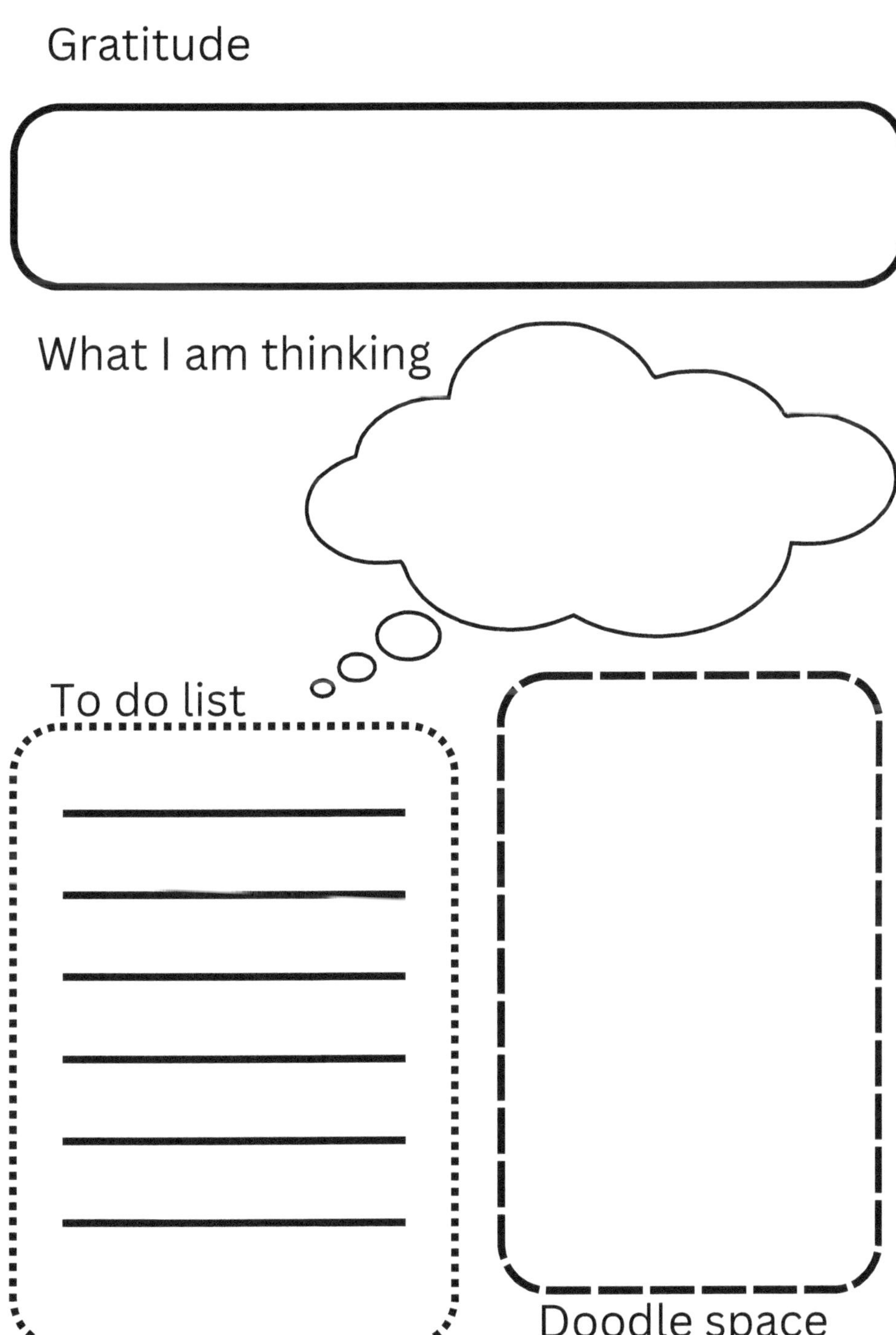

Date:..............
Gratitude
What I am thinking
To do list
Doodle space

Date:..............

Date:..............

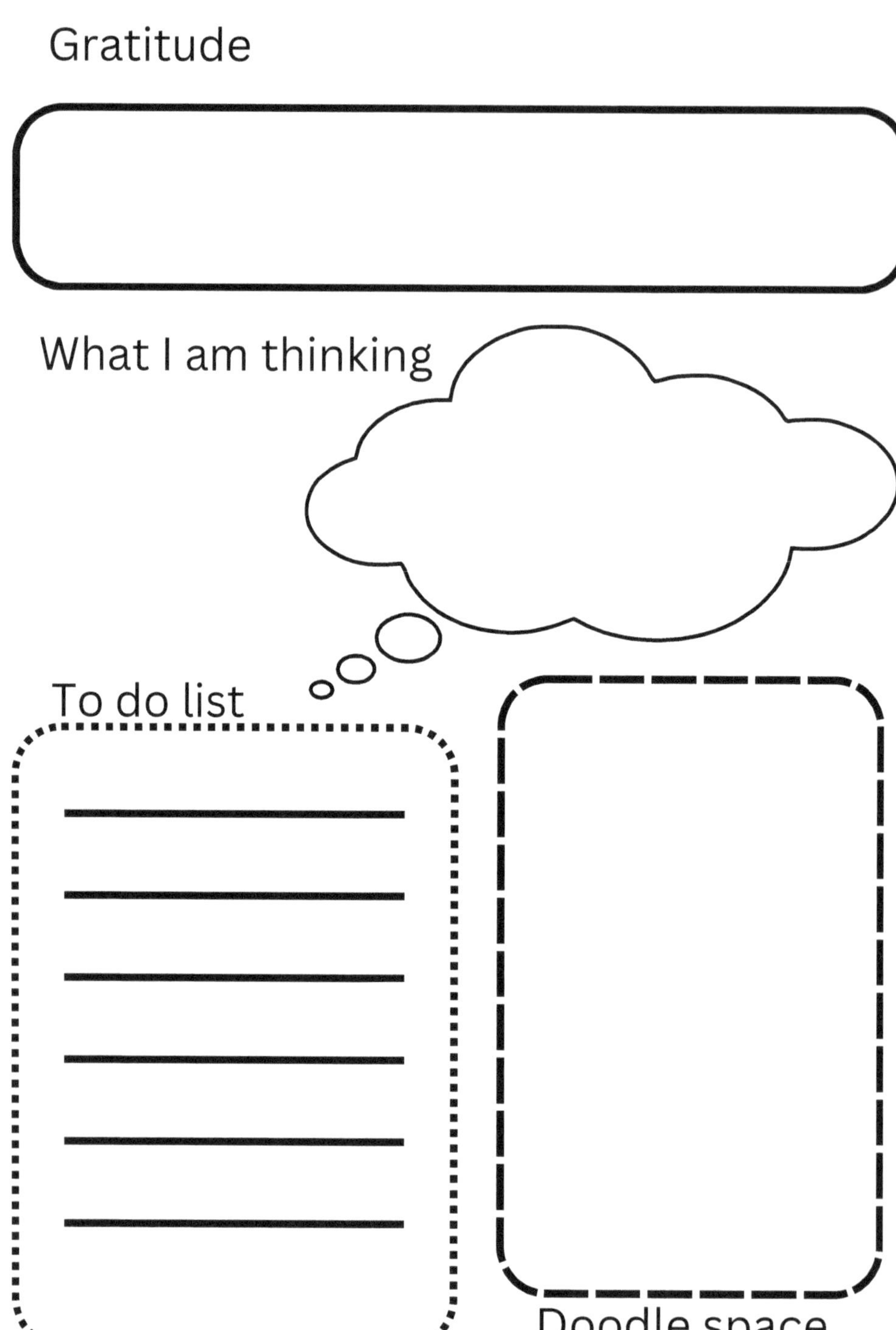

Date:...............

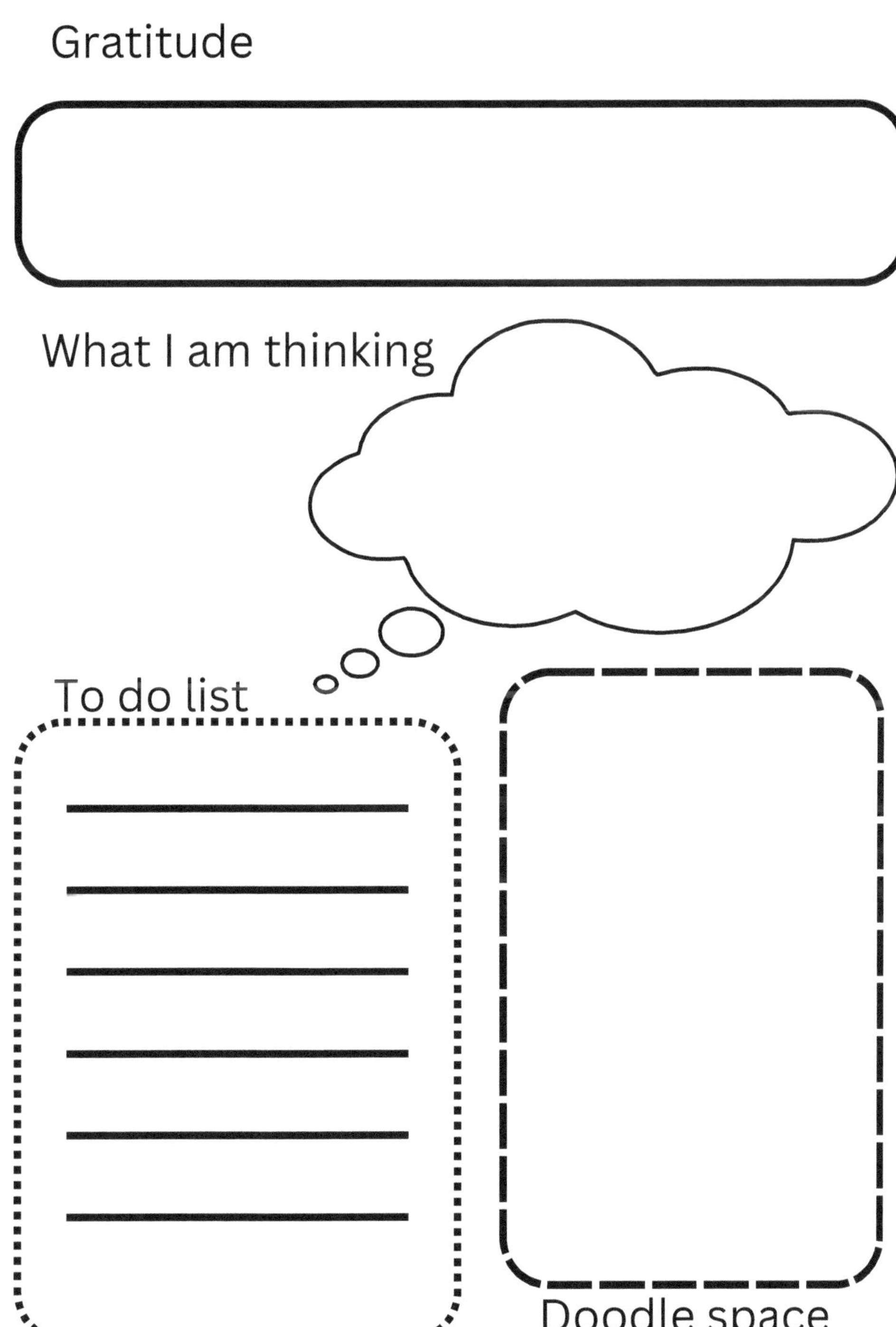

Weekly planner

Date:..../.../.....to..../.../....

MON

TUE

WED

THU

FRI

SAT

SUN

Date:..............

Date:..............

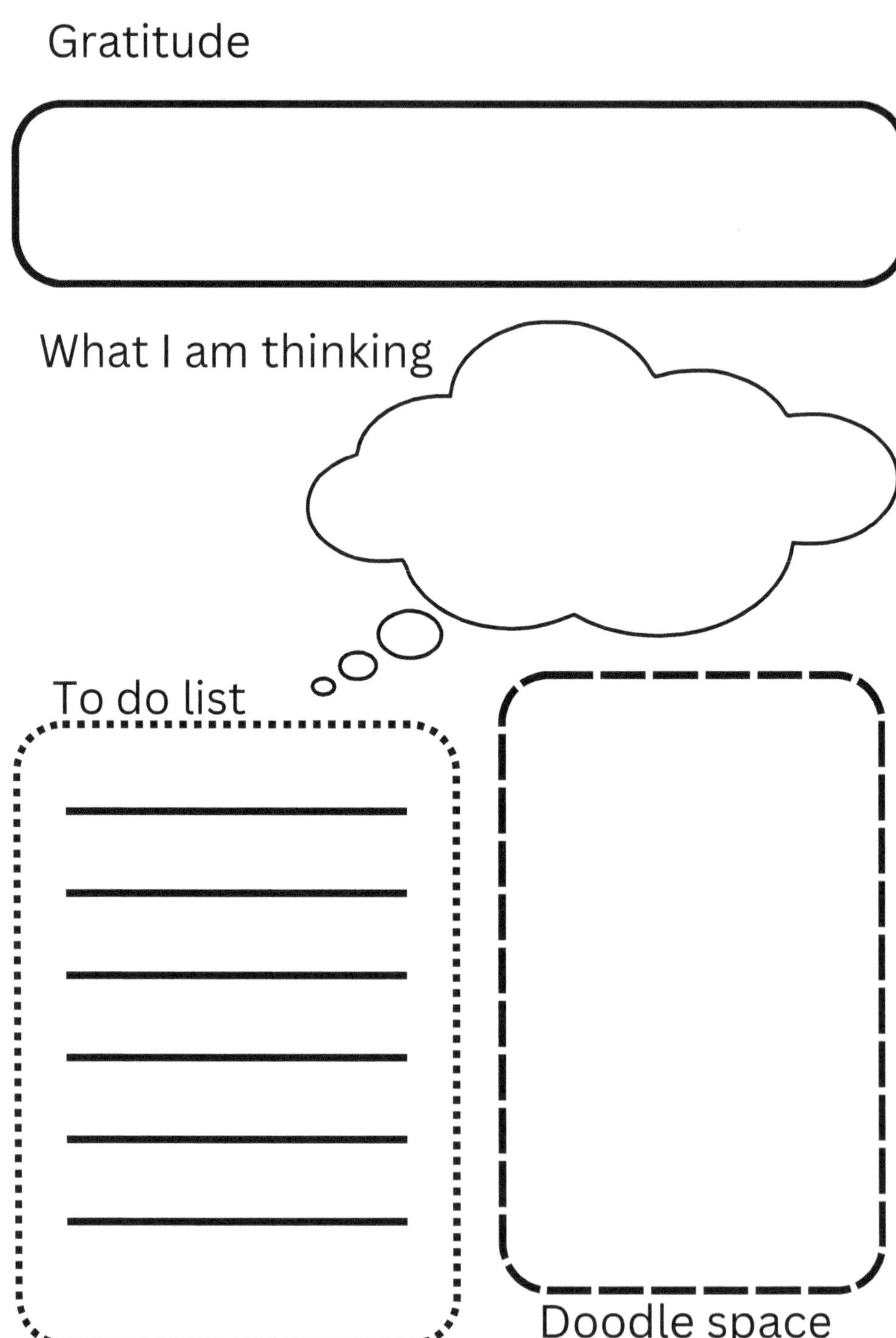

Date:..............

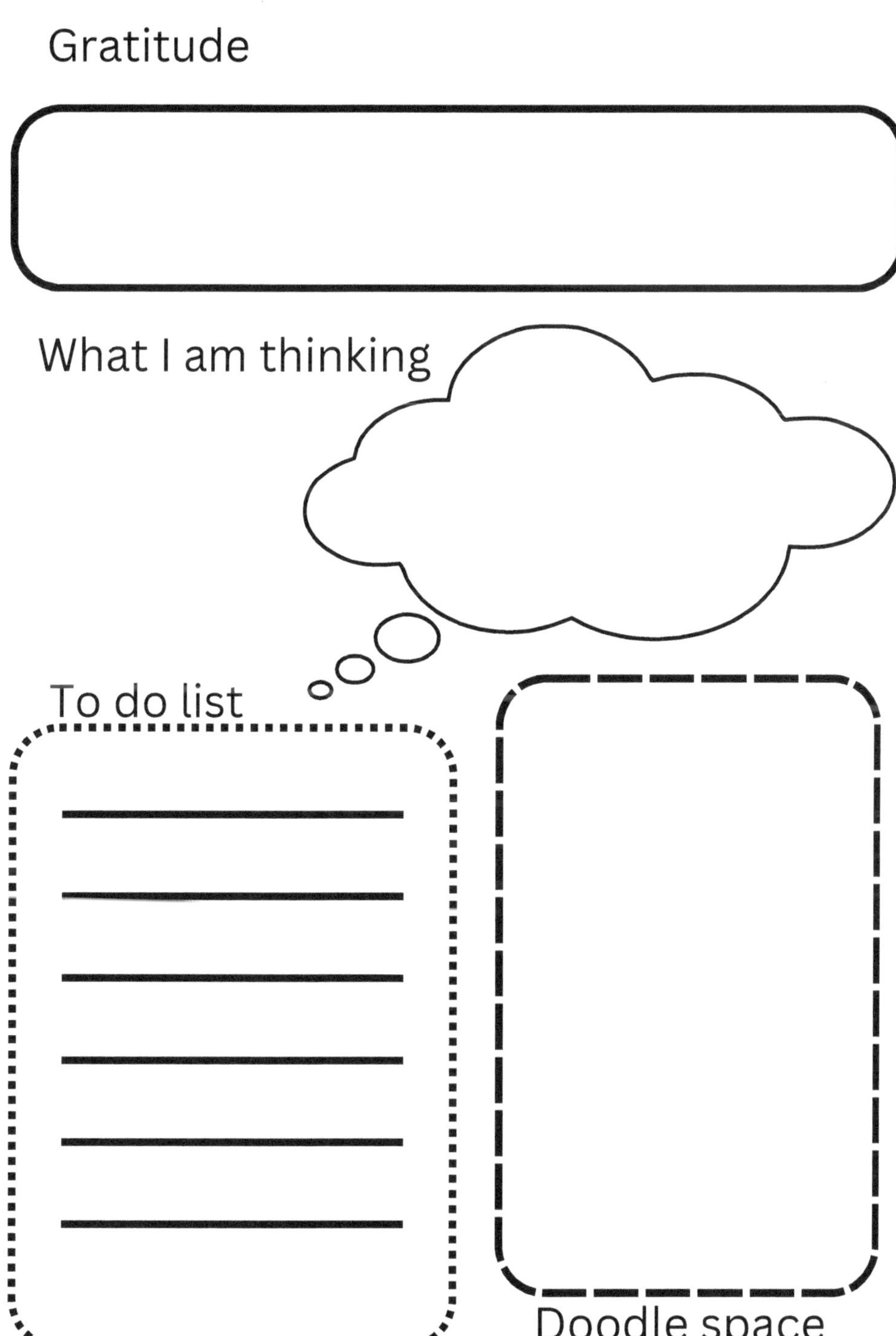

Date:..............

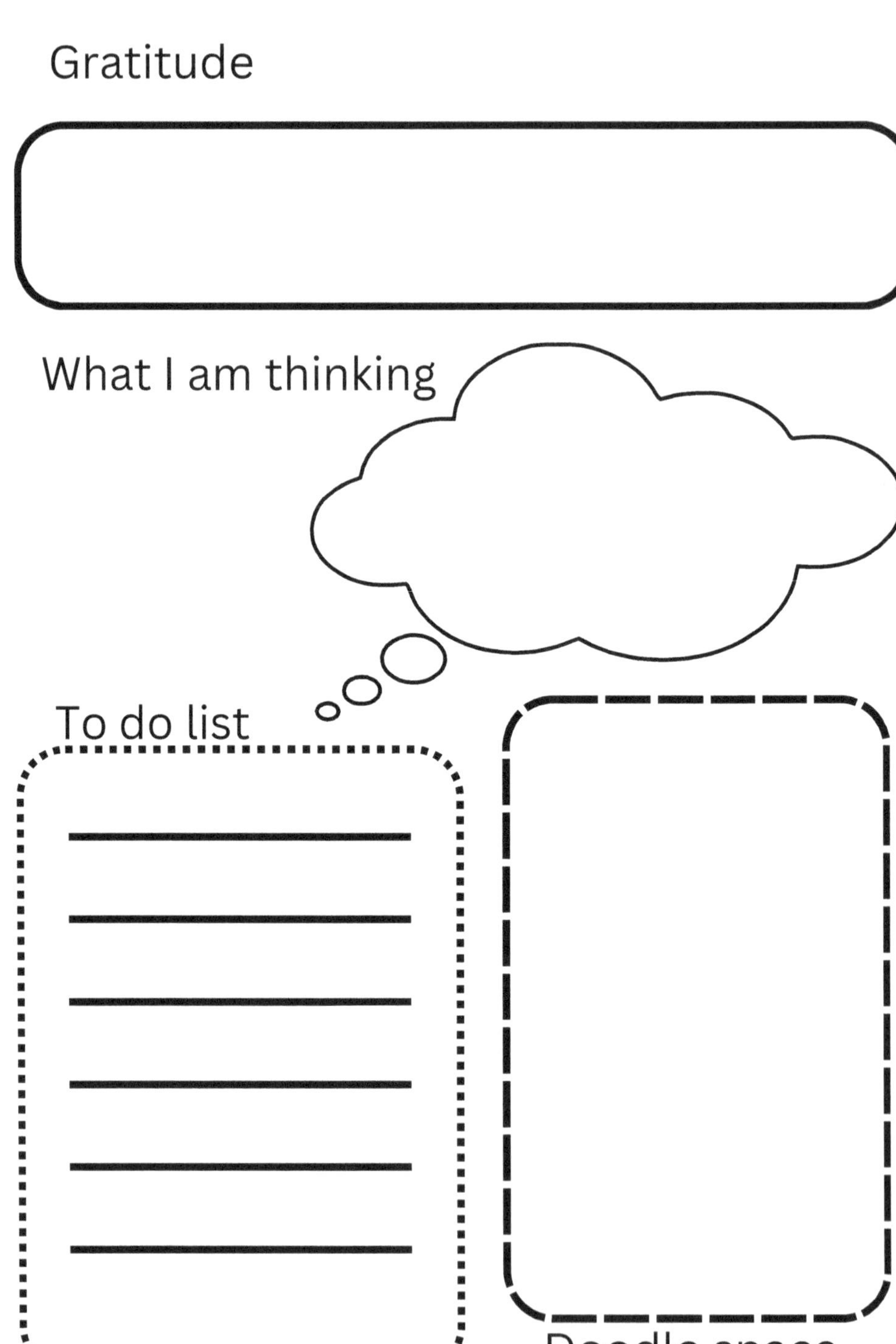

Date:..............

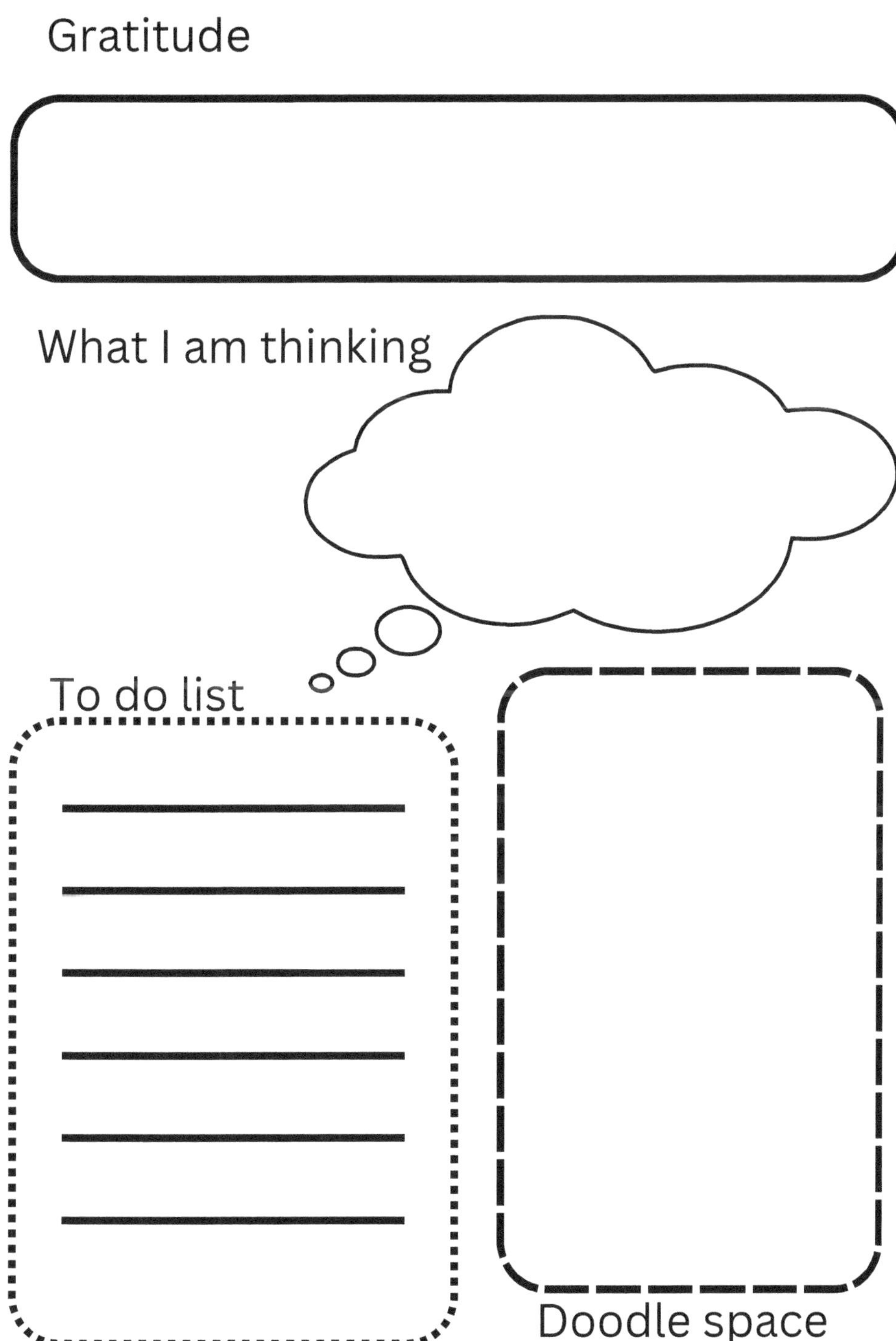

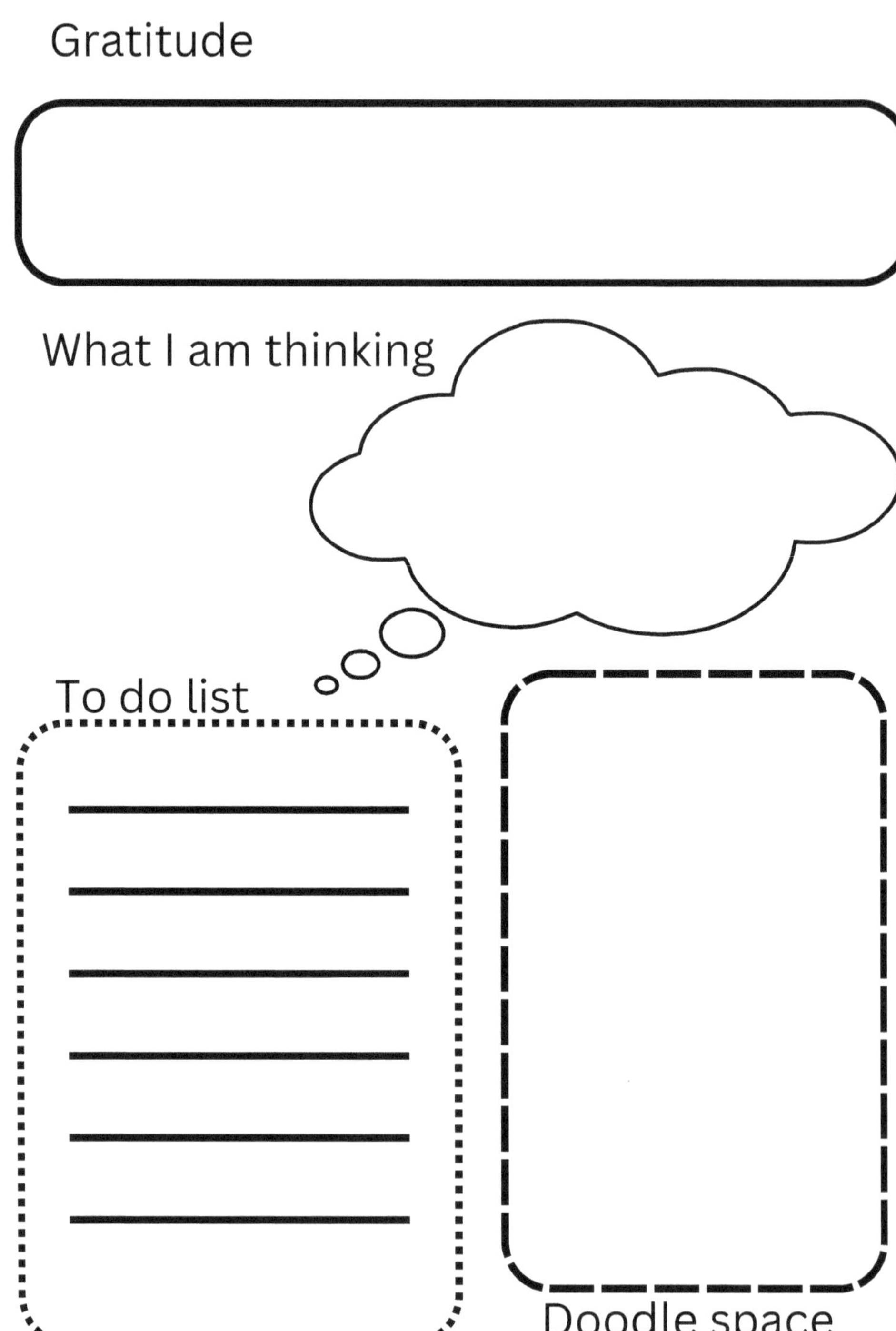
Date:...............
Gratitude
What I am thinking
To do list
Doodle space

Date:..............

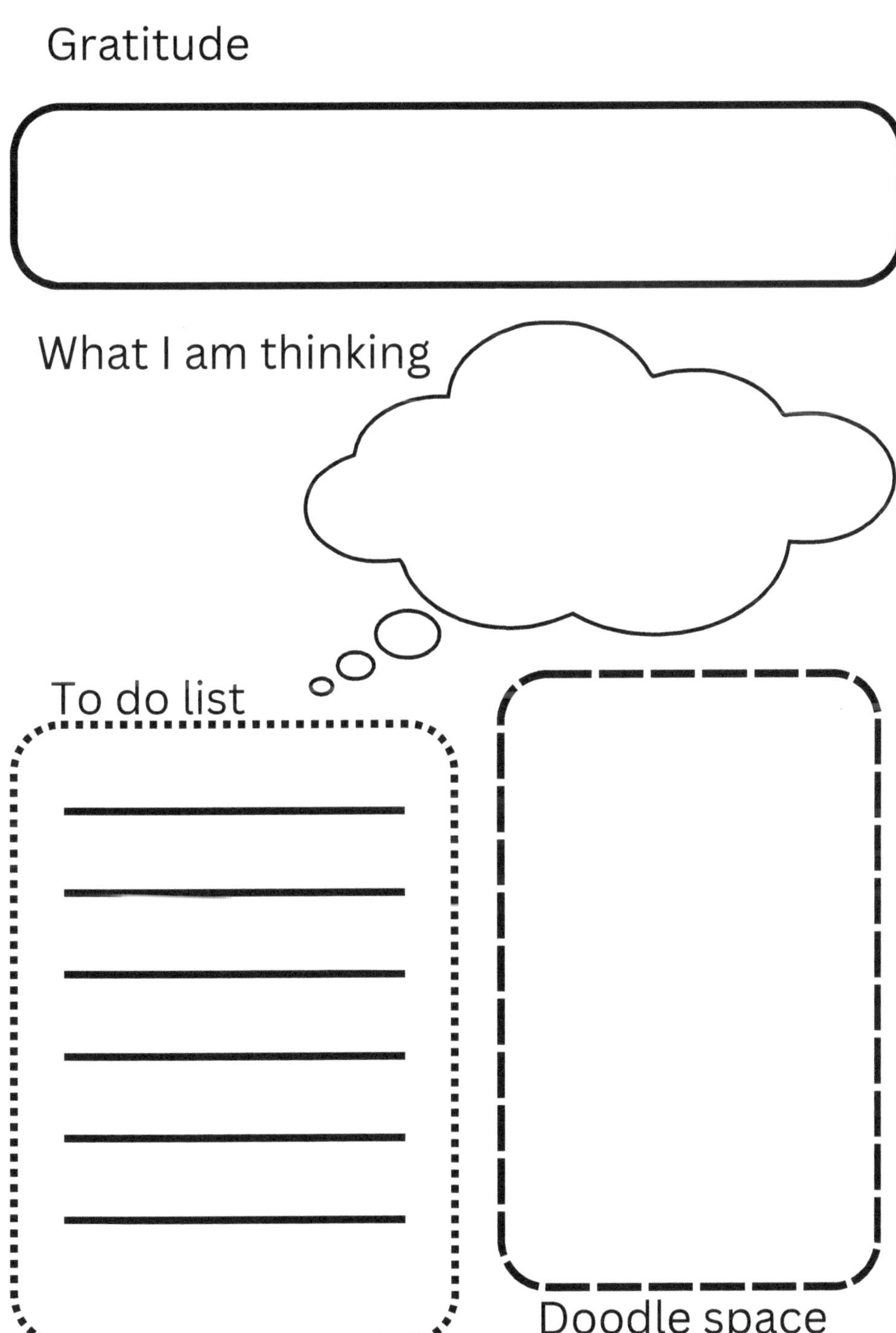

Weekly planner

Date:..../.../.....to..../.../....

MON

TUE

WED

THU

FRI

SAT

SUN

Date:.............

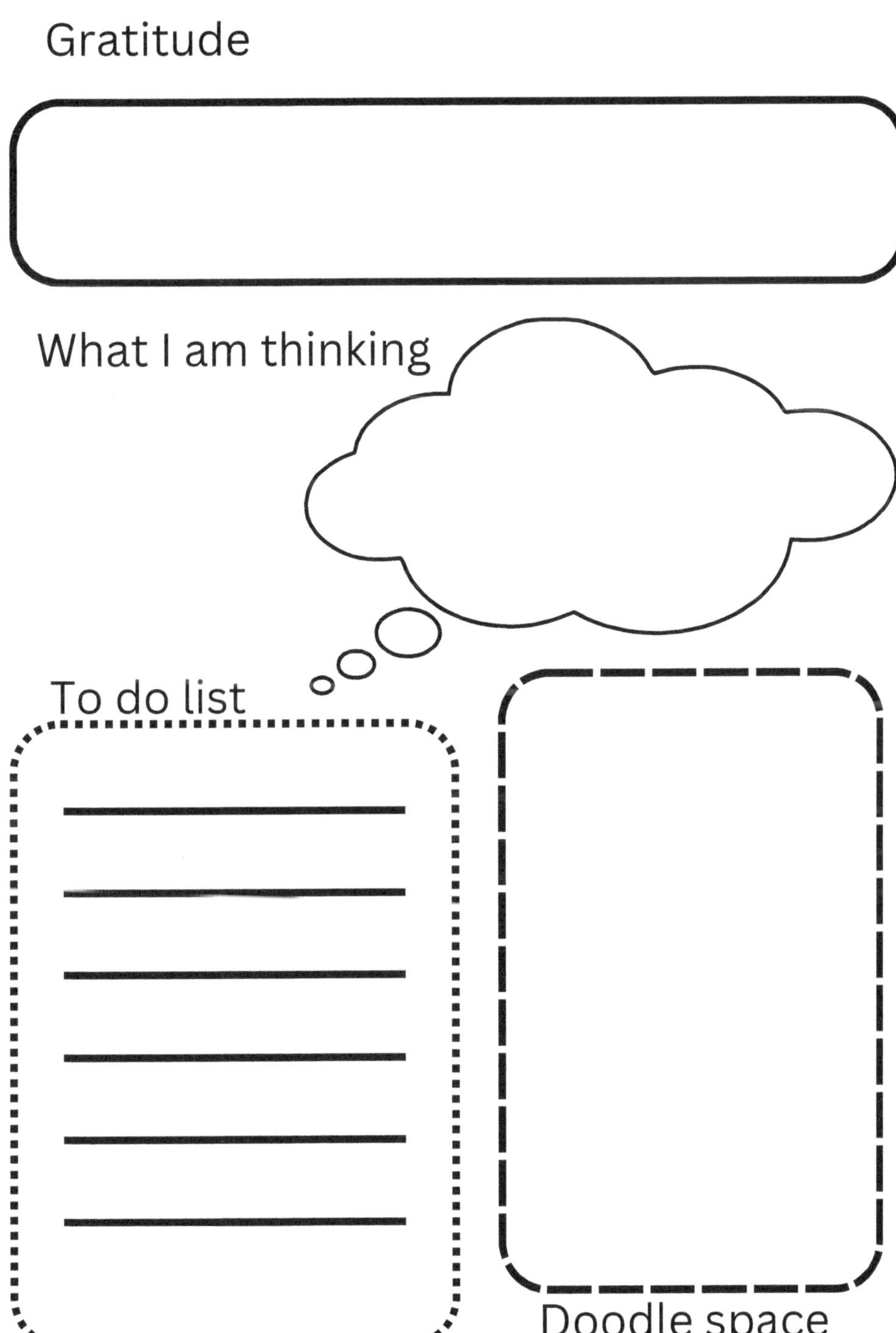

Date:..............

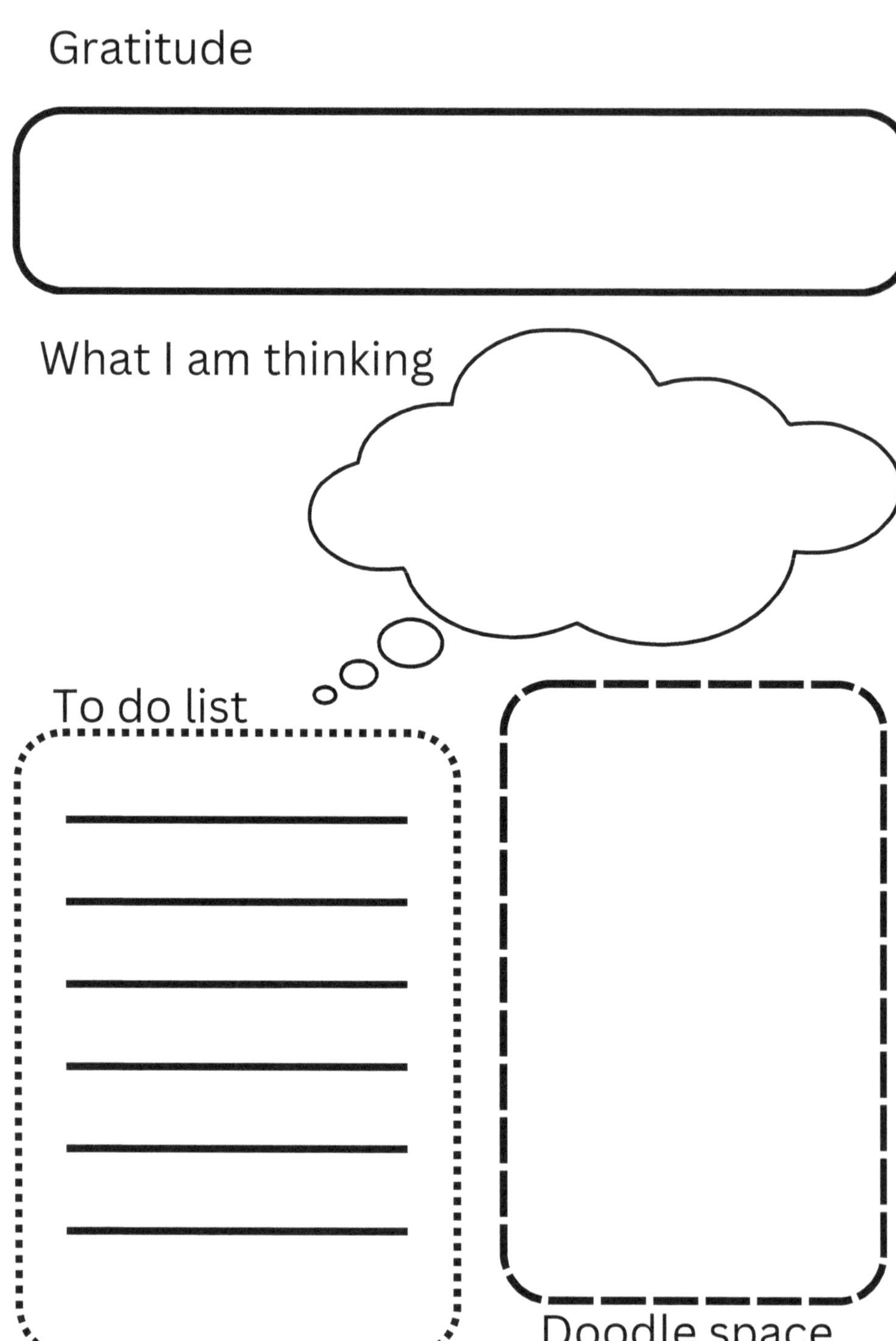

Date:..............

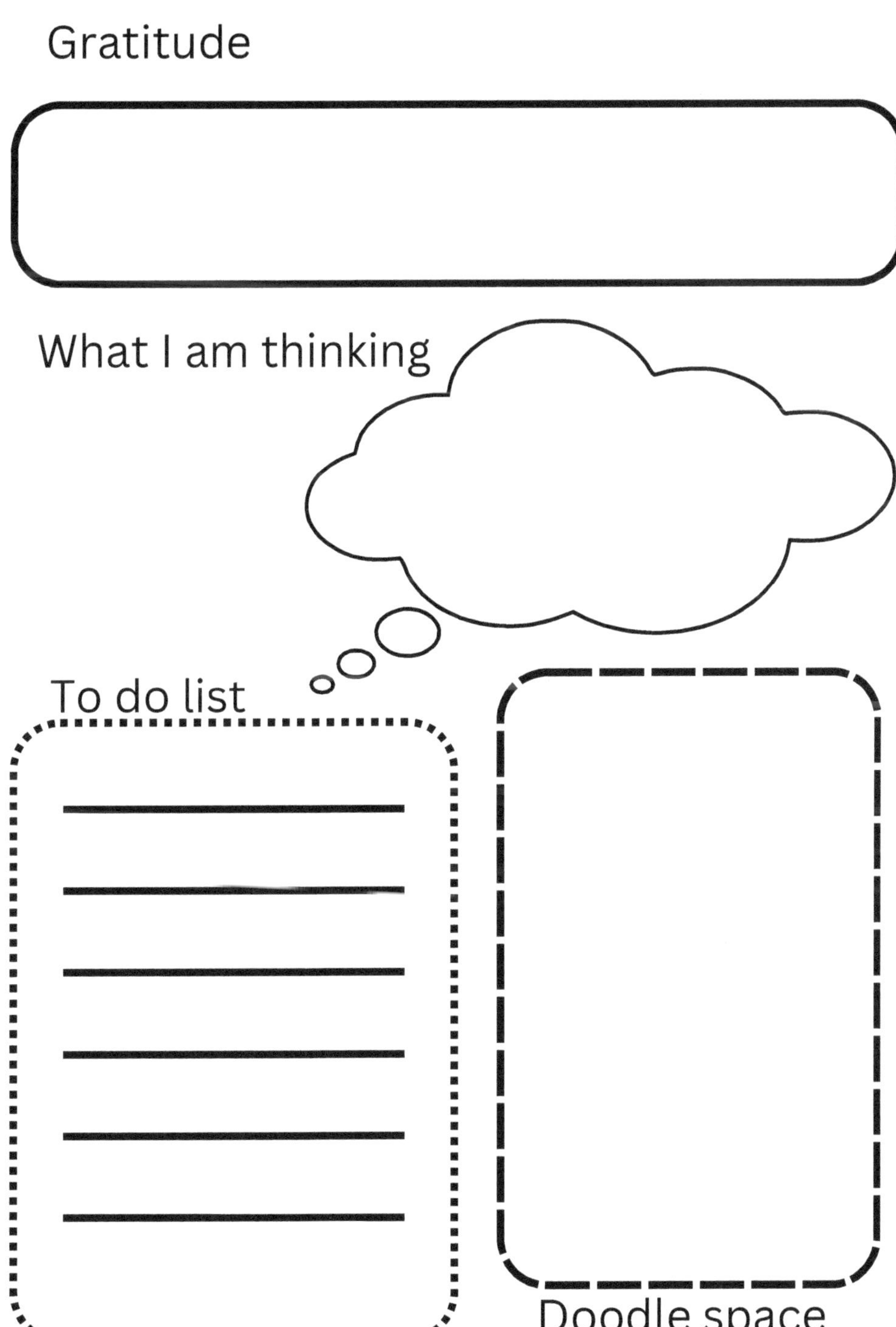

Date:..............

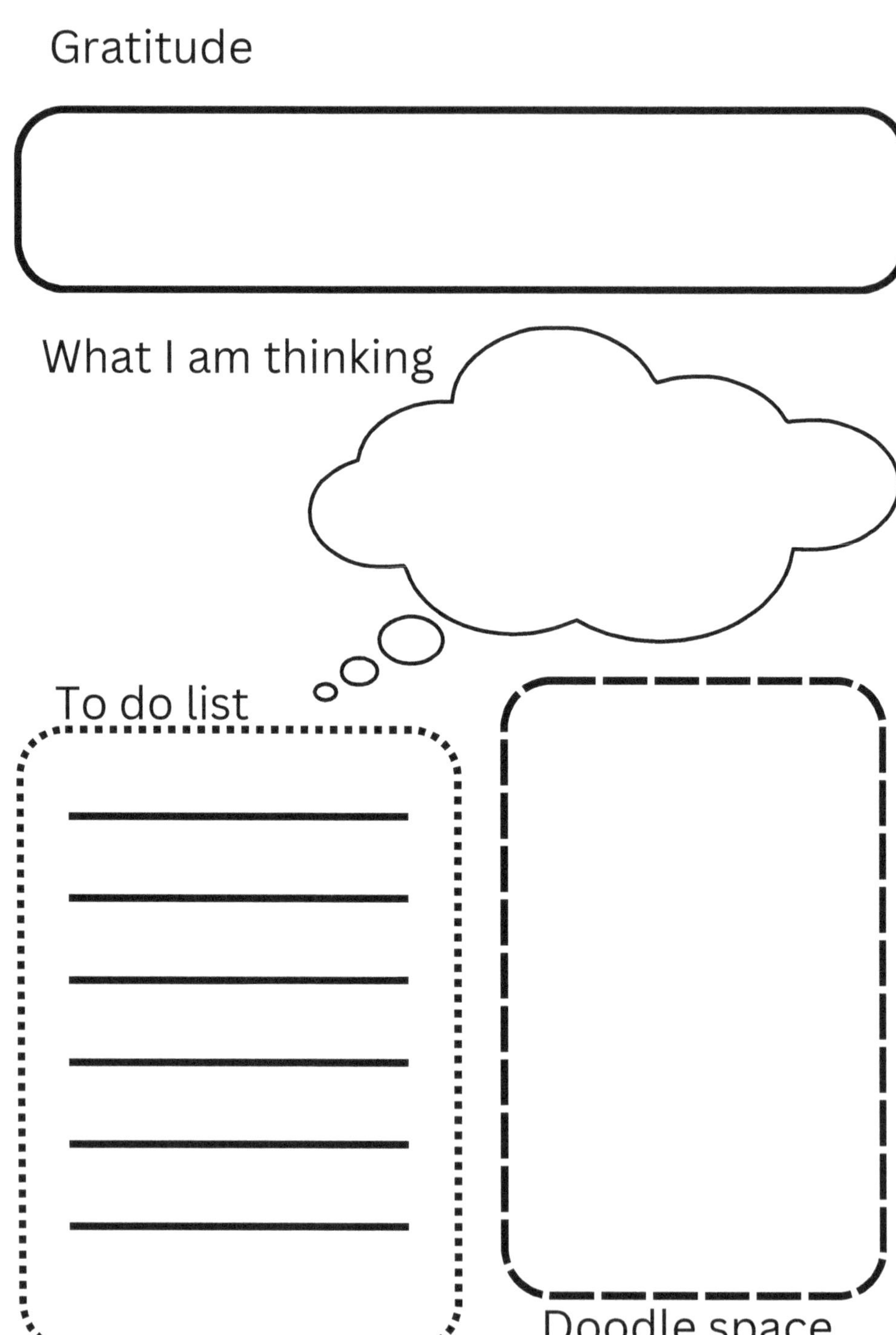

Date:..............

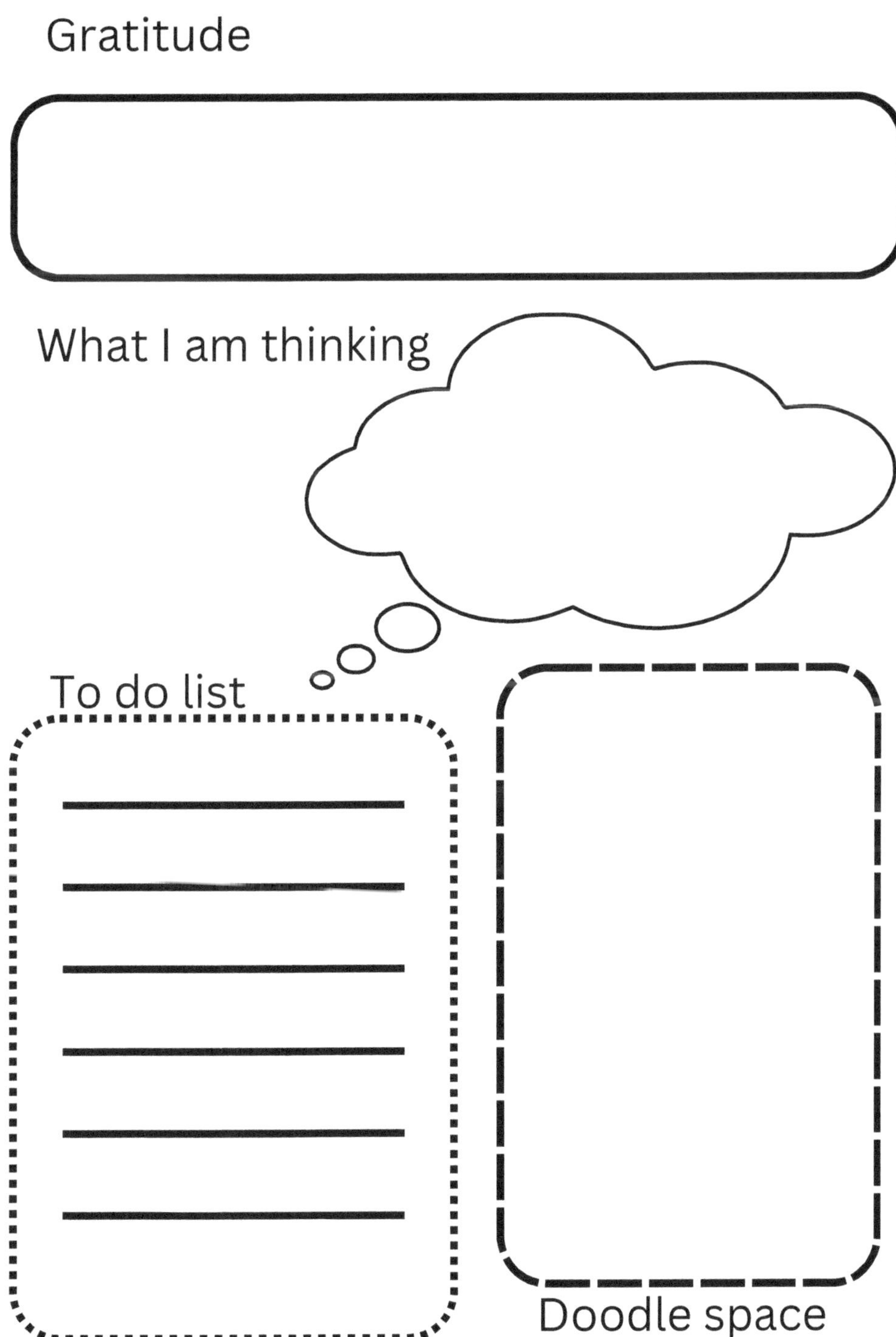

Date:..............

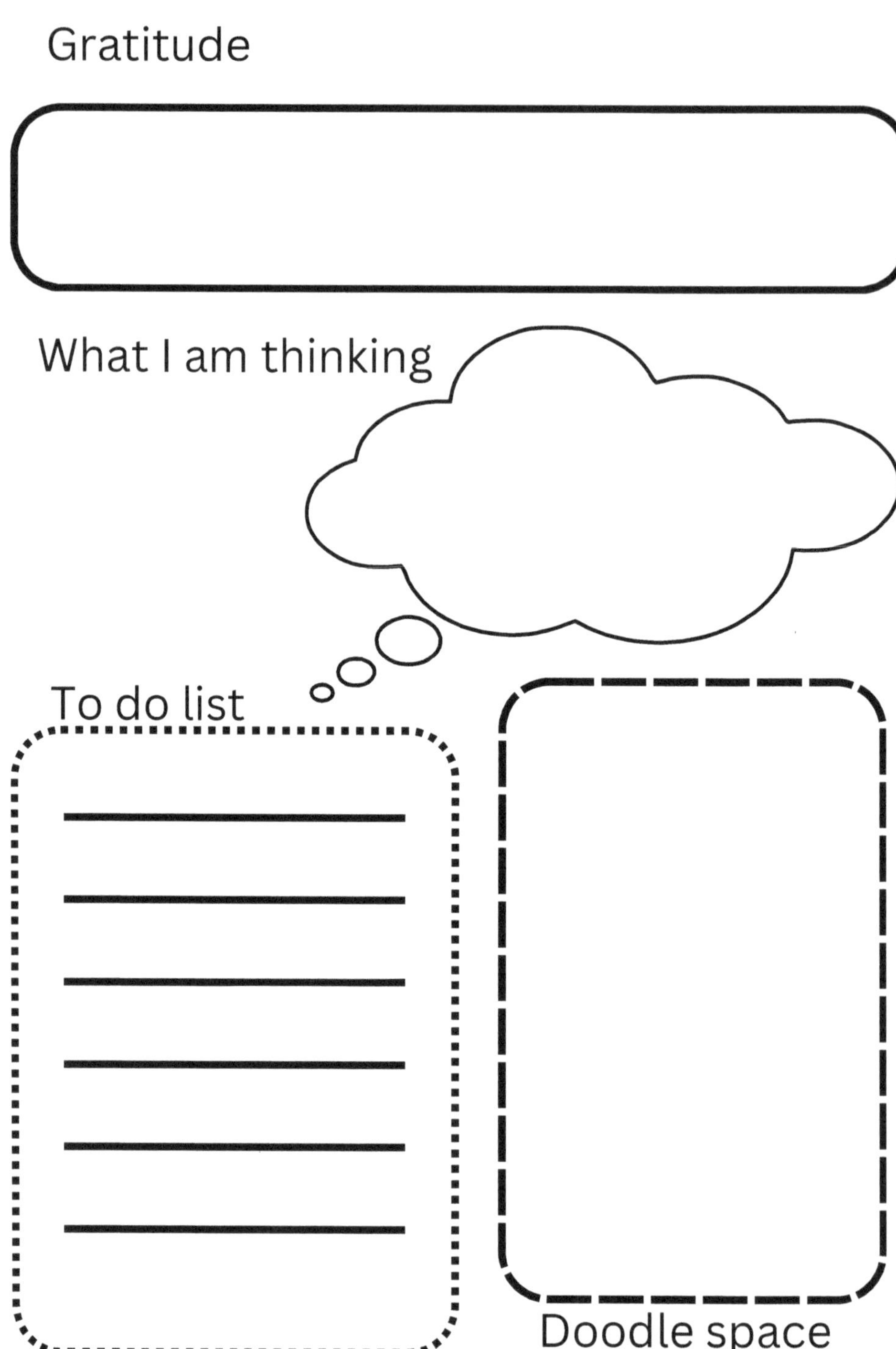

Date:..............

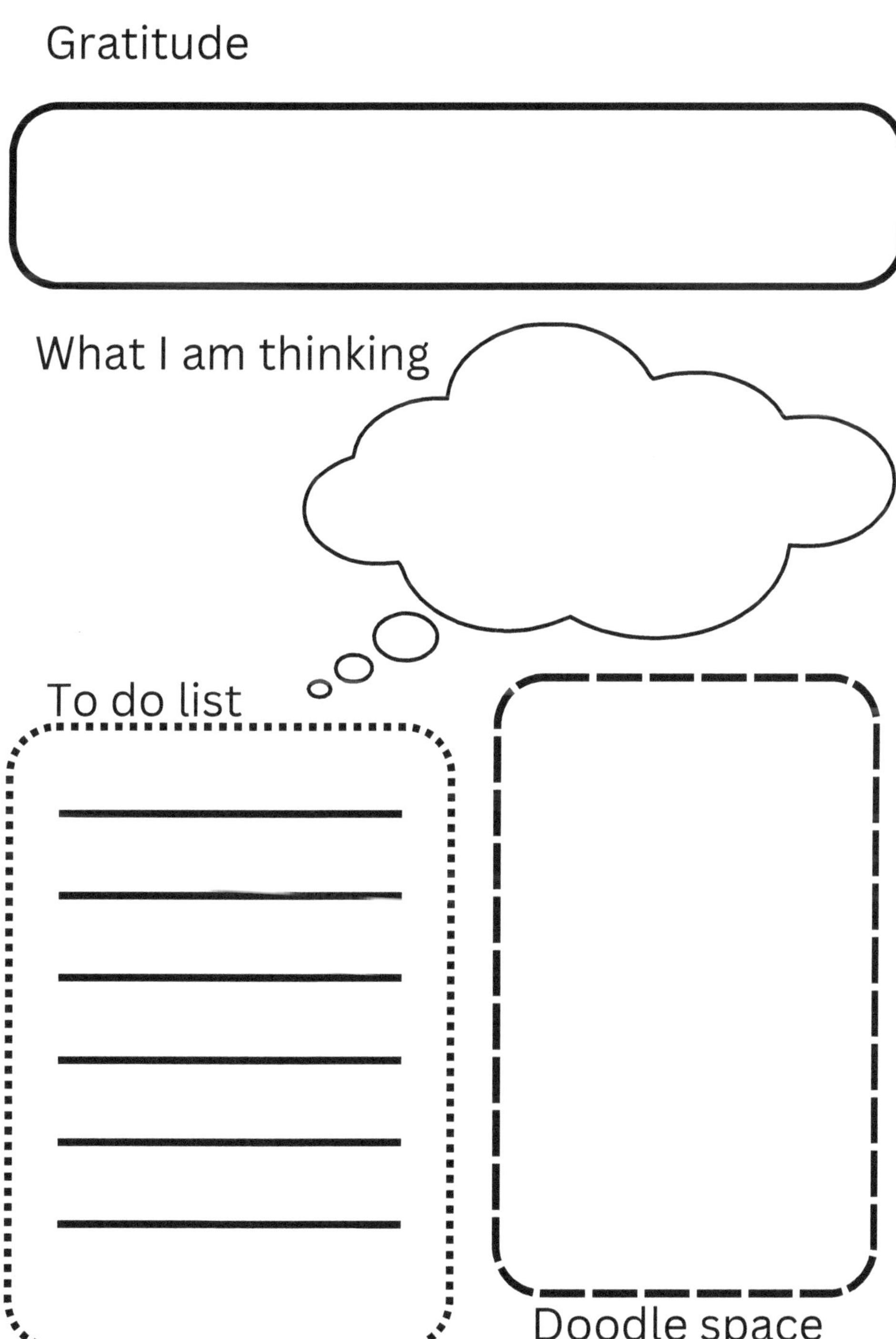

Weekly planner

Date:..../.../.....to..../.../....

MON

TUE

WED

THU

FRI

SAT

SUN

Date:..............

Date:..............

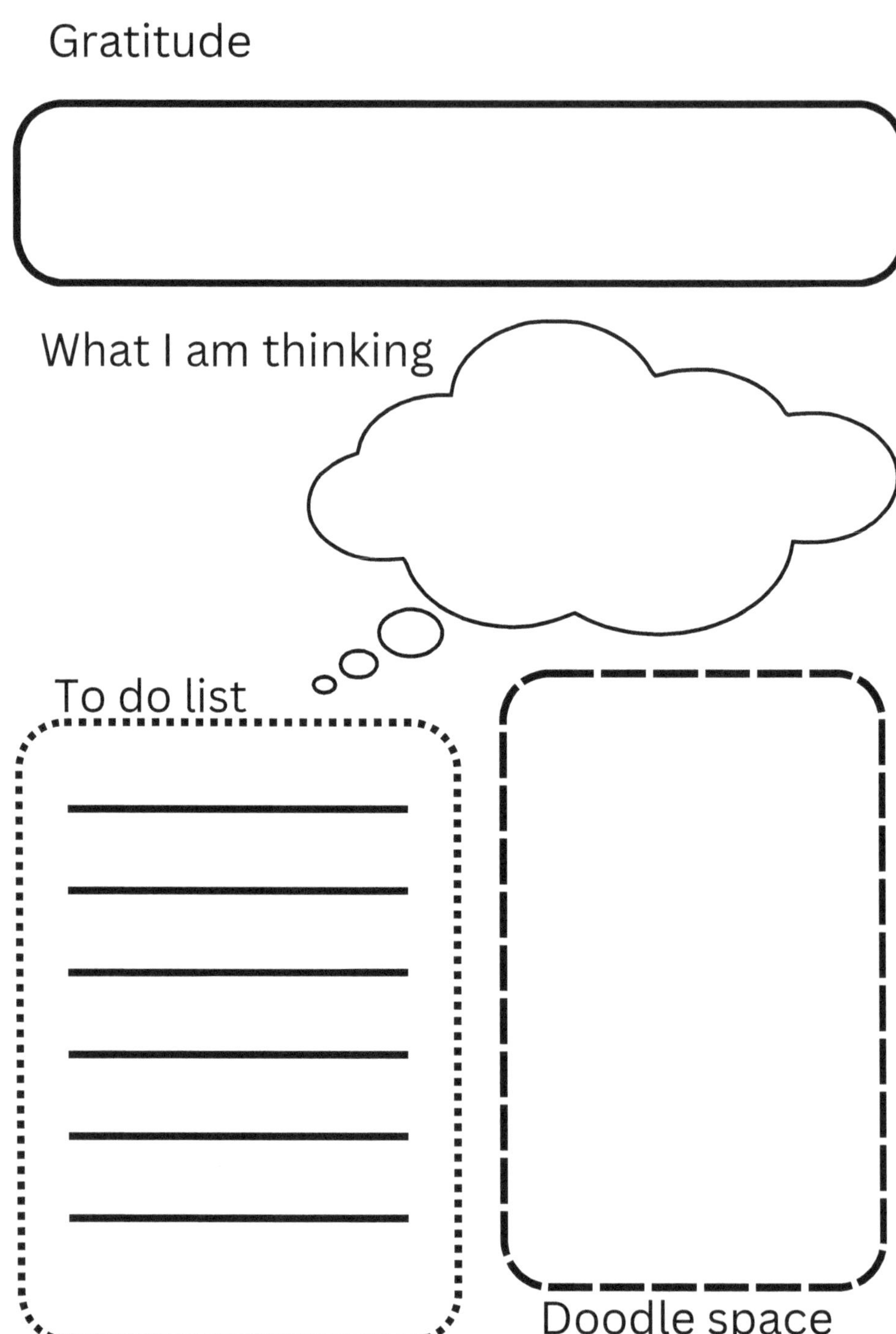

Date:..............

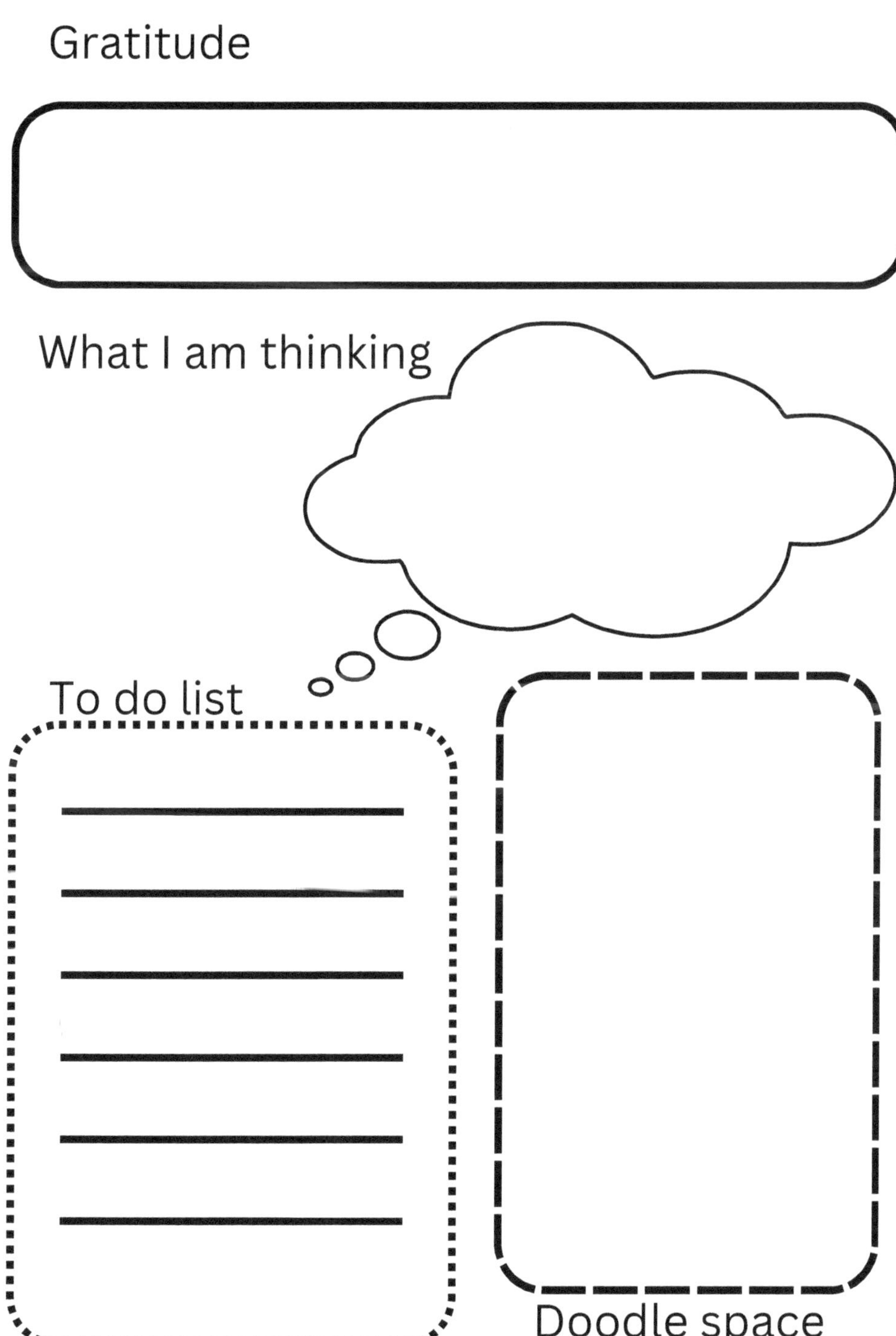

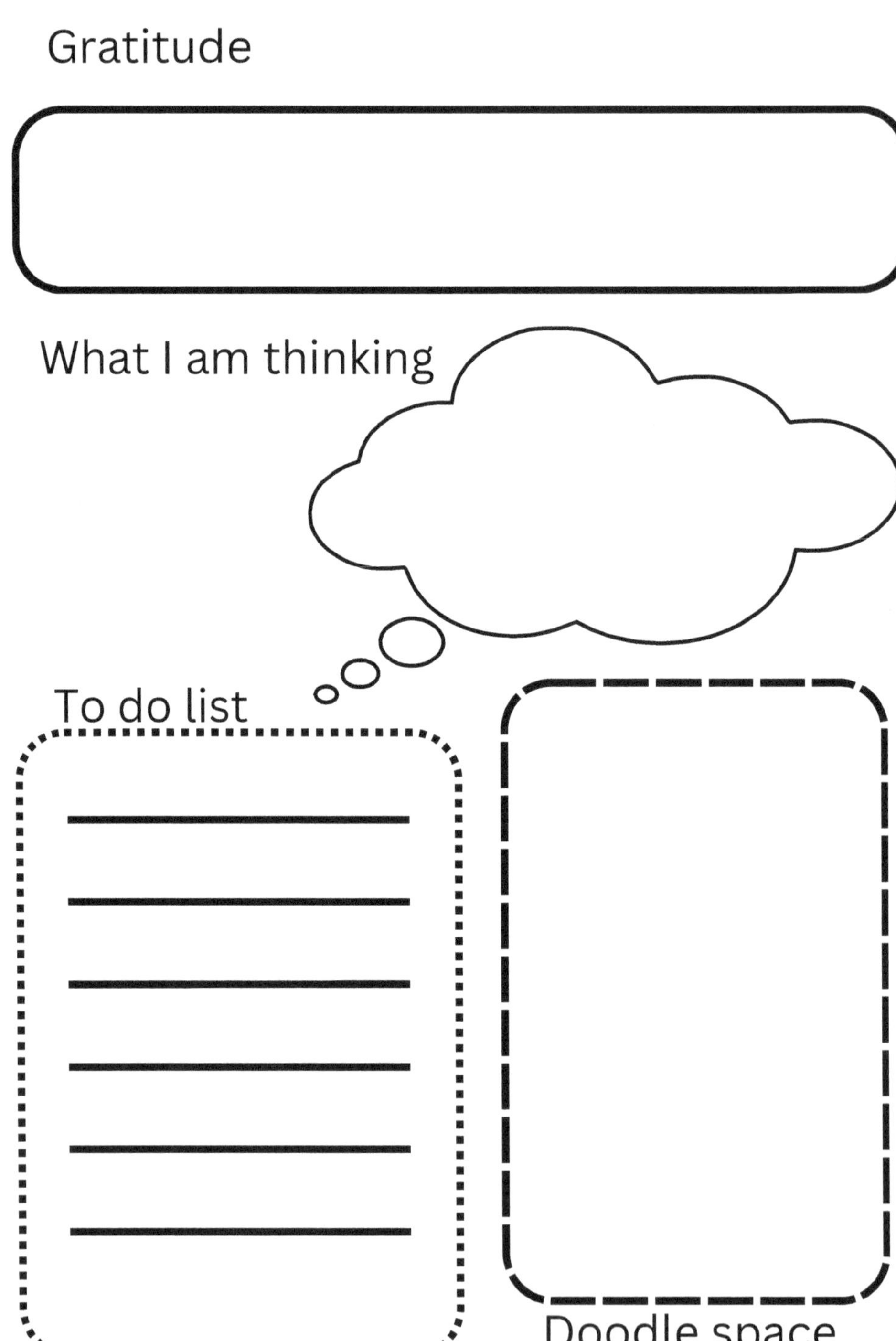
Date:..............
Gratitude
What I am thinking
To do list
Doodle space

Date:..............

Date:..............

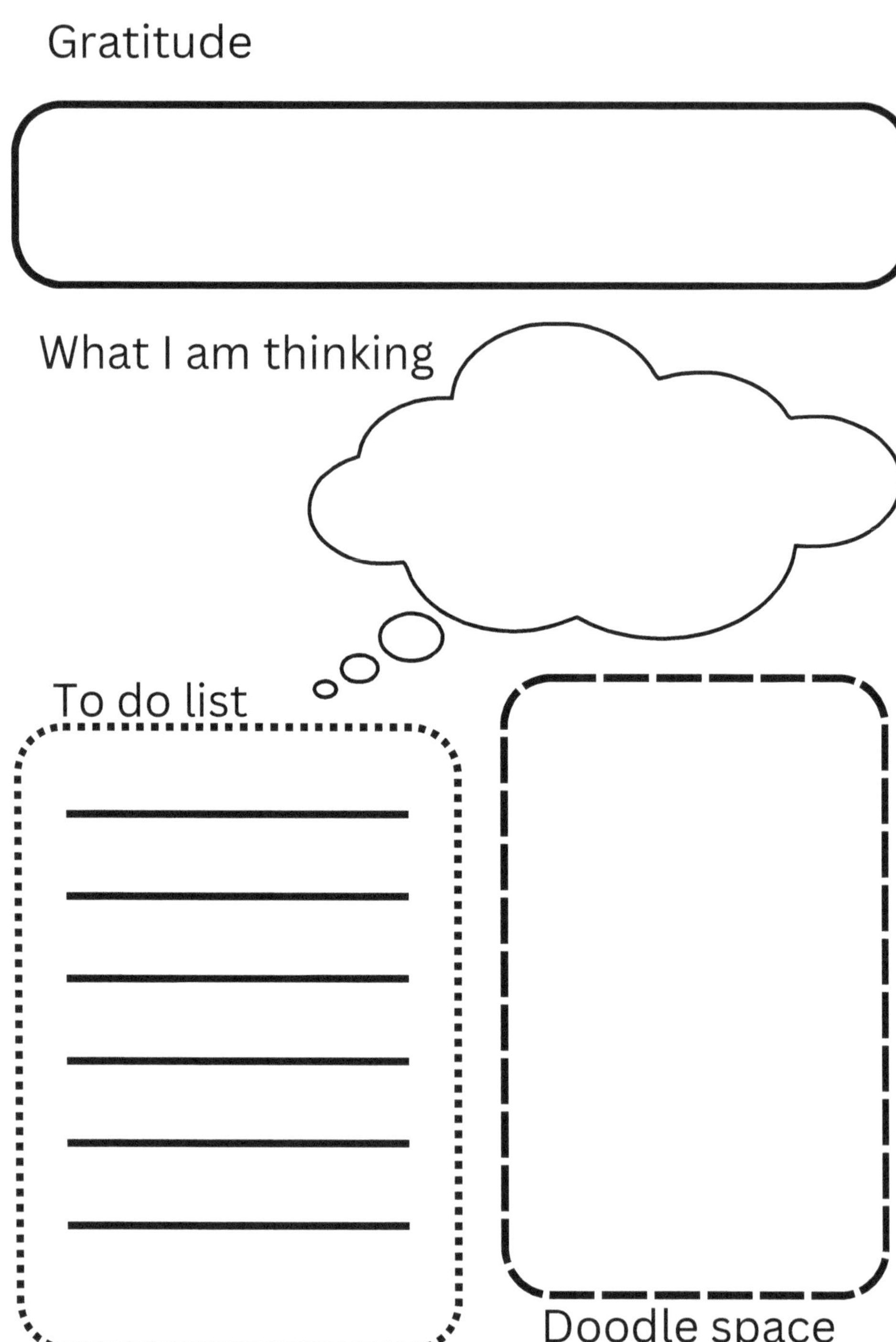

Date:..............

Weekly planner

Date:..../.../...../to..../.../....

MON

TUE

WED

THU

FRI

SAT

SUN

Date:..............

Date:..............

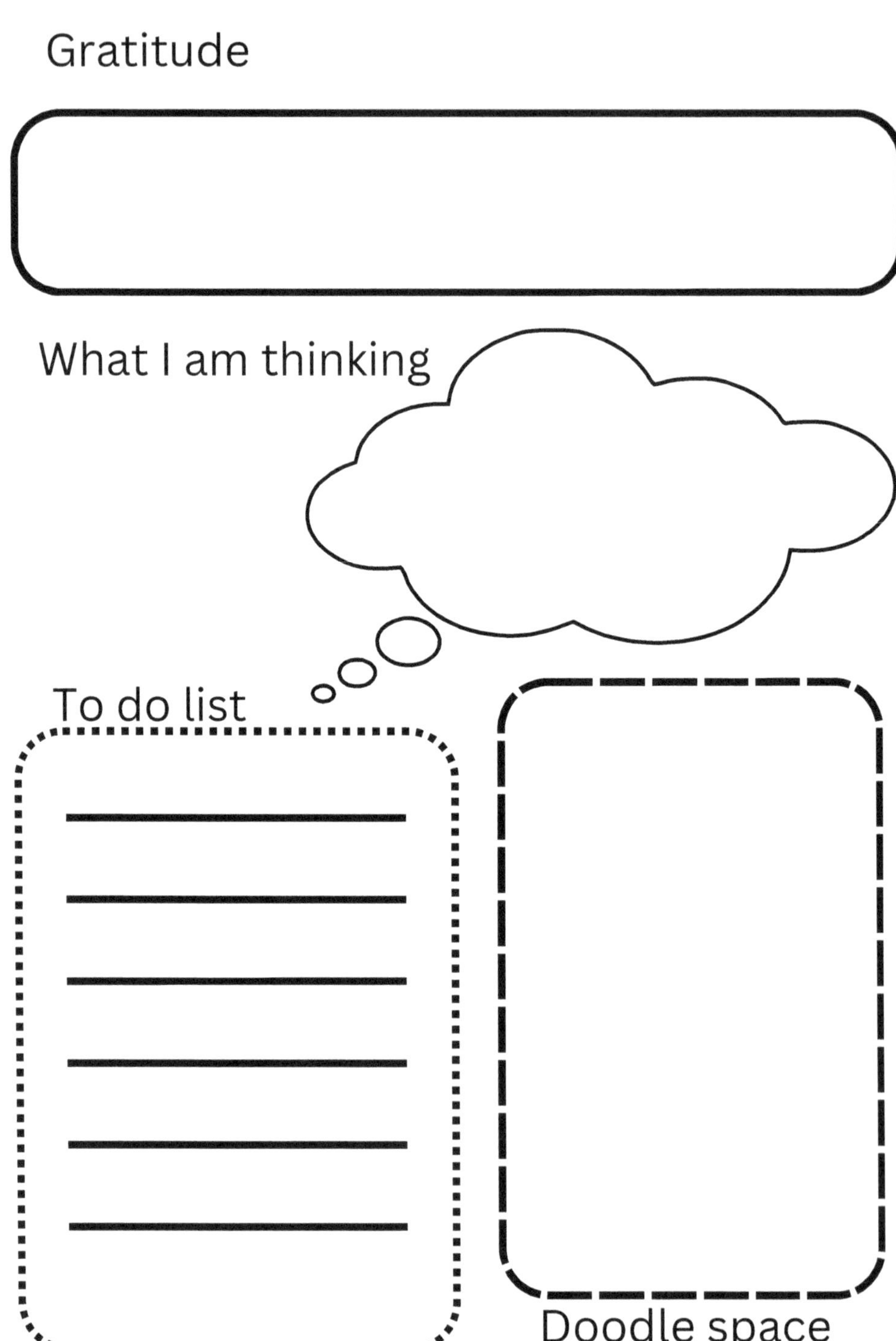

Date:..............

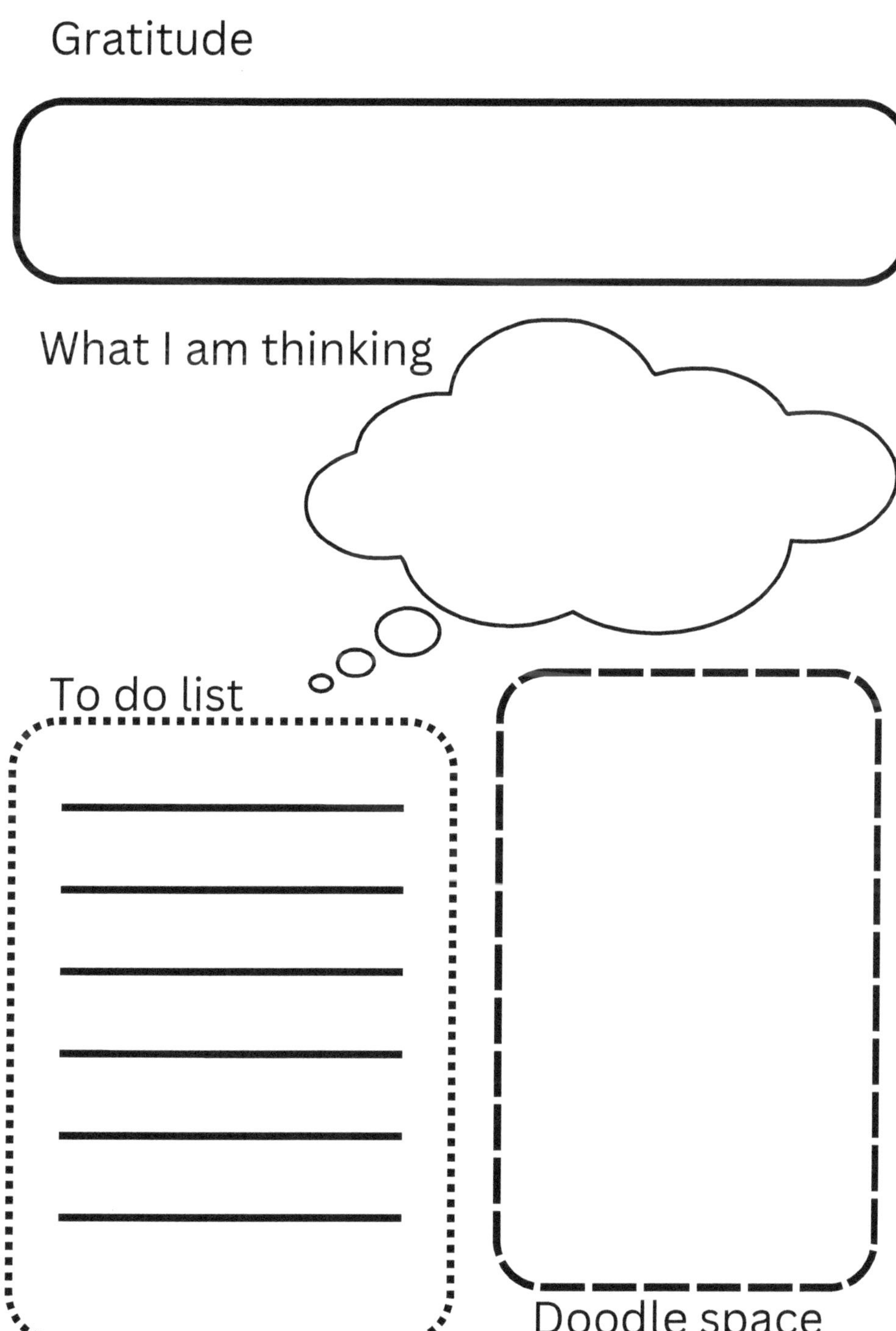

Date:..............

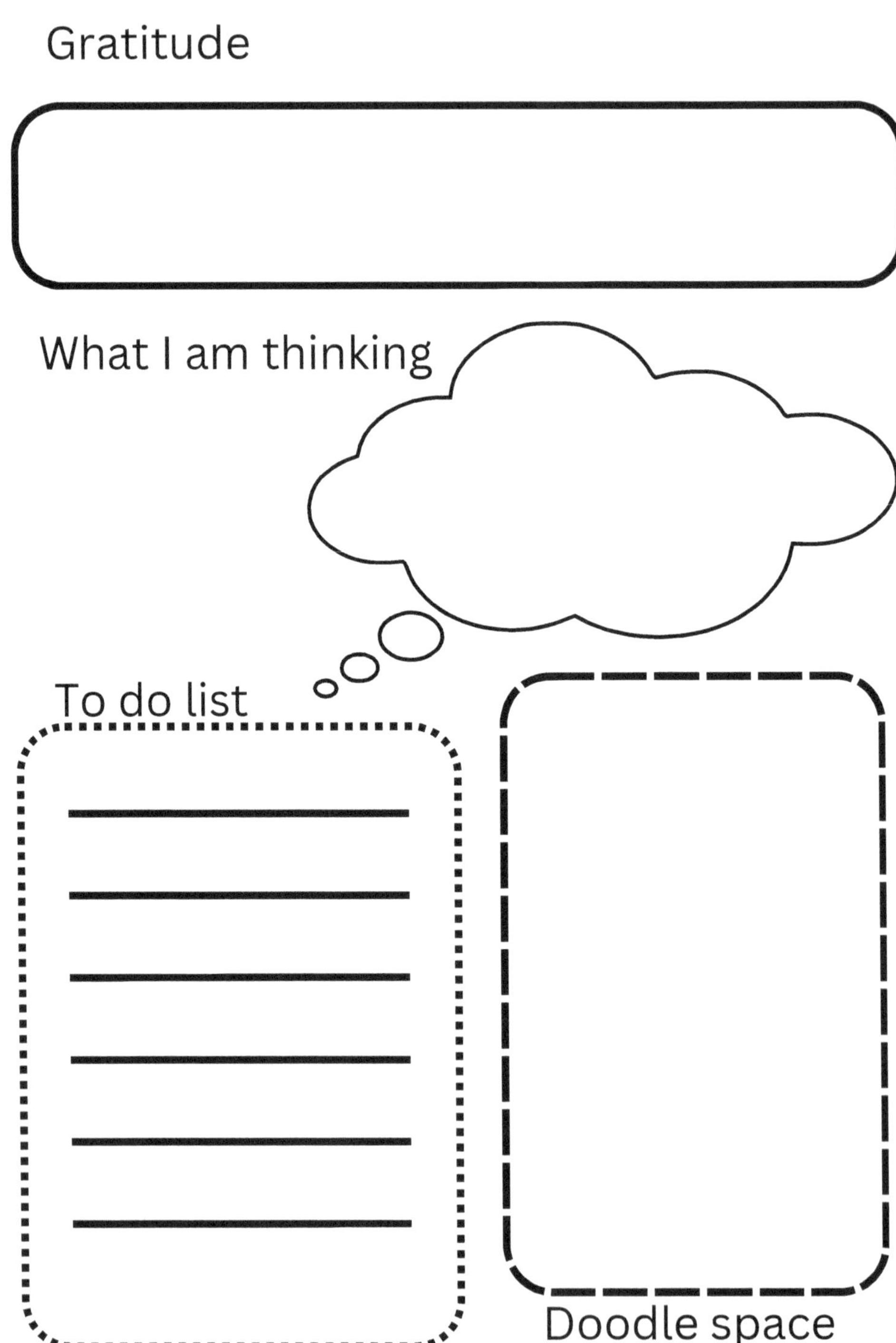

Date:..............

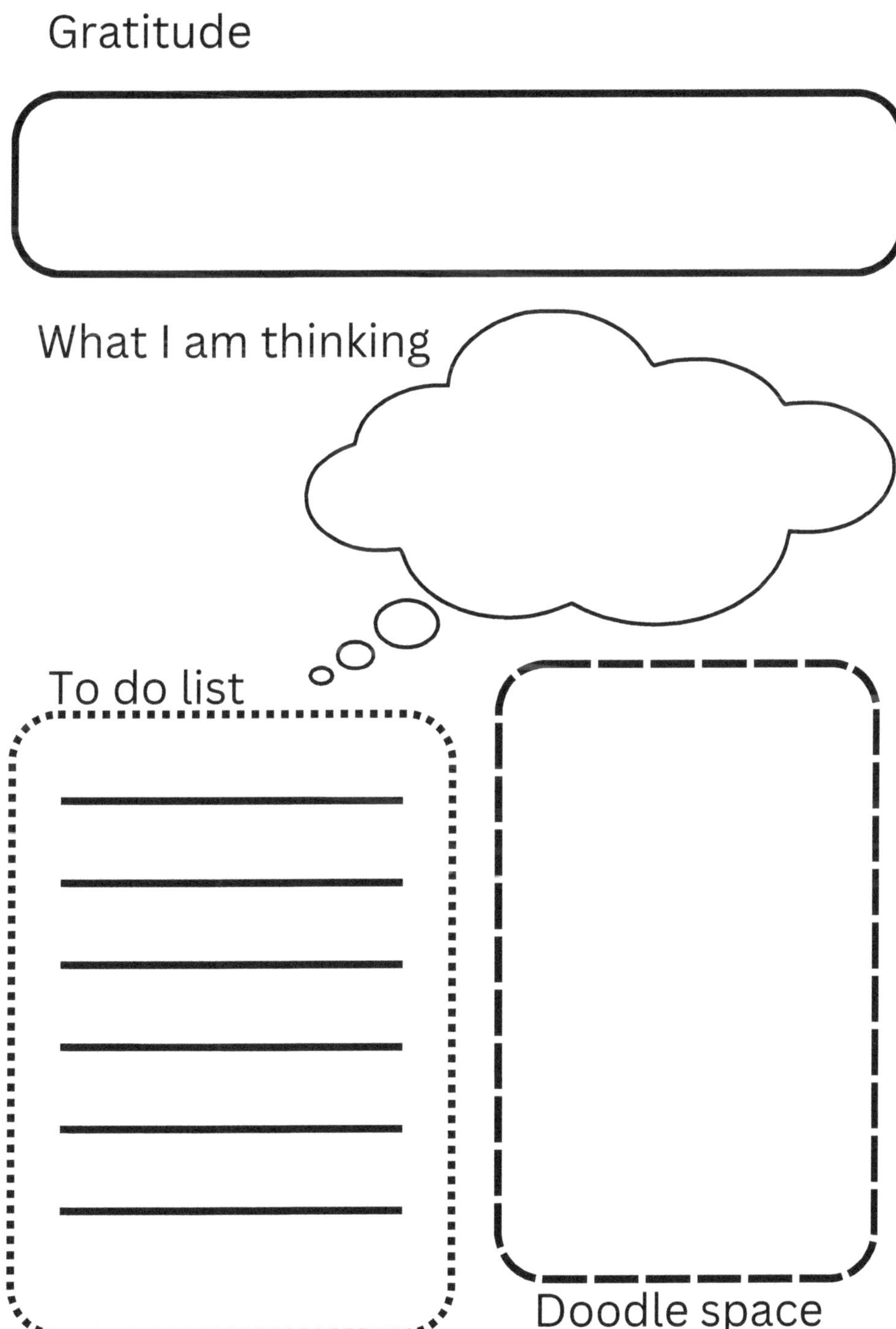

Date:..............

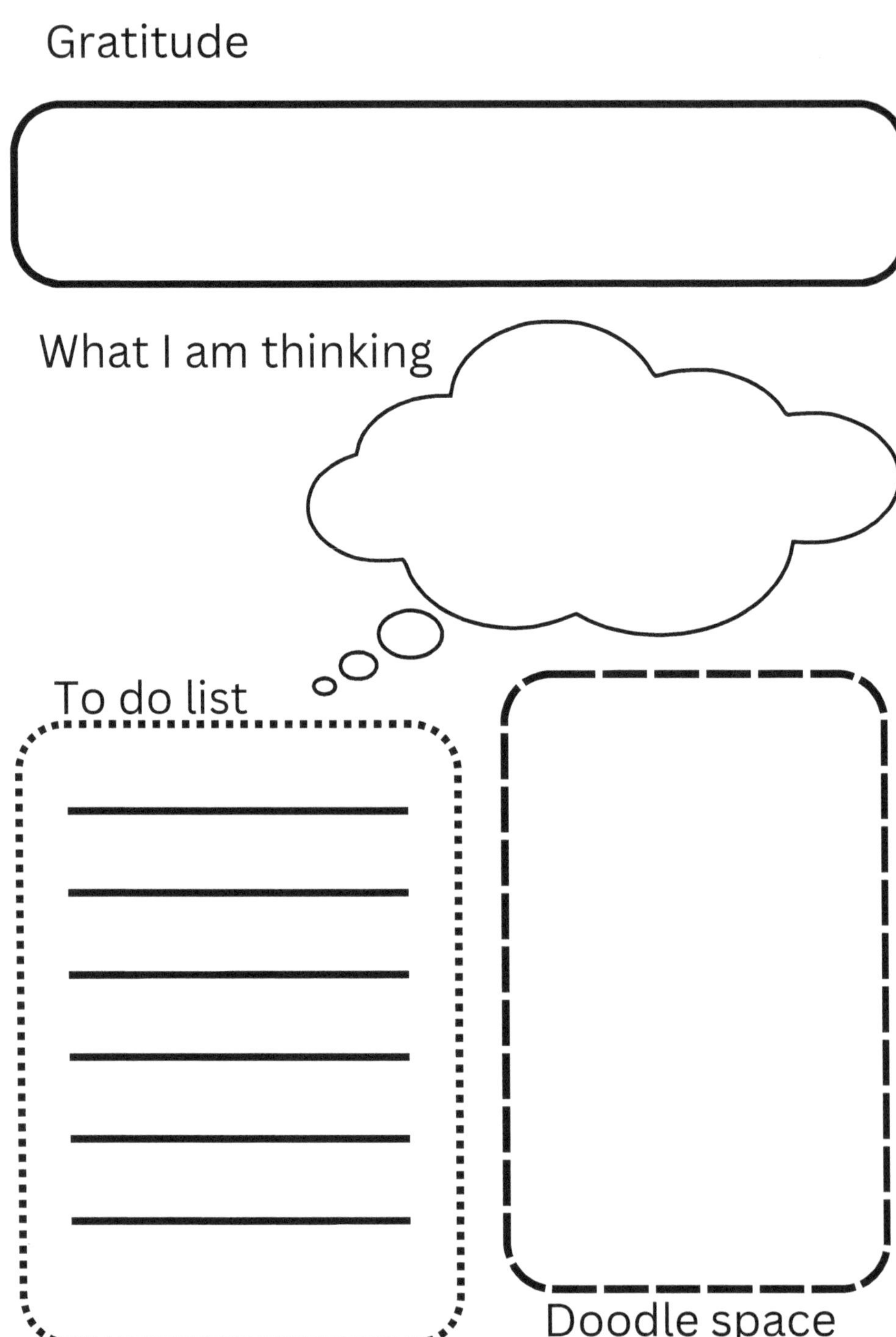

Date:..............

www.ingramcontent.com/pod-product-compliance
Ingram Content Group UK Ltd.
Pitfield, Milton Keynes, MK11 3LW, UK
UKHW062310290726
14090UKWH00018B/990

9 798892 770637